PINBALL WIZARDS

JACKPOTS, DRAINS, AND THE CULT OF THE SILVER BALL

ADAM RUBEN

CHICAGO
REVIEW
PRESS

Copyright © 2018 by Adam Ruben
All rights reserved
Published by Chicago Review Press Incorporated
814 North Franklin Street
Chicago, Illinois 60610
ISBN 978-1-61373-591-6

Library of Congress Cataloging-in-Publication Data
Names: Ruben, Adam, author.
Title: Pinball wizards: jackpots, drains, and the cult of the silver ball /
    Adam Ruben.
Description: Chicago, Illinois : Chicago Review Press, [2018] | Includes
    index.
Identifiers: LCCN 2017012377 (print) | LCCN 2017013283 (ebook) | ISBN
    9781613735923 (pdf) | ISBN 9781613735930 (epub) | ISBN 9781613735947
    (kindle) | ISBN 9781613735916 (pbk. : alk. paper)
Subjects: LCSH: Pinball machines.
Classification: LCC GV1311.P5 (ebook) | LCC GV1311.P5 R84 2017 (print)
    DDC 794.7/5—dc23
LC record available at https://lccn.loc.gov/2017012377

Cover design: Jeremy John Parker
Cover photograph: Darron Fick
Typesetting: Nord Compo

Printed in the United States of America
5 4 3 2 1

For my children, Maya and Benjamin,
who will one day love pinball, and for my wife, Marina,
who will then be outnumbered

Contents

Introduction

Ever Since I Was a Young Boy, I Played the Silver Ball

I LOVE PINBALL.

It is a bizarre, intricate game that has no valid reason to exist. Just think of the absurdity of someone inventing this thing from scratch, designing the 3,500 individual pieces that compose today's games, meticulously assembling and decorating every square inch, programming a complicated set of rules, then putting it in a bar for strangers to slap. Pinball machines almost look like attempts at what's kindly called outsider art, the sort you'd find at a specialized museum next to a placard reading: *This machine, and the adjacent toothpick model of the Burj Khalifa, were built by hand over a span of twenty years by a high-functioning chimpanzee trapped in a municipal steam turbine.*

Once, in graduate school, I mentioned the word "pinball" to a classmate, and she asked, "Pinball? Is that, like, the game with the Ping-Pong ball and paddles?" I explained that, no, the game with the Ping-Pong ball and paddles was called Ping-Pong. I then described pinball in excruciating detail, until I realized that she had stopped listening because she thought I was describing a video game.

In actual pinball, the ball is about the size of an egg yolk but with a nice weight to it—like if you held it in your hand, you'd think momentarily about lobbing it through a windowpane just to hear that satisfying crash. Only you can't hold it in your hand, because it's trapped inside a machine called a "cabinet," which looks like a coffin on legs.

With your right hand, you pull back a rod on a spring (the "plunger"), then release it to smack the little silver sphere onto the playfield, a mostly flat, lacquered expanse as jam-packed with flashing gadgets as sanity and cost constraints will allow.

The object of the game is to keep the ball on the playfield, where it can boing around scoring points—registered on a display board called the "backglass" in the upright "backbox"—as long as possible. The playfield, however, is tilted ever so slightly downward, toward you, so that the ball inevitably succumbs to gravity, rolling down the polished wood surface and into the drain.

Yes, the hole right in front of you—the hole you struggle to keep the ball the hell away from—is called the "drain." When the ball drops in there, it's gone, and some frustrated cursing and machine shoving may occur.

If that was the whole game, I'd never play it. What I've just described is like those little plastic toys with the tiny ball bearings, where you shoot the balls and try to catch them in U-shaped cups with point values attached, the kind that provides literally minutes of entertainment when a child selects one from the treasure chest in the dentist's office. And for years, pinball was just that: plunge and pray. Score points on your ball's brief trip from plunger to drain, then exclaim something 1930s-ish, like "Humdinger!," and head to the Odeon to pay a dime for the double-feature newsreel.

Then, in 1947, a game called *Humpty Dumpty* introduced a bold new concept: button-operated flippers.* (The ads for *Humpty Dumpty*, with its "New Type Skill Flippers," boasted that "The Player will Laugh! The Spectator will Roar! The Operator will be Thrilled!")

Flippers. Two flat, rubber-lined paddles like pinky fingers, just above the drain, and if you press buttons on the side of the cabinet, the flippers flick upward, knocking your ball away from the drain and back toward the enchanting gadgets, where it can continue to accumulate points. With the flippers, you can actually aim the ball, trying to hit a particular target, or send the ball zipping up a plastic ramp. You can call your shot and feel like a little Babe Ruth.

But the gadgets. Oh, the gadgets.

Big, swirly ramps that swoosh the ball satisfyingly around the playfield. Squat, round "pop bumpers" that ping the ball away quickly and unpredictably. "Drop targets," which are exactly what they sound like (targets that drop when hit with the ball). "VUKs," or "vertical up-kickers"—shoot the ball in a shallow hole, and the VUK will K the ball V-ly U into another gadget. "Rollovers," buttons that activate when rolled over. Even extra flippers, positioned high up the playfield for hitting distant targets or side ramps. Holes that swallow the ball and suddenly send it out elsewhere, like when Pac-Man munches off the left side of the screen and magically appears at the right—only this, and all of this, is happening with an actual, physical ball. And not only do you get to watch it all happen, you get to control it, to

---

* *Humpty Dumpty* had a fairy tale theme, though the relevance of the six bikini-clad maidens depicted on the backglass throwing ribbons at Humpty is debatable. All pinball machines have themes, from box office tie-ins (*Maverick the Movie*, 1994; *The Lord of the Rings*, 2003; *James Cameron's Avatar*, 2010) to general historical time periods and activities (*Joker Poker*, 1978; *Volcano*, 1981; *Medieval Madness*, 1997) to popular bands (*Kiss*, 1979 and 2015; *Guns N' Roses*, 1994; *AC/DC*, 2012) to sports (*Surf Champ*, 1976; *World Cup Soccer*, 1994; *Big Hurt*, 1995) to television shows (*Doctor Who*, 1992; *Twilight Zone*, 1993; *The Simpsons Pinball Party*, 2003) to the vague and inscrutable (*Hooey-Ball*, 1932; *Daffie*, 1968; *Dipsy Doodle*, 1970).

conduct the mechanical symphony of this idealized world, to direct a hundred tiny mechanisms to function in harmony. It's like a Rube Goldberg machine in real time, a universe of physics and fast choices and skill and luck and angles and sounds and flashing lights and steel and plastic and varnished wood and complicated rules and rewards and consequences and heartbreaking drains and magnificent saves and brilliance and glory.

I love pinball.

My first exposure to pinball came during childhood, when it was just one component of the greatest time and place the universe had to offer: summer nights at Funland amusement park in Rehoboth Beach, Delaware.

Like many visitors "down shore," my family spent fifty-one weeks a year in northern Delaware and one glorious week in southern Delaware, at the beach. Delaware boasts a handful of beach towns, of which Rehoboth is the largest. My family would rent a little house in one of the smaller towns—Lewes or Bethany—and spend a week in a kids' paradise.

During the day, we'd play in the ocean or on the sand, eating a lunch of local sweet corn and canned tuna on the porch. At night, we'd drive to Rehoboth, where we could hear the screams from the Ferris wheel and paraglider the moment we opened our car doors. My dad would feed the parking meter quarters we'd brought in black plastic film canisters, grumbling about how a quarter used to buy you half an hour, and now it was twenty minutes.

"This gives us until 9:40," he'd say, and my sister Rachel and I would beg for just one more quarter, a little more bought time, twenty more of the most treasured minutes we knew.

Funland was—and still is, I'm happy to report—a wonderful little family-owned amusement park on the Rehoboth boardwalk. There were rides. There were win-a-stuffed-animal games, but not the impossible kind ("Throw a basketball through a hoop slightly smaller than a basketball!"). And always—sitting in the same spot between the shooting gallery and the carousel, just beside the toddler boats and with a clear view of Super Goblet Toss—there was pinball.

At the end of the night, arms full of new stuffed animals that needed names, we'd amble down the boardwalk, the Atlantic crashing softly on one side and the bright saltwater taffy shops on the other, buy frozen custard, and count the hours—or if it was the week's final trip to Funland, the months—until we could return.

My wife, Marina, says I overromanticize Rehoboth, that it's really just another hot and crowded beach town with cheap pizza and henna tattoos. Maybe that's true. But whatever neural processes lock a place and time into one's memory as heaven on earth have locked it into mine. Even now, more than thirty-five years since our initial visit to the shore, my family has returned every summer, spouses and grandkids and all. Rachel's then boyfriend, now her husband, proposed to her during one of these trips. One of my happiest moments was watching my daughter, Maya, ride the toddler boats in 2013, just like I did in 1981—possibly even without the boats having been repainted in the interim.

For years, pinball embodied everything I loved about the beach, but it remained strictly a beach activity. I didn't hang out in arcades, and even when a restaurant or bowling alley had a pinball machine, it held no special sway beyond "I know what that is."

Then, during college, I dated a woman who loved pinball. When we were camp counselors together, we'd play whenever possible, usually on the 1992 *Fish Tales* machine in the cafeteria, until a destructive camper leaned a little too hard on the playfield glass, taking *Fish Tales* out of commission for the rest of the summer.

Some aspect of her affinity for pinball must have stayed with me, and the affinity grew into an obsession. If I saw a pinball machine, I had to play it. Leaving it untouched would be like walking past an exquisite sunset, saying, "Meh. There'll be another one tomorrow."

There's just something about pinball. It's not like a video game. Pinball is a kinetic sculpture, like the one in the lobby of the Franklin Institute, Philadelphia's science museum, that I used to stare at endlessly during class field trips. It's a shiny, blinking, flipping, bouncing, shooting, cracking overabundance of stimuli. It is, however, only a game.

Or so I thought. Then I joined a pinball league.

In grad school, I had a friend named Mike. Mike delights in two things above all else: playing tricks on his friends that make them feel worthless and frustrated and buying his friends wonderful, incisive gifts. The gifts don't exist without the tricks; that's part of his charm. Actually, it may be all of his charm.

Mike and I had a ritual of playing *Theatre of Magic* (1995) at a local bar on Tuesday nights. Mike excelled at all sports, from racquetball to martial arts, but pinball was *my thing*. I think that's why he played it with me so often—when he won, on occasion, he'd have the extra gloat power of beating me at something I was good at.

For my twenty-fourth birthday, Mike's gift was simple. He had the foresight to Google two words it somehow had never occurred to me to Google, and those words were "pinball league." Mike paid my forty-dollar entry into the summer 2003 season of the Free State Pinball Association, and for me, the world would never be the same.

People often ask me what a pinball league is. Actually, they ask what the *hell* a pinball league is, and they ask it while chuckling, because everyone's hobby—be it tropical fish care or *sous vide* cooking or old-time bicycle repair—sounds like a hilarious waste of time to everyone else.

A pinball league is a group of people who play a set number of pinball games on preselected machines. Highest scorers are awarded "league points," and after several weekly games (in our case it was ten weeks, four games per week), those with the most league points face off for prizes. My first season, I won third place in the lower division and took home a beautiful piece of cabinet artwork from a soccer-themed European game called *Flipper Football* (1996).

As the years passed, I learned from my competitors. I picked up advanced techniques, like the hold pass (holding the ball with one flipper, then passing it to the other), the bounce pass (letting the ball bounce off a lowered flipper to catch it with the other one), and the chill maneuver (doing nothing but chilling while the ball rockets down the middle, relying on the benevolence of the center peg for rescue). The list of machines whose rules I knew grew, and according to the Professional and Amateur Pinball Association Advanced Rating System (PARS), I rose as high as eightieth in the world.

In the *world*.

I put it on my résumé.

Seriously, I did, at the very bottom, under "Other Interests and Activities." An interviewer even asked about it once. "Oh sure," I said, nonchalantly exhaling onto my fingernails, "I dabble a bit."

I don't play sports. I have a physique like an Ethernet cable. Pass me a basketball, and I feel helpless. Put me on the volleyball court, and I'm counting the seconds until I can rotate off. But give me two quarters and a 1997 *Medieval Madness*, and suddenly the rhythm of the world makes sense.

Which is why I felt the physical symptoms of withdrawal when I stopped playing pinball for four years. I could pretend I dropped out of my league and stopped traveling to competitions because I wanted to retire at the top of my game. I could offer a respectable excuse, like carpal tunnel syndrome. But the real reason I stopped playing is far more common among men who suddenly quit the leisure activities they used to enjoy: I had a baby, and my wife wouldn't let me.

The other pinball players understood. They even threw me a surprise baby shower, including an awesome pinball machine–shaped cake. When the spring 2011 league ended, for the first time in eight years, I didn't submit my name for the summer season.

Don't get me wrong. I love my family, and I'd stop playing pinball forever if that would somehow avert some disaster from befalling them. Still, I missed the excitement of competition, the anticipation before releasing the plunger, the thrill of knowing I need to hit the left ramp *and I've just hit the left ramp.*

One day, in the tiny Belgian seaside town of Ostend, Marina and my almost toddler daughter and I randomly passed a glitzy arcade called Pinball Fun.

"I just want to look inside for a second," I told them. There, a trio of pinball machines sneered at me, including one of my favorites, *The Simpsons Pinball Party* (2003).

"Yeah," they seemed to say, "you know you want to play us. Your family can wait fifteen minutes. Your wife might tell you that you didn't fly four thousand miles to play pinball, but you know what? We say you didn't fly four thousand miles to *not* play pinball." I didn't play.

Shortly after my daughter turned three, my son was born. *Now that's it,* I thought. *With two kids, I can scarcely justify a trip to the bathroom, let alone a night at pinball league or a weekend at a tournament. Pinball is history, and I'll just have to take up another hobby, like nothing. Yes, that's what I'll replace pinball with: nothing.*

Then something wonderful happened. For years, I'd dreamed of writing this book, but I kept procrastinating—not for any good reason, but just because writing a book is a lot of work, even when it's about something you love. To help me out, Marina, who is nothing if not a proponent of professional development, offered a deal: "If you write that book you keep talking about," she said, "you can play all the pinball you want."

I should emphasize that she said this out of the blue. Caught me completely off guard. I probably stammered with my tongue on the floor, cartoonlike, wondering what the trick was. Was this one of those things where women want you to resist to show you care?

"But I don't want to play pinball!" she was expecting me to say. "I only love you and the children and laundry!" I then concluded she must be having an affair.

But no. The offer was genuine. In that wonderful way that spouses know exactly what their partners require to succeed, she had intuited my need for external motivation to write a book. I could play pinball, free and clear. And I could start with a triumphant return to the World Pinball Championships.

I knew I wasn't going to take the pinball world by storm, to suddenly kick ass and clean house and dominate the competition, screaming to the heavens while gripping the first-place trophy with my bleeding flipper fingers. That wasn't the point. The point of my project was to see if it could be done *someday*. If I, an ordinary person with a modicum of experience, stood any chance of becoming a world pinball champion.

The World Pinball Championships, run by the Professional and Amateur Pinball Association (PAPA), are held outside Pittsburgh every year in a warehouse arcade of over five hundred pinball machines. Over the course of the next year, I would travel from my home in Washington, DC, to compete in the World Pinball Championships three times—PAPA17, PAPA18, and PAPA19.

Between the World Pinball Championships, I would rejoin my pinball league for a season, not only to see if I'd lost my touch, but also to see how pinball had changed. The country is currently enjoying a pinball renaissance; not only is the game's popularity back on the rise after a multidecade drop, but the industry itself—which nearly disappeared off the face of the earth on four different occasions—is reinventing itself in risky, interesting ways.

I would learn the fascinating history of the game, which began in a much simpler form, then so irked the establishment that New York City mayor Fiorello La Guardia publicly smashed pinball machines with a sledgehammer and dumped them in the Hudson River. I would meet Roger Sharpe, the man who helped relegalize the game and whose sons currently oversee the more than forty thousand players in the International Flipper Pinball Association (IFPA).

I would visit pinball arcades and barcades, pinball museums, and the factories where pinball machines are still built. I would talk to the people keeping the sport alive, including competitive pinball champions, game designers who sweat for months over the exact placement of a ramp, and the CEOs of pinball manufacturing companies, from the largest and oldest to the upstart start-ups trying, and sometimes failing, to make and sell new pinball machines from their garages. I would fly to Chicago for Pinball Expo, where vendors show off their newest innovations and fans get to find out what future, if any, pinball can look forward to.

And maybe, just maybe, throughout all of this, I'd stay married.

1

Admirable Occupations for Reasonable Creatures

———

IN A WAY, the existence of modern pinball mirrors the arguments in favor of creationism: How could something so complex, with so many independently functional components, have evolved organically? Isn't it easier to believe that pinball arrived fully formed, in a Boardwalk arcade on Coney Island, in a cloud of sawdust and pulverized rubber, glowing and electrified and flashing its START button?

The world's most popular sports can generally be reduced to variations on a simple task. Baseball, cricket, tennis, Ping-Pong, badminton, racquetball: use stick or paddle to hit ball into area defended by opponents. Soccer, field hockey, golf, football, rugby, basketball, billiards: move ball into hole or goal. Running, cycling, horse racing, car racing, swimming, skiing, sailing, rowing: go fast. You can picture these sports beginning with two bored cavemen and a rock, or maybe a rock and a branch.

But pinball is a different animal. If soccer is arithmetic, pinball is calculus.

Theoretically, one could say that modern pinball machines evolved from any game in which players competed to move balls to specific places in exchange for points, and the list of games that contributed conceptually to pinball includes antiquated amusements called nine pins, rocks of Sicily, scoring pockets, and trou madame.

Many of these were some variety of miniature wooden table that could be enjoyed inside a reasonably sized room—variations on bowling, billiards, and/or golf, but logistically simpler than any of them. Trou madame, for example, consists of a long, flat ramp leading to a wall of several wooden archways, each with a number painted above the door. Players rolled a wooden puck on its edge down the ramp and could earn points based on the doorway through which it passed. Also, "trou madame" roughly translates as "pit woman." If you ever travel to France, call someone "trou madame" and see what happens. I'm curious.

Since the sixteenth century, lawn games such as croquet and bocce had been widely enjoyed; billiards and its variants represented attempts to bring the experience indoors. But somehow, over the course of two hundred years, shooting balls into pockets soon grew tiresome. So clever game builders kept things lively by adding obstacles between the ball and its destination—scoring pockets, for example, was a 1710 billiards variant with pins sticking out of the table in front of the pockets. But it was a French adaptation that removed the ball's path a bit farther from the hole, a tilted table on which players used a cue to hit an ivory billiard ball, not at some kind of scoring pockets, but up a clear lane on the right-hand side, after which the ball would circle its way around into numbered holes.

If there's any step in pinball's evolution that the origin stories have in common, it's this one: the game of bagatelle.* Some trace bagatelle's origins to ancient Greece, noting that the game was abandoned

---

* If you're into semiantiquated idioms, you may have heard the word "bagatelle" not as a game of balls and scoring holes but as an example of something trifling: "a mere bagatelle," as in, "In Marina's opinion, my need to play pinball is a mere bagatelle."

during the Dark Ages (wasn't everything?) and repopularized in the eighteenth century. Most pinball historians—yes, that's a thing—prefer to say that the story really begins when bagatelle became popular in the court of King Louis XVI. That's when it earned its name, a moniker honoring the king's younger brother, the gambling-loving Comte d'Artois, whose new Château Bagatelle—essentially an adult playground—included a *salon de jeu*, or game room.

It seems that one evening in 1777 there was a fete honoring the king and queen, and the beau monde enjoyed its first exposure to the bagatelle table. Apparently seeing something at a party in the eighteenth century was enough to kick-start its popularity, because soon afterward the game swept through France, most likely crossing the ocean into the only very recently united States sometime during the American Revolution.

Over the next century, bagatelle spread and changed.* A small tabletop version was created for kids (aww), and shooting either a full-size billiard ball or a tiny marble up onto a pockmarked, angled table gave children and adults alike a small to moderate amount of fun.

It's hard, in an age when our greatest dread is boredom, to comprehend just how insignificant and foreign the concept of pleasant relaxation was in the eighteenth and nineteenth centuries. The Comte d'Artois could certainly slot bagatelle into his idle hours, but for everyday folks, who the hell had time for games? Maybe that's why, when the middle class began to emerge, its description of enjoyable pursuits took on an air of self-congratulation.

For example, as reprinted in a 1992 *New York Times* article tracing the history of my dad's favorite card game, an English doctor named James Paget, most famous for discovering an eponymous bone disease, wrote a letter to his fiancée in 1843 in which he described how he

---

* According to the documentary *Pleasure Machines*, the British version of bagatelle was called "cockamaroo." The British have an endless capacity for converting lyrical French words into their looniest-sounding cognates.

and his companions "improved our minds in the intellectual games of bagatelle and bridge for about two hours—admirable occupations for reasonable creatures."

Reasonable creatures enjoyed their admirable occupations for decades, and bagatelle was in fact so well known that it became the central metaphor of an 1864 political cartoon, a sketch famous among pinball historians and now somewhat impenetrable for the rest of us. The drawing shows Abraham Lincoln, cue stick labeled "BALTIMORE" in hand, bent over a bagatelle table stamped "THE UNION BOARD." It's one of those intricate old comics intended to convey, without subtlety, the specific political positions of about half a dozen different bearded men, each speaking nearly a full paragraph in speech bubbles that pour out of their closed mouths like gravity-immune puddles of drool.

"O see here. We cant stand this!" cries a long-coated man with tiny feet who is apparently Lincoln's running mate in the upcoming election, Senator "Gentleman George" Pendleton. "Old Abe's getting in all the pots on the board, this game will have to be played over again or there'll be a fight, THAT'S CERTAIN."

"This cue 'is too heavy and the' platform's 'shakey!! O! O! I want to go back in the yard!" says General George McClellan, dressed in children's clothing and looking a bit like a disgruntled Ron Swanson from *Parks and Recreation* as he tumbles from a box marked "Chicago Platform." As though the scene was not crowded enough, two rats run under the bagatelle table, while a black dog and a cat with the words "MISS CEGE-NATION" printed on its fur are tied to both a tea kettle and each other.

Complicated times, those.

Then, in 1871, something happened that made pinball pinball. A British inventor named Montague Redgrave, having relocated to Cincinnati two years previous to build bagatelle tables,* devised and

---

* One of his bagatelle machines was actually titled *Is Marriage a Failure?* I guess some themes are timeless.

patented a series of improvements to his bagatelles. In his patent, he called the invention—wait for it—*Improvements in Bagatelles.*

The game from Redgrave's original patent model, which I've seen on display at the Smithsonian's National Museum of American History, looks wholly unremarkable by today's standards. I've played pinball for days straight and wanted to play more, but I'd probably tire of Redgrave's game in ten minutes. Then again, I'm not a child of 1871 whose most fun toys are a battledore and shuttlecock.*

Redgrave's patent, number 115,357, from the quaint old days when patent numbers had just tipped over into six digits, begins with great triumph and fanfare: "Be it known that I, MONTAGUE REDGRAVE, of Cincinnati, in the county of Hamilton and State of Ohio, have invented a new and Improved Parlor Bagatelle." Sometimes I wish we could return to those halcyon days when one could begin a sentence with "Be it known."

Be it known that numbered holes dot Redgrave's playfield, and balls launched in pretty much the modern manner—via a spring-loaded plunger on the far right side of the game—roll downward toward the player, possibly settling in a numbered cup to earn points or else falling all the way to the bottom. The most valuable cups are surrounded by circles of pins and can only be entered via tunnels like miniature croquet hoops. Some will even strike, and ring, dome-shaped metal please-ring-for-service bells.

The patentable part of Redgrave's invention, says his patent, "consists in combining gravity with muscular power to act as antagonistical forces, the one tending to carry the ball in one direction and the other in an opposite direction; the one impelling it against the action of the other until the muscular power is spent, when gravity takes it in hand and moves it until arrested." Redgrave claimed

---

* According to the Internet, these are racquetball implements that existed in the 1870s. Either that or they're lesser-known houses of Hogwarts.

four distinct improvements over traditional bagatelle: the increased incline of the board, curved walls at the base of the holes, gates above the holes, and finally the metal spring itself—the ability to wrap a steel wire into a spring was at the time a new concept. Of that last element, the spring, Redgrave declared rather floridly that "with it all the mathematical science may be possessed without the firmness of nerve necessary to execute and without the ability to impart that exactitude of force which is the foundation of success in this game." In other words, someone who couldn't launch a ball skillfully using a cue might be able to do so with a spring. Either that or he had solved the mystery of dark matter—with Redgrave's prose, it's hard to tell.*

"It made gravity the enemy," pinball historian David Marston says of Redgrave's invention. Redgrave's seemingly simple idea to slope the machine, and give the player a means besides a cue stick of propelling the ball onto the playfield, introduced qualities that have remained central to pinball to this day.

In 1880, Sicking Manufacturing, also of Cincinnati, introduced a tabletop bagatelle game called *Log Cabin*—the first bagatelle game to be coin operated. With the ability to collect money, games could now move from the parlor to the pub, providing a specific motivation for business owners to purchase them. Much more than modern pinball tables, the game bore its most striking resemblance to the *Price Is Right* game Plinko, in which the player drops an object through a field of pins and, fingers crossed, sees where it lands. Looking at older games, it's easy to see where the name "pinball" came from—the pins are actually *pins*, the thin kind used for sewing, pushed into the playfield to redirect the ball.

---

* Searching patents is really fun. Since 1976, there have been no fewer than 230 US patents issued with the word "pinball" in the title, including #4,243,222 ("Seesaw Targets Apparatus for Pinball Game"), #5,938,195 ("Serpentine Ramp for a Pinball Game"), and one I haven't quite figured out—#4,382,597 ("Pinball Game Employing Liquid").

Pinball persisted—at least in some form that involved pins, balls, and a plunger to launch them—alongside other coin-operated amusements like fortune-tellers and love testers for the next forty years, but no one seemed to care much. In 1929, an advertising rep named John Sloan decided to go all retro and begin, once more, to mass-produce bagatelles. For whatever reason, the nation may not have been ready to welcome back the tabletop bagatelle craze, but it was *almost* ready.

Sloan's own business failed, but other would-be manufacturers soon took the reins, including a young Chicagoan named Harry Williams. Williams invested in several successful games, and as his coin-op empire grew, he began experimenting with new machine designs, starting with a game called *Advance* (1933).

One day, Williams watched a man in a drugstore play *Advance* and earn himself a nice high score—not by playing well but by smacking the game's underside to nudge balls where he wanted them to go. Williams's innovative response must have been born of anger: he took the game back and hammered in a field of nails whose sharp tips protruded through the bottom of the machine, not just deterring cheating but also administering instant stigmata.

Williams knew, however, that in order to prevent players from cheating without actually piercing their flesh, he'd need a new device. So he invented what he called a "stool pigeon"—presumably so named because it ratted out the offending player—that sat in a nonplayable corner of the game. The stool pigeon consisted of a small ball resting atop a post, like a marble on a golf tee. Shaking the game too roughly dislodged the ball, which would land on a metal ring, complete an electrical connection, and end the player's game.

Back in the drugstore, Williams watched the cheating patron lose when the ball fell off the tee, and according to Roger Sharpe's 1977 book *Pinball!*, he said, "Oh, look, I hit it and it TILTED.'" Thus the stool pigeon earned a new name: the tilt mechanism.

For the most part, the stool pigeon is no longer in use today, but its immediate descendent—which Williams introduced in 1935—still is, amazingly. The "tilt bob," also called a "plumb bob" or "pendulum tilt," worked so well that it's remained virtually unchanged.

The tilt bob is a short metal rod with a weight at the end, dangling unseen inside the pinball cabinet, right through the center of a wide metal ring. When a player shakes the game too violently, the pendulum sways and contacts the ring, completing a circuit that either issues a warning or shuts the game off immediately, depending on the machine. Modern games tend to wait until the third infraction to kill power to the flippers and drain the ball.

The brilliant quality of the tilt bob is that it does allow *some* shaking before it completes the circuit, and that little bit of shaking reinforces the difference between skill and luck in pinball. The top players in the world, then, have three specific skills: knowledge of rule sets, ability to aim shots with the flippers, and ability to shake the machine just enough to save the ball but not enough to tilt. With the tilt mechanism in place, shaking, nudging, or bumping the machine is officially not cheating, since shaking too aggressively results in a penalty.* Basically, it's allowed if the machine says it's allowed. Still, you don't want to go completely nuts, especially if you're playing a public machine and the game's owner is watching. Acceptable gameplay is one thing, but you can understand why some operators might get nervous if you, pardon the expression, shake their moneymaker.

In the early '30s, people were going great guns for any mechanical amusement, and the proof is in a very popular 1930 device called

---

* If you ever happen across a pinball machine with a broken tilt bob, you can play for a long, long time, especially if that machine is on a slick, flat, uncarpeted surface. Without the possibility of tilting, you can swing the game several feet in any direction to save your ball. I once found a *Sopranos* (2005) machine with a nonfunctional tilt bob inside a mall arcade in Scranton, Pennsylvania. I played one game for over an hour, much to the delight of the local junior high school boys who gathered to watch, squealing about how mad someone named Earl would be that I had displaced his high score. Sorry, Earl.

Little Whirlwind, in which players rocketed balls up into a metal spiral to earn points based on where the balls landed. The game weighed only eleven pounds and took up a mere nine inches of space front to back—about the size of a large dictionary standing up—making it a simple addition for bars and display counters. *Little Whirlwind* wasn't exactly a pinball game, but it showed bar owners that, for a reasonable price, they could add a mechanical diversion that would entertain patrons without any significant investment of effort or real estate on their part.

Pinball during the Great Depression owes its surprising success to the American economy's surprising failure. The masses craved affordable entertainment, and lo and behold, here were these festively painted, polished, electrically juiced pinball machines that could be played for small coins. It's the same reason McDonald's thrived during the most recent economic recession: people may stop splurging on big luxuries, but surely they can treat themselves to a Big Mac. Surely they can drop a few pennies in the bagatelle.

The four faces on pinball's Mount Rushmore, if there were one, would have to include both Redgrave and Williams. In the more modern-era Teddy Roosevelt slot, many would argue for the inclusion of Roger Sharpe, the man who would save pinball in 1976. The fourth position—either Lincoln or Jefferson, since Redgrave is Washington—has to go to Milwaukee-born David Gottlieb.

In 1931, his manufacturing business D. Gottlieb and Company introduced *Baffle Ball*, the first mass-produced and mass-marketed pinball machine.* For a penny, players had seven chances to shoot marbles onto a playfield painted like a baseball diamond, earning points based on where the balls landed. A March 1932 ad in Billboard, the

---

* As Jay Stafford, senior editor of the comprehensive Internet Pinball Database (IPDB) reminds me, we all laud *Baffle Ball* as the first pinball machine, but *Baffle Ball* was preceded by a few "bat games," wooden toys in which players swung a tiny baseball bat at balls launched onto a playfield.

coin-operated machine industry's trade magazine, boasts that the game "Pays for Itself FIRST WEEK," although according to *Pleasure Machines*, it would often pay for itself in a weekend. In less than six months, Gottlieb sold more than fifty thousand machines. To put this figure in context, in the early 1990s, a game's success would be considered legendary if it sold over ten thousand units over its entire manufacturing run. Today a game selling more than five thousand units is a blockbuster.

For a public intent on distracting itself from the Great Depression, *Baffle Ball* wasn't enough. Gottlieb was churning out four hundred machines a day, but demand exceeded supply—a fact not lost on one of Gottlieb's marketers, Ray Moloney, who probably deserves the fourth spot on Mount Rushmore if Sharpe doesn't want it.

At the beginning of 1932, Moloney founded Bally Manufacturing with a simple mission: do what Gottlieb was doing.

And indeed he did. His first game, *Ballyhoo*, helped by its bright patchwork paint job and its catchy slogan ("What'll we play in '32? *Ball-y-hoo!*") sold over fifty thousand units in seven months.

In that early era, pinball owed its success to one indisputable consequence of the Great Depression: a lot of men with a lot of free time. "Sitting in a bar," writes Paul Verlag in the 1992 book *Pinball** "making a beer last a whole afternoon and playing this new game were a great way of whiling away the time at no great expense."

Since imitation is the sincerest form of American entrepreneurship, what happened after '32 (*Ball-y-hoo!*) shouldn't be surprising. Dozens of other tycoons-to-be started manufacturing their own "pin games," the collective name given to bagatelle and pinball, hoping to catch a piece of the craze—and at one point there were more than 145 independent manufacturers. It's a ubiquity unthinkable today, when the number of pinball makers between 2000 and 2016 can be counted on one hand.

---

* Not to be confused with Roger Sharpe's book, whose title includes an exclamation point.

Yet for all of their variety, mechanical pin games didn't change a whole lot in the early '30s. Sure, some had clever gadgets and gimmicks, but for the most part they were all variations on plunger, holes, and pins. Even flippers were a decade and a half in the future, and players had to keep their own score—a process I found perplexing when I played a vintage *Jig-Saw* (1933) pinball machine for a penny at a Pittsburgh-area museum called Pinball Perfection. (Unhelpfully, *Jig-Saw*'s marquee cards displayed a complicated scoring rubric that includes instructions like "INCOMPLETED JIGSAW w/o DOUBLE SCORE with two blocks open . . . . 5 pts." How patrons tallied their own scores a few beers into the afternoon, I'll never know.)

Amid the tiny mechanical arms race, the man to credit with moving pinball to its next plateau was none other than Harry Williams again. Pin games at the time had no lights, no sounds, and no autonomous moving parts. Why not, Williams wondered, add electricity?

He started simple. Williams attached a solenoid to a 1933 game called *Contact*. A solenoid is a metal rod with a wire coiled around it; when electricity runs through the wire, the rod punches out the end of the coil.

In *Contact*, if a ball fell into a hole, it stayed there until a second ball could be shot into another hole, completing a circuit that ejected the first ball. "This spelled the end for the gravity-controlled machines," says the narrator of the documentary *Pleasure Machines*, observing that pinballs could now travel *up* as well as down a playfield—at least a little bit.

Like most "first of its kind" stories, this one may be somewhat apocryphal. Harry Williams invented the first pin game to use electricity in the same way that Alexander Graham Bell invented the telephone: the credit and the glory, along with the patent, may belong to Bell, but to this day many argue that Italian inventor Antonio Meucci's *telettrofono* scooped Bell by more than a decade and a half.

Similarly, some older bagatelle machines did use electricity, but Williams's *Contact* popularized the possibility for pinball.

The door was now open for electrical gimmicks. Williams rigged up a ringing bell—initially, he later told Sharpe, to prank his business partner Fred McClellan, who would leave the game to go answer the phone every time it rang. The bell was deemed a keeper, as were a handful of other gizmos. That electricity came from batteries until 1935, when games were developed that could be plugged into wall sockets.*

Bumpers,† those squat knobs that rocket the ball around, would come in 1937, thanks to a Bally employee named Nick Nelson. Some early, nonelectrified versions were fairly gentle but still gave the ball's trajectory a nice jolt of unpredictability. Illuminated scoreboards would follow in 1938, and the gimmicks became as bright as pinball's future as a source of amusement.

So let's see. With electricity, pin games could now make sounds, light up, and shoot balls in various directions. What else could they do that players might appreciate?

Hey, dispense money.

What could go wrong?

---

* Today's pinball machines include both power cables and batteries, with the latter acting as a backup in the event of an electrical outage—that way the high scores aren't sacrificed every time the game is unplugged. The battery-enabled retention of the high score made possible a 1998 episode of *Seinfeld*, in which George Costanza tries to move an unplugged *Frogger* arcade game before the batteries drain and his high score disappears.

† Throughout their history, and depending on the manufacturer, pop bumpers have also been called "jet bumpers," "percussion bumpers," "power bumpers," "cyclonic bumpers," "kicking bumpers," and "thumper bumpers." I suppose that's what happens when people try to think of a name for something novel and strange with no apparent use outside of the niche for which it was invented. And prewar Germans called them, for some very prewar German reason, "bombers."

2

A Vicious Form of Amusement

———

I DON'T WANT TO DRAW UNFAIR CONCLUSIONS, but based on everything I've read, at least as far as pinball is concerned, Fiorello La Guardia was kind of a douche. I say that not only as a pinball fan who cringes at press photos of a New York mayor smashing pinball machines with a sledgehammer but also as a concerned citizen who feels that unease is not an overreaction any time a politician publicly smashes things he dislikes with a sledgehammer.

A complicated figure with an occasional penchant for authoritarianism, New York's ninety-ninth mayor helped the city recover from the Great Depression, but he also imposed his own fundamentalist sensibilities on industries that offended him. Pinball offended him.

La Guardia's anti-pinball crusade was, at least nominally, part of his pre–World War II crackdown on organized crime, but he had no compunction about expanding that crackdown to suppress any activity he deemed evil: pinball, roulette wheels, jukeboxes, pool tables, burlesque houses, and—see if you can guess—artichokes. (La Guardia's artichoke embargo had more to do with accusations of Mob-driven price-fixing than with any animosity toward artichokes in particular, but I'll grant him that if there is such a thing as an evil vegetable, it's an artichoke. I can't eat you unless I steam you? Get over yourself.) The Mob had a stranglehold on his city, controlling more than a lot of people were comfortable with, and La Guardia was determined to save New York's soul. But . . . pinball?

Before 1934, the New York City Police Department had a huge job on its hands: slot machines were proliferating throughout the city, and unless officers could absolutely prove that they were being used for gambling—a more difficult task than it sounds—they could do nothing. Meanwhile, according to police commissioner Lewis J. Valentine, the slots bred worse vices, and the primary obstacle to eliminating them was political will. In the first couple of months of 1934, La Guardia mustered that political will, and about two thousand slot machines were seized, half owned by Mob boss Frank Costello, effectively wiping the city clean of the offending one-armed bandits. Pin games rushed in to fill the void, flourishing in all of the corners previously occupied by slots.

"Let's drive the bums out of town," La Guardia famously declared in a radio address, broadly—and problematically—implicating non-specific bums.

Mob connections aside, to the casual observer, it's easy to assume pinball was banned simply because it was a game—a frivolous amusement, a time and money waster for a serious generation that could spare neither. But the reality was a lot messier.

Pinball manufacturers had begun blurring the line between pinball machines and gambling devices. For example, even though games like *Contact* easily took in pennies and nickels in exchange for a fun few minutes, their true competition for patrons' coins—slot machines—offered automatic payouts for lucky pulls. So Bally debuted *Rocket* (1933), a handsome, art deco pinball table that paid players for high scores, making it essentially a slot machine plus physics. The advertising flyer boasted that it could "OPERATE IN 'OPEN' OR 'CLOSED' TERRITORY," meaning that the payout door was lockable, converting it back when necessary to what they called a "novelty" game, one played purely for enjoyment.

It didn't help that many of the machines set to give cash payouts were the type known as "one-balls," games that consisted of launching a single ball, seeing what happened, then either collecting or not collecting coins. What's the difference, really, between pulling a slot machine lever and watching reels randomly spin and pulling a pinball machine plunger and watching a ball randomly drift into one hole or another?

Indeed, one difference, pointed out by "dad, programmer, amateur astronomer, [and] geek" Jim West on his WestWorld Pinball web page, was that players may have perceived the physics of a pinball machine as a much *fairer* way of assigning a payout than the slots—which many people thought were rigged.

The pinball boom scared La Guardia, who watched the public's growing addiction to pin games with concern. Store owners, he learned, were lowering the price of pinball from a nickel to a penny during school hours, presumably in order to attract students on their lunch breaks—and, as some claimed, to encourage truancy.

To those who opposed pinball, the assertion that skill played a role in the game must have sounded ridiculously unlikely. "The final results obtainable from these games depend entirely upon the force of gravity, over which the operator has no absolute control," wrote assistant engineer of the New York City Police Department John T. Gibala. "The operator of the machine can and does have limited control over the decelerated velocity with which the ball ascends up the inclined plane through the runway, but all further control and guidance of the ball on its journey towards the completion of its cycle is automatically removed from him the moment the ball passes through the one-way exit gate at the upper end of the runway." In other words, after the initial spring-loaded release of the ball, since flippers still hadn't been invented, pinball was essentially a dice roll.

On July 4, 1935, the *New York Times* reported on a high-court decision regarding "the legality of the game of bagatelle, or the pin game." The court case arose when city commissioner of licenses Paul Moss refused to issue a license for "a Brooklyn amusement place." The dispute, as it remained until a dramatic event in 1976, was over whether the pin game was a pin game of skill or a pin game of chance.

The *Times* subheadlines are unambiguous, declaring in all caps "SKILL RULED NO FACTOR" and quoting the judge's decision that the "device relies on 'Innate Gambling Spirit.'"

To be fair, the machines in question made only a token effort (literally) to distinguish themselves from gambling devices, dispensing tokens rather than actual money—tokens that, Moss argued, a proprietor could arrange to exchange for prizes or cash. Still, it's quite a gray area. If you find yourself agreeing that a machine giving out jackpots of tokens is essentially gambling, you should probably ask whether the awarding of prize tickets at Chuck E. Cheese's or Dave and Buster's is truly any different.*

Using pinball as a gambling device was kind of like downloading MP3 files on Napster in that it was a vice so universally practiced at the time that no one gave a second thought to its legality—until the authorities started issuing fines to random users and shut it down.

---

* In September 2015, *Wired* profiled Jon Hauser, one of the "Ticket Kings" who can earn up to $50 an hour by playing redemption machines at Dave and Buster's, earning tickets toward prizes like iPads, then selling the prizes on eBay. The only true difference, then, between the estimated fifteen hundred "advantage players" who make their living this way and professional gamblers is the fact that Hauser and his colleagues have two additional hurdles: exchanging tickets for prizes and then exchanging prizes for cash. The lesson here, as with fantasy football and online poker, is that outlawing gambling adds steps to make it more inconvenient but doesn't really stop gambling.

The unlucky individuals in the crosshairs were nineteen-year-old Sidney Turner and thirty-eight-year-old Sadie Billet, both of whom violated their city-issued pinball licenses by offering payouts to lucky patrons. As with any legal decision, the conviction of Turner and Billet—each of whom had to pay a fine of fifty dollars or earn its equivalent in what the *New York Times* called a "ten-day work house"—did more than punish the defendants. It provided the legal precedent that would send pinball into back rooms for the next four decades.

"The licenses issued by the city for these machines stipulate they are to be used merely for purposes of amusement," said assistant district attorney Maurice Spalter. "This clear-cut conviction should mean that all similar places in this city ought to be closed up by the police."

Jacob Mirowsky, the proprietor of a stationery and candy store in the Bronx, found himself in court in 1935, accused of running an illegal gambling room. Mirowsky's defense included a logical but risky proposition: bring in three skilled bagatelle players, and if they consistently score higher than an amateur, bagatelle must be a game of skill. If not, it's a game of luck and therefore a gambling device.

Think about that. Think about how confident Mirowsky must have felt that his experts would play the chancy bagatelle machines well enough to outscore a beginner. Think of the pressure on the three players, and imagine if a similar challenge had been issued to, say, golf. "Tiger Woods," a judge would say, "if you can sink this next putt, golf must be a game of skill. If you miss, well, clearly it's a game of luck." If it was really Tiger Woods on the green, he might well have sunk the putt—but he could just as easily have choked.

That, unfortunately for the pin game, is exactly what happened. "The youths, known to their friends as successful shooters of the little balls in the pin game, had been called by the defense in an effort to show that bagatelle is a game of skill," reported the *New York Times*. "For a long time the little balls rattled around and fell into the holes on the board, and bells rang as lucky shots were made. But it all came to nothing. None of the youths made a score better than 11,500, the lowest winning figure, and they could not place the balls where the justices told them to, as a test of their control." To add insult to injury, a detective with no apparent bagatelle skill stepped up to play, and he scored about the same as the so-called experts.

This outcome could not have been too surprising. According to the Brooklyn Public Library's blog, in a post beautifully titled "Pinball Gets Blackballed," a New York University professor in 1936 sought to test the skill question with brute-force academic rigor. His students tallied their scores during a whopping 67,800 unskilled plays on pinball machines, sometimes playing blindly, with the machines obscured, plus another 30,000 games played by department assistants assigned to develop their skills. The skilled players did demonstrate an improved chance at winning—but only between 2 percent and 9 percent of the time.

Certainly assistant engineer Gibala hadn't seen any evidence of skill influencing pinball. He wrote, "My reasons for believing that the pin game referred to is one in which chance predominates or in which the outcome is unpredictable by even the most skillful in the art—phantomly so—is because no one skilled has yet been produced, viz., one who can consistently obtain, let us say, the same most profitable combination in 4 out of 5 plays, like a gunner hitting a bullseye or a bowler getting a strike or even a golfer consistently scoring below or even par."

Even in modern times, with flippers and other skill-related additions to the game, pinball would not necessarily stand up to such a challenge. If you put a champion-level player in front of a pinball machine, he or she would probably trounce an opponent who knew little about pinball—or maybe not. Even the experts ultimately end up losing every ball, and sometimes they lose that ball early.

I'm reminded of a moment during my bachelor party, most of which I spent playing pinball with a few friends. (I'm serious about that. Pinball, bowling, and steak. The only scantily clad women were the ones on the pinball backglasses.) My friend Mike, who had paid my way into pinball league a few years before, suddenly declared that the next game of *Funhouse* (1990) would be for bragging rights. I'd been a league player for years at that point, exercising my flipper fingers for hours a week, and Mike was basically an amateur—yet he beat me by a significant margin. Mike was insufferable for the rest of the weekend.

For his part, La Guardia relished the appellate court's verdict, classifying bagatelle and pinball as the "big brothers of the slot machine" and calling the decision "highly gratifying to me." Practically overnight, pinball became verboten. Possession of even one illegal machine at an establishment was an egregious enough violation for Commissioner Moss to refuse licenses for its neighboring legal machines. That policy took effect when Moss announced that on January 13, 1936, he was suspending licenses for what might today be considered arcades, including places with names like Sportsland and Playland, where pin games were just one of many attractions. The *Times* even reported that, in addition to the ignominy of being shut down, arcade owners had to deal with a sudden rush of thousands of winners who had been saving their coupons for "silk stockings, cigarettes, and other merchandise [who] have been besieging the establishments demanding that their coupons be liquidated." It wasn't quite Chuck E. Cheese's— I don't know many kids who express interest in exchanging their Skee-Ball tickets for silk stockings—but it wasn't exactly high-stakes baccarat, either.

The Times Amusement Corporation, which owned arcades from Faber's Sportland on Broadway to the Gramad Amusement Corporation in Brooklyn, fought back, appealing the New York State Supreme Court's decision and taking Moss to court for revoking their license. The commissioner's office, which had issued licenses on a per-machine basis, now found itself having to defend the shuttering of an entire corporation, when they could simply have outlawed certain machines and permitted others. To the beleaguered arcade owners, Moss's actions were blatantly a backdoor means of shutting down any venue, bagatelle based or otherwise, that offered prizes for games of chance.

Moss, who *Time* magazine described in 1937 as "a big, grey-haired Jew . . . as notable for his integrity as for his dapper dress," was a perfect sidekick for La Guardia. In addition to cracking down on pinball, he hit unscrupulous ice sellers, smutty magazines, and burlesque houses with the full weight of the city's licensing office. That may not sound like a lot of weight, but as *Time* noted, "the power to license is the power to reform." Anything Moss didn't like was either denied a license or had its license revoked. On May 1, 1937, he made headlines by opting not to renew the licenses for any of the city's fourteen burlesque houses, immediately putting more than two thousand people out of work in what La Guardia called "the beginning of the end of incorporated filth."

Max Schaffer, president of the Amusement Men's Association, who represented the Times Amusement Corporation, not to mention around fifty Sportland owners, felt blindsided by Moss's confiscation of his businesses' licenses. In his affidavit, he described the suddenness of Moss's actions, especially considering that awarding prizes in arcades had been, until that moment, perfectly legal. "These business enterprises were built up gradually," he wrote, "and so built with the knowledge and encouragement of the Government of the City of New York—particularly the Department of Licenses."

Moss had his counterargument ready: "I have heretofore issued licenses for amusement centers in the belief, induced by the representations of amusement center operators and their attorneys, that the pin ball games submitted to my department for approval are games of skill and did not violate any provisions of the Penal Law because of the award of prizes." In other words, it was those sleazy arcade operators who had bamboozled Moss, and he was shocked—*shocked*—to find that gambling was going on in there.

Bagatelle and pin games weren't the only ones on the chopping block, and when it came to the distinction between illicit gambling and harmless amusement, Moss was a "know it when I see it" kind of guy. "I also warned them," said Moss, "that I would not countenance the use in any amusement center of the so-called 'crane claw and digger machine.'* This machine has never been licensed by my department because I am convinced that it is inherently a gambling device, dishonest and corrupt." Consider that the next time your child maneuvers the joystick to try to grab a stuffed Scooby-Doo.

The game for which Moss was pleased to deny a license in the Times Amusement Corporation case was called *The Sportsman* (1934), an electromechanical hunting-themed game manufactured by O. D. Jennings and Company. For a nickel, players would launch ten balls, one at a time, across a playfield painted with fields and streams, then watch each ball tinkle down through a region of diverters like tiny pins and staples, ultimately landing in one of thirty holes with point values and pictures of birds, rabbits, or squirrels, or else skipping the holes and landing in a large region at the bottom labeled "MISSED."

Interestingly, a *Coin Game Journal* ad for *The Sportsman*, aside from bragging that "the mechanism works a thousand times out of a thousand," strove to be clear about the game's legality: "*The Sportsman* has been pronounced a game of skill by a multitude of legal judges, an attorney general and others with authority to speak. They say there is no difference between a skill table such as *The Sportsman*

---

* Digger machines were similar to claw machines, except instead of trying to win one large item, players controlled a miniature excavator that scooped up a few small items—gum or candy, for example. Or, as Moss no doubt despised, coins. Some gaming establishments, not bold enough to stock the diggers with coins but aware that their clients weren't there for the gum or candy, instead used a standard buyback program. One patron described using a digger machine to win a small clock, which he handed over to a clerk, who "looked at a card and advised me that he would give me 75 cents for the clock."

which pays out rewards automatically, and an ordinary pin table on which rewards are paid over the counter." This was completely true. Thus, Moss decided, if *The Sportsman* was indistinguishable from an "ordinary pin table," one needed simply to outlaw an ordinary pin table. And everything remotely like it.

It's not even clear that the distinction between luck and skill was all that important to Moss. Murray Goldstein, secretary of the Amusement Men's Association, wrote in his affidavit about a conversation he observed in the office of the license commissioner between Moss and the owner of a Sportland location:

Moss: Just a minute, do you award prizes?

Owner: Yes, for skill, according to skill.

Moss: Then your license is revoked.

Here's the loophole that *The Sportsman*, and so many similar games, had been using. Instead of coins, the machine might pay out tokens or nickel-sized slugs, non-legal-tender currency that you could use to play again. Phrased that way, it almost sounds like an innocent work-around to award free games in an era when machines couldn't handle something so complex—instead of displaying "Credits: 1" and flashing the START button to indicate a free game, the machine would simply give the player a few tokens to reinsert.

Or, like tickets at Chuck E. Cheese's, the tokens could be exchanged for prizes.

Or, unlike at Chuck E. Cheese's, the tokens could be exchanged for cash.*

So pinball and its operators couldn't claim full innocence, a fact that did not escape Moss. Sounding like a stereotypical sourpuss, Moss harrumphed, insofar as an affidavit can harrumph, that "Chapter 317

---

* Not for the first or the last time, Europeans in the 1930s simply looked at Americans and shrugged. Some pinball machines there dispensed free game tokens, but the fact that tokens were tokens and money was money appears to have settled the whole business in Europe.

of the Laws of 1934 was passed to protect our citizens against"—and I love this next part—"this vicious form of amusement."

"If it is claimed that this game is a 'game of skill,'" continued Moss, "then why are not all holes marked with birds and tokens and why are not the slugs and tokens returned to the player, no matter what hole the ball finally rests in?" If the point of the game is amusement, he wondered, why does it cost money at all? I'm not positive, but I believe the answer to his question can be found in Economics 101.

In addition to the sin of offering a chance outcome, Police Commissioner Valentine argued, the games were rigged to give the house an advantage (well, duh), rendering them not just a gamble but a rip-off. "Not only is the score made exceptionally high before a prize is awarded," added New York assistant superintendent of schools Anthony Pugliese, "but the presence of the obstructing pins in front of and around the holes makes it expressly unprofitable for the player, with the result that very few prizes are given in proportion to the number of efforts made by the player." That is, the pinball machines were not only games of chance but also games of chance that couldn't reliably be won.

What I find most fascinating about this period of pinball's history, however, is a claim Valentine made in his affidavit that "if the dominating element in a pin game was skill, the amusement centers and other operators of such machines could not survive." That, ladies and gentlemen, is how foreign the concept of "fun" was in the 1930s—there was an undeniable incredulity that anyone would spend their hard-earned nickel to watch balls bounce around. The idea must have sounded like a slot machine in which coins are inserted, a lever is pulled, and reels spin, but no money ultimately comes out. Who are these people who feed coins into the slot to watch pictures of cherries going around—idiots?

The novelty of "leisure" in lean times, when schoolchildren frequently had to work to put food on their families' tables—my own grandfather and his siblings were selling cantaloupes on the streets of Cleveland at the time—must have made pinball instantly suspect. But its Mob connections put the nail in the proverbial cement-lined coffin.

Justice Frederick L. Hackenburg of the Court of Special Sessions, in his conviction of Mirowsky, the stationery and candy store owner in the Bronx, got right to the point—or, rather, got right far beyond the point when discussing the trinkets players could win: "There is a central place for people to go to for prizes. [The Mob] control[s] the entire game in the County through the central place. The next thing, they will be allotting territories, 20 central places. The next thing, when somebody walks across the boundary of the territory, we will find somebody in Bronx Park with five bullets in his head. It is an incipient racket. Before that racket grows I am going to step down on it."

The ban on pinball was also born of a "trouble in River City" attitude, a general disquiet among adults regarding the irascible youth who must be up to no good. But the adults worried La Guardia more; he felt that if a fully grown man was playing a game, there was either something wrong with the man or something unwholesomely addictive about the game.

"It's a perfect target," Roger Sharpe told me, and it's a topic he knows a lot about, since he's the one personally responsible for upending the New York City pinball ban in 1976. "It's just a game. It's not as if there's a person standing by it, taking money. It's just standing there on the corner." He recalled his own mother happily giving him $1.35 every week to pay for his junior bowling league but making him swear he'd never go upstairs in the bowling alley. And what was upstairs? Just people playing pool. Bowling: large ball, wooden lane, knock down pins. Pool: small balls, felt-covered table, get the balls in the holes. Yet the former had the air of purity and innocence, and the latter, seediness.

Assistant engineer Gibala's testimony in the Times Amusement Corporation case exemplifies this paranoia. Gibala described the ball as "tumbling to and fro in a distorted zigzag path through the laby-rinth of passages, much, of course, to the possible amusement of the player, with results in the hands of destiny and not in his," bouncing off pins and gadgets that are "apparently so tranquil and harmless, like a crack regiment on the parade ground" but were clearly "designed and determined by master-minds trained in the science and wiles of subterfuge."

Though they spelled the termination of many livelihoods at the time, the affidavits in the case have unintentional comic value today, as they use the most vaunted of legal language to describe a bunch of people playing pinball. For example, police officer Michael Duff reported that he "returned to the said premises 550 Bergen Avenue at about 8:30 P. M. of said November 19th, 1934, and again played the said 'Drop Kick' machine thirty times and made a total score of 159 points, for which deponent [Officer Duff] received coupons indicating such score. Upon presenting all of the coupons, that is, those received in the afternoon and those received in the evening, deponent received a prize, to wit, a bread box."

An article in *Automatic Age* advertising *Drop Kick* (1934) bills it as "the most thrilling action ever seen in a pin game." Presumably the most thrilling action for D. Lee Plume, whose amusement cen-ter awarded Officer Duff the bread box, came when Duff promptly arrested him for running an illegal gambling establishment.

The Times Amusement Corporation case was one of several, and in just a few years, La Guardia successfully transitioned his position from "refuse licenses for pinball machines" to "ban pinball machines" to "smash pinball machines." On January 21, 1942, when America probably had better things to worry about, he signed an order allowing police officers to greet pinball machines with sledgehammers.

Historical photo archives show men in suits and hats burying implements of destruction inside the offending games, their faces full of self-righteous determination. Games were purged from the city, their remnants hauled off in barges and dumped unceremoniously in the Hudson River.

In one instance, before 3,710 smashed machines were dumped in the Hudson, La Guardia even repurposed more than 2,000 of their wooden legs as—and it's hard to get more blatantly symbolic than this—police billy clubs. By the end of his term as mayor, La Guardia would go on to order the destruction of more than 11,000 pinball machines.

Around the same time, the federal government enacted the Salvage for Victory campaign, a recycling drive that urged all patriotic Americans to contribute scrap metal, wood, and even rags to the war effort. Pinball machines were, of course, made of metal and wood, so the Salvage for Victory campaign forced average Americans to ask themselves, "Do I *really* need this thing more than our soldiers would need its components?" Sorry, troops, no gunboats for you because we need the wood to make distracting time-wasters for kids, but if it's any consolation, we'll give some of the time-wasters wartime themes! In such a context, it's easy to see how pinball machines, otherwise meaningless diversions, could seem downright unpatriotic.

Once something is outlawed, it's hard to reinstate. Pinball remained illegal in New York for more than a generation, and across the continent, similar bans proved difficult to revoke.

In California, Oakland's prohibition on pinball, for example, enacted in the 1930s, wasn't repealed until the summer of—seriously—2014. Before opening in January 2016, the owners of a Montreal bar called North Star Pinball (motto on their website: PLAY PINBALL. DRINK.) had to convince city authorities to ignore still-active anti-pinball statutes. And as I learned from a 2009 *Popular Mechanics* article, in Ocean City, New Jersey, it's still illegal to play pinball on Sundays.*

---

* This last bit of trivia struck me as unlikely, since Ocean City is home to Jilly's Arcade, which has included pinball since 1976. So I contacted journalist and pinball expert Seth Porges, who wrote the *Popular Mechanics* piece, and he happened to be in the middle of

Across the country, the legal community was all over the place with pinball, and a midcentury transcontinental drive would have taken one through jurisdictions of not only varying strictness but also varying friendliness to loopholes. In some places, the spring-loaded plunger was illegal, but the rest of the machine was fine. In others, players were not allowed to win free games, but extra balls were okay. It was kind of like trying to park in a modern-day metropolis, where every block has its own set of parking restrictions—two-hour parking from here to the curb, weekdays from 7:00 AM to midnight, except Zone 12 stickers, but you can park indefinitely on holidays, and you can't park at all during a snow emergency. The variety was hard for players—but harder for manufacturers who had to churn out machines that they could legally sell in all of these places.

Efforts to comply with or sidestep or invent around these rules yielded a few innovations of necessity that remain with pinball to this day. Manufacturer Harry Williams, for example, knew he could reinforce pinball's role as pure amusement simply by removing the payout mechanism—but he knew players preferred a tangible reward they could win. How could Williams's pinball machines offer a legally acceptable prize? What's the unit of currency of fun?

The answer came from a mechanically inclined teenager in Williams's employ named Bill Bellah. He devised a gadget that allowed customers to accumulate free games: landing the ball in a certain saucer would rotate a number wheel, and as long as the number displayed wasn't zero, pushing the empty coin acceptor later started a new game. Today free games are a natural, though rarer, part of the

---

filming a minidocumentary for the *New York Times* investigating that very topic. The result: it turns out the law, which is indeed still on the books, only applies to pinball machines inside businesses that *aren't* arcades—so Jilly's is operating legally, much to the relief of director of operations Jody Levchuk, whom I think I scared with an e-mail asking if he knew whether Jilly's was violating the law.

pinball and video game universe, but they began as a very specific solution to a legislative problem.

One of the first games to use free play was *Quick Silver* (1935), whose ad in *Automatic Age* magazine listed ten reasons for operators to purchase the game, finishing by reminding potential customers that "QUICK SILVER *legally* performs every function of the slot machine and pay-out pin table"—emphasis theirs.

Here's what this meant in reality: the number of earned free games on the scoring wheel could easily be converted, under the table, to a cash reward. So a patron would win, say, twelve free games, but instead of playing them, he'd cash out—the operator would buy the free games from the patron and reset the scoring wheel. There were even machines that could count up to 999 free games awarded, in retrospect an obvious sign that people weren't necessarily *playing* the replays they'd earned. And some machines combined free play and payouts in the same game—no wonder it was difficult to figure out whether anyone was breaking any laws.

If a payout of free games—which was soon viewed as gambling and banned in many locations—was a half-assed version of a cash pay-out, it would not be until 1960 that pinball manufacturer David Gottlieb's son Alvin helped develop a half-assed version of *that*, a reward even more ephemeral and piddling than a free game: an extra ball.

This may sound insignificant. In modern pinball machines, an extra ball is listed alongside other rewards a player can earn, such as a few million points or starting multiball. But Alvin Gottlieb's "add-a-ball," as he called it,* gave the player a reward that no one would mistake for gambling.

---

* The distinction between "extra ball" and "add-a-ball" is purely semantic but vitally important. Bingo machines, which looked somewhat like pinball machines but were unquestionably gambling devices, had been using the term "extra ball" liberally—so the term "add-a-ball" was coined, so to speak, to emphasize the distinction. Pinball historians will refer to a particular location by the type of pinball that was legal there—for example, saying something like, "Wisconsin was an add-a-ball state."

"I wanted to give a little extra play to the game," he told Sharpe in *Pinball!*, "but when the game was over, I wanted it to be over."

And that's exactly what pinball's future looked like in 1942: game over.

●   ●   ●

La Guardia was certain pinball could contribute nothing positive to society. If only he could have seen Project Pinball.

I've encountered representatives of Project Pinball at nearly every national pinball event I've attended. They're easy to spot in their neon-green T-shirts as they run charity tournaments, solicit donations, and try to advance a cause that makes the uninitiated say, "Wait, you want to do *what*?"

According to their mission statement, Project Pinball "places pinball machines in children's hospitals," thus making it one of the most hyperspecific 501(c)(3) charities imaginable. This unique endeavor started with Daniel Spolar, who runs an arcade called Pinball Asylum in Fort Meyers, Florida. Spolar is tall and clean-cut—picture *Spider-Man*'s newspaper editor J. Jonah Jameson without the mustache.

Incidentally, the first machine Spolar rehabbed (pardon the hospital pun) happened to be a *Spider-Man* (2007). He found the game in complete disrepair at Golisano Children's Hospital of Southwest Florida; it had been donated to the hospital by the family of an eleven-year-old boy who passed away. Unfortunately, the usefulness of this generous gesture had expired when the game broke, and Spolar wanted to set things right. He spent over 112 hours and $1,000 to restore the game, then donated it back to the hospital. When he visited to clean and repair the machine two and a half years later, he found that it had been played *almost sixty thousand times*—the equivalent of a new game played every half hour, twenty-four hours a day. The right flipper alone, he says, had logged over 1.5 million flips, which told Spolar that *Spider-Man* was definitely not sitting in a corner gathering cobwebs.

At last count, there are 334 children's hospitals in the United States. Spolar's goal is as straightforward as it is ambitious: place a pinball machine in all of them.

As of this writing, he's almost reached two dozen hospitals across the country, with each game purchased using donations and maintained by a local volunteer. Spolar showed me a photo of sixteen kids crowded around a car racing–themed pinball machine called *Mustang* (2014) at Palm Beach Children's Hospital at St. Mary's Medical Center in West Palm Beach, Florida, each child connected to an IV pole, all blissfully distracted by the game.

He tells a story of a boy who needed recurring chemotherapy, which he hated, because it always made him ill. One day, when it was time to drive to the hospital for treatment, his mother searched the house but couldn't find him—it turned out he was already in the car, eager to go to the hospital for chemo, because he could play pinball there.

Up yours, La Guardia.

And it's not just kids who enjoy the machines, Spolar says. The games usually sit in the family waiting room, giving parents, and occasionally doctors and nurses, an opportunity to relieve stress.

Project Pinball's list of successes keeps growing: *Star Trek* (2013) at St. Louis Children's Hospital. *Iron Man* (2010) at Advocate Children's Hospital in Oak Lawn, Illinois, and Johns Hopkins Hospital in Baltimore. *The Wizard of Oz* (2013) at UNC Children's in Chapel Hill, North Carolina. *Shrek* (2008) at Omaha Children's Hospital. At the Oak Lawn dedication, Spolar recalls, so many Stern Pinball employees attended the dedication ceremony that Stern had to temporarily close its factory. All of the machines, of course, are set to Free Play—no quarters required.

Still, thanks to pinball's reputation, Spolar says it's not easy to convince hospitals to welcome a pinball machine. Project Pinball constantly finds itself fighting the perception that pinball is old, large, loud, smoky, and inappropriate for kids.

Spolar has learned to arm himself against these criticisms. He brings a large, specially cut piece of vinyl to hospitals and lays it on the floor to show the relatively small footprint of a typical pinball machine and distributes literature touting the family-friendly themes of the machines he selects.

In the decades since La Guardia and other temperance-minded types ran pinball out of town, it has returned as a force for good. And Project Pinball is far from the only pinball charity. In Frederick, Maryland, for example, another impassioned player, Joe Said, founded Pinball EDU, with the mission of opening a Pinball Education Center, where he can offer STEM education and pinball therapy to children diagnosed with conditions like autism and cerebral palsy. The idea may sound strange, but as Pinball EDU's web page reminds visitors, pinball is a play-based multisensory exercise that has already made a therapeutic difference in many kids' lives—among them, autistic Canadian pinball prodigy Robert Gagno, who consistently ranks among the best in the world.

Then there's the Pinball Outreach Project, a public charity in Portland, Oregon, that aims "to improve the lives of children by sharing the history and excitement of the game of pinball," according to its mission statement. In practice, this means bringing pinball machines to hospitals and schools temporarily and allowing other nonprofits to use their arcade space for fundraisers.

Even PAPA, inside the mega-arcade that hosts the World Pinball Championships, used to hold an annual tournament called Cupids and Canines, inviting the Western Pennsylvania Humane Society to bring puppies to the Carnegie facility and donating entry fees to the charity. The idea was that pinball players would compete in a tournament while their long-suffering spouses snuggled with puppies. I dragged Marina to one of these before the kids were born. As I recall, the pinball competition lasted long beyond the time when the puppies had to return to the Humane Society in their crates, and the weekend ended up with me playing pinball after midnight while Marina resentfully fell asleep in a chair.

"Hey," I said, gently nudging her awake. "It's 1:00 AM. The competition's over."

"Did you win?"

"No, I didn't win," I laughed. That was a relief to Marina, since first prize was a pinball machine. "But . . . I did come in third."

"Great," she mumbled, extricating herself from the chair and blinking to moisten her desiccated contact lenses.

"So, uh, I won something else," I admitted as we walked toward the door. I showed Marina a small card. "I get to enter the next World Pinball Championships for free. Want to come back here in August?"

She did not, and I returned in August alone.

That was 2009. Five years later, in August 2014, I pushed open the doors of a nondescript warehouse in Carnegie, Pennsylvania, to reveal a bright panorama of pinball, pinball, pinball. In the years since I'd stopped playing, my worldwide ranking had plummeted from 80th place all the way down to 9,938th.

I'm back, I thought. *Ready to rock this thing.*

Boy was I wrong.

3

Come to PAPA

––––––––

S TEVE EPSTEIN DIDN'T INVENT PINBALL, but he did help make
it competitive. He certainly had ample opportunity to play as he
ran the family business, a crowded midtown Manhattan hangout called
Broadway Arcade. In today's era of Virgin Megastores and ritzy multi-
story bazaars defining their global presence with flagship Times Square
retail destinations, it's quaint to think that a true arcade could thrive in
New York's priciest zone. Yet thrive it did, starting as Sportland in the
1930s and happily siphoning coins from the local population until 1997.

Broadway Arcade's demise coincided with a decidedly "virtual
reality is the future, clanging metal parts are the past" vibe that nearly
killed pinball entirely. In 1997, I held a summer job at a lackluster
indoor amusement park, so I can vouch for the sudden ridiculous
obsession with virtual reality helmets and motion-simulated theaters.

The pinball community wept for Broadway Arcade, as immortalized in archived postings from the Rec.Games.Pinball newsgroup
in 1997. "Say it ain't so!" wailed an enthusiast from Atlanta, while
another player replied with only mild hyperbole, "This is quite possibly the worst thing I have ever read."

Before the Broadway Arcade shut down, however, Epstein made one last contribution to the pinball scene, an idea that would slowly blossom and develop into a worldwide institution with tens of thousands of adherents. Along with his friend Roger Sharpe, Epstein essentially invented the notion of *competitive* pinball.

In some ways, pinball has always been competitive. You can play a multiplayer game, essentially alternating balls, then seeing whose score is highest at the end. Epstein and Sharpe's idea was to make that victory only one in a series—in other words, to establish a metascoring system that would do for pinball what league play did for bowling.

In the process, in the mid-1980s, Epstein and Sharpe founded the Professional and Amateur Pinball Association (PAPA), the organization that would oversee some of the world's largest pinball tournaments. Soon pinball leagues and competitions began popping up around the country, with most adopting the PAPA scoring system that Epstein and Sharpe invented.

Everything seemed to be going well. From 1991 through 1995, Epstein ran PAPA's annual tournament at the Omni Park Central Hotel in New York. Then Broadway Arcade went under, and despite a brief attempt at one more tournament in Las Vegas in 1998, PAPA's scoring system lived on, but the big PAPA competition took an indefinite hiatus.

We should pause for just a second here to acknowledge the slight awkwardness of that acronym, especially when it leads to phrases like "big PAPA competition." It's an awkwardness I discovered myself when a fellow pinball player asked me, grinning, "You wanna come to PAPA?"

Enter Kevin Martin, a pinball fan with a massive bankroll from his web-hosting business, Pair Networks. In 2004, Martin had the determination to restart PAPA as pinball's foremost championship, but he had something else as well—something amazing, something wonderful, something Epstein would have loved. Martin had hundreds of pinball machines.

Yes, his own collection. Yes, hundreds. Martin purchased a century-old, thirty-thousand-square-foot warehouse in Carnegie, Pennsylvania, just outside Pittsburgh. The building was a sprawling, high-ceilinged, cement block begging to be rehabilitated and filled with pinball machines. Since if you build it, they will come, Martin had the walls painted, had most of the floor carpeted, and installed amenities like restrooms, lockers, a café area, and an information desk. They came.

In September 2004, the seventh tournament run by PAPA (called, creatively, PAPA7) helped inaugurate Martin's dream facility. Much pinball was played. The title went to Keith Elwin, who racked up more than 1.3 billion points on *Theatre of Magic* in the finals. A good time was had by all, and the competitors returned to their ordinary lives afterward, with no idea what horror would soon descend upon Martin's gleaming pinball Mecca.

A mere five days later, Hurricane Ivan dropped nearly six inches of rain on Carnegie in one day, swelling the adjacent Chartiers Creek well above its hundred-year flood line and—it still pains me to write this—right into PAPA headquarters. We're not just talking about a little water. We're talking about multiple feet of water containing "silt, debris, sewage, and diesel fuel," according to a lament on the PAPA website. If you're imagining a field of pinball machines with their metal legs covered in standing water, you're imagining an outcome kinder than what actually occurred. Add a few more feet of contaminated water to what you're imagining.

Every machine's wooden playfield was soaked with sludge. Every machine's electronics were destroyed. I still remember sitting at my computer in Baltimore, scrolling through photo after photo on Flickr of waterlogged pinball machines, bellies submerged in brownish mire, brand-new machines and machines that had seen decades of play, never to be turned on again. In all, 232 pinball machines went to that Great Arcade in the Sky, along with about a dozen classic video games and, as can be seen in the gut-wrenching photos, a black Corvette in the parking lot.

PAPA itself might have disappeared after Hurricane Ivan, because who wants to rebuild after such thorough devastation? Then, Hanuk-kah-style, a great miracle occurred. The pinball community rallied around the remains of Martin's Mecca (to completely mix religious metaphors). Floors were cleaned, parts were salvaged, and new machines made their way to Carnegie. Flood insurance helped.

"Once you're crazy/determined enough to build the place," Martin would later tell *The Pinball Blog*, "rebuilding it is only a few percent-age points crazier." The facility opened its doors once again in August 2005, just in time for PAPA8—with 277 functioning machines.

As for Epstein—who lost his own Times Square arcade not by an act of God but through the more powerful forces of gentrification and changing public preferences—he's found a home at the helm of a new Manhattan arcade in the Rose Hill neighborhood a couple blocks from Baruch College. Modern Pinball NYC opened its doors in 2013, and Epstein has watched pinball players enjoy their unlimited play—ten dollars for one hour, or twenty for the whole damn day.

The old Broadway Arcade "wasn't for kids," Epstein told me. I didn't press him on what that meant, but I gather that at the time, much of New York City "wasn't for kids." At Modern Pinball NYC, however, he's spoken to several parents who specifically bring their kids to offer an alternative to video games. (Of course, books are an alternative to video games, too, but there's only so far you can push kids.) The arcade is even a registered vendor of the New York City Department of Education, hosting field trips for kids to learn about art, physics, and electricity.

"I think there's a return to live-action entertainment," Epstein said, gazing at his little room of flashing lights—not in Times Square but certainly not in Timbuktu—"and you get that kind of entertain-ment on a pinball machine."

• • •

On a Friday in August, I leave my office in Rockville, Maryland, at the end of the day—but instead of driving home, I point my Saturn northwest, through the Appalachian Mountains, watching the sun sink lower and disappear. It's an exhausting drive, not because of the distance—five hours—but because my new son, Benjamin, is a month old, which means I haven't had a night of uninterrupted sleep in a while. I briefly entertain the possibility of driving straight to my hotel to rest, but that's not going to happen. That's insane. There's pinball to be played.

PAPA dwells in an unlikely location. Driving by, you'd think it was a large, solid, but decrepit warehouse with weeds sprouting from the asphalt in a faded parking lot. Actually, you wouldn't think anything, because the facility is the epitome of the word "nondescript." And actually, you wouldn't drive by, unless you happen to conduct business at one of the adjacent industrial warehouses: NORD-Lock, Bisco Refractories, or the thrillingly named Heat Exchange and Transfer.

Having added a second contest in the spring, PAPA is open exactly twice a year, at which points it converts from a characterless concrete monolith to a characterless concrete monolith with an overflowing parking lot. I park illegally in a weed-choked alley, as it seems most people have done, and step inside.

How to describe the sensation of entering PAPA? (Again, the acronym is less than ideal.) For someone whose mood is instantly lifted by finding a random functional pinball machine in a bus station, the elation is overwhelming. Here at PAPA's 2014 competition (PAPA17) are not one, not ten, not fifty, but more than *five hundred* pinball machines in Martin's ever-growing collection, all playable, and me with nothing but tokens and time.

Hell, the PAPA collection even includes woodrails, those pre-midcentury contraptions built from unpainted wood, before LED displays, before scores could be tallied by rotating number wheels—before it was even a given that a pinball machine might use electricity.

On the inside, the concrete walls have been painted purple and yellow. Banners bearing the names of past champions—mostly Keith Elwin, Bowen Kerins, or Lyman Sheats—hang from the steel rafters. It almost feels like a casino, loud and windowless and unapologetically alluring, but a casino forced to display its splendor in a high school gym.

And there's security. Which makes sense—lots of people, lots of cash—but imagine being hired to keep the peace at a pinball competition. It's probably an easier day than most. The security guards look bored out of their minds, or maybe they're constantly tormented by the attractive pinball machines on all sides that they're not allowed to play.

Who travels to Carnegie, Pennsylvania, to play pinball on a Friday night? All types of people. Competitive pinball players are a varied bunch, which is a nice way of saying that they're interesting, which is a nice way of saying that many of them look like your uncle who attends *Battlestar Galactica* conventions. Yes, there are middle-aged men, those dependable engines that keep the various hobby industries chugging along. But there are also kids and grandparents. The inescapably nerdy and those who meld well with crowds. Athletic shoes, sandals, combat boots, and work boots. Ponytails aplenty, for both genders. People who look like they just emerged from a biker bar, and people who look like they just came from their jobs as patent examiners. Guys who look like the Lone Gunmen from *The X-Files* (which is itself a 1997 pinball machine).

I see a man stare intently at a machine, then wipe the sweat off the flipper buttons with his "HARDEST PART OF MY DAY IS MULTI-BALL" T-shirt, stretch his neck in that cracky way that bodyguards and bouncers can pull off, and enter *the zone*. A willowy blonde woman with large glasses plays wearing white golf gloves. And there's a squat man in cargo shorts and a fishing hat, looking a bit like Rick Moranis with square glasses, also wearing golf gloves. Are golf gloves a thing in pinball now? Are they trying to improve their grip on the buttons? Or are they, like the T-shirt man, protecting themselves from the finger sweat of hundreds of strangers?

Upon further observation, they appear to be friendly with each other. They're probably a married couple, though I think I prefer the possibility that they just met and fell in love that afternoon over shared interests.

Him: "Hey, nice golf gloves!"

Her: "Look, pal, they protect me from the sweat—oh! You have them, too! I never imagined I'd find that perfect someone!"

Him: "You wanna, you know, play a multiplayer game?"

And then a pun about balls that's not even worth writing.

Sixty machines have been roped off for the competition, but the remaining hundreds sit in neat rows, ready to be played by anyone for fun. I take ten dollars in tokens to the nearest interesting-looking machine, which happens to be *Transformers*, a 2011 game I've barely played before. On my first try, I surpass the score required for a free game and do a little internal dance. This is going to be a good weekend.

For most pinball machines, that's the reward for a high-scoring game: you get to play another game for free. The reward for pinball is *more pinball*. Sometimes a very high score will earn you multiple free games. I still remember earning more free games in college than I could reasonably play on the *Medieval Madness* in the student center basement, then walking away with the display reading "Credits: 5," feeling like Robin Hood.

With gambling so integral a part of pinball's past, it's kind of funny that we've come full circle and figured out a way to once again monetize the game: first prize in PAPA's top bracket, A Division, is $10,000. Additional cash prizes for lower finishes, in the lesser B and C Divisions, and for minitournaments and random contests, bring

PAPA's total prize package to more than $45,000—not to mention trophies the size of mountain lions.

There are two stages of the competition. In the first, you purchase an entry, which lets you play any five games from a designated group and receive a composite score based on how well your games rank against everyone else's. The metascoring rubric rewards consistency, so it's not enough to play one good game on an entry ticket—you need a few. The number of entries a player can purchase is limited only by the constraints of time (qualifying opportunities begin on Thursday morning and end at midnight on Saturday) and financing, which is partly how the prize package can be so lucrative.

The second stage is the finals, played on Sunday by the top twenty-four players in each division. I've never made it to the finals.

PAPA has grown every year, and this year there are more than 150 players competing in C Division alone. They wait for machines to become available, arms crossed, lanyards with their player numbers hanging from their necks.

Under the right circumstances, anyone can look menacing. In my mind, they're all secret pinball wizards capable of directing the silver ball wherever they want, and what the hell chance do I have?

But I have a secret weapon. His occupation: mnemonic courier. His cargo: three hundred and twenty gigabytes of data wet-wired directly to his brain. His name: Johnny.

Johnny Mnemonic (1995), the only pinball machine I've ever owned, is fairly unremarkable, especially considering that it was released during an era that birthed some of the greatest machines ever manufactured. Often a pinball machine's theme must be determined before anyone knows whether the movie on which it's based will be a dud—such was the case with 1994's *The Shadow*, based on the unfortunate Alec Baldwin film—and the less said about the *Flintstones* pinball machine from the same year, the better. There's even a saying in the pinball industry: "Great games, bad movies."

Johnny Mnemonic is a dystopian 1995 film starring everyone's favorite block of wood, Keanu Reeves, as a "mnemonic courier" who had to jettison memories of his childhood in order to carry 320 gigabytes of data in his brain for a wealthy client. Along the way he meets radical J-Bone (Ice-T), a street preacher (Dolph Lundgren), and a sassy dolphin named Jones. Yeah. It's as good as you'd think.

While *The Shadow* might have flopped at the box office, the pinball version is nicely complicated and well planned. The same cannot be said, unfortunately, for *Johnny Mnemonic*, which falls into the bad game, bad movie category. Apart from a weird bonus multiball grid and modes that don't mean anything, *Johnny* has a single goal—something called the super spinner—that awards such an unbalanced number of points that it dwarfs all other strategies on the game. If you light the super spinner, a single shot to the circular spinner target can be worth more than the rest of your entire game.

I know about the super spinner shot; then again, so do half the people at PAPA. But because I owned *Johnny Mnemonic* for a few years in grad school, I also know every nuance of the machine—yes, it was a lackluster game, but it was a lackluster game *in my house*.

And at PAPA, it's one of the ten games in C Division.

I head straight to my old companion and put up a great score, more than 1.2 billion points. If I can rock four other machines, I'll be doing great.

But with abysmal scores on *Batman* (2008), *Attack from Mars* (1995), *Jack*Bot* (1995), and *Corvette* (1994), I don't rock any other machine. My skill set is too limited and specific, like a baseball pitcher with a dynamite fastball who can't bat, run, or field.

"Tap here when you've verified your scores are correct," says a volunteer holding a mini–Nexus tablet. As frustrated as I am with my performance, I can't help feeling impressed by the technology. Five years ago, this was all done with paper tickets, and an army of volunteers typed all day and night to keep the leader boards up to date. Now with one tap on a tablet, I've registered my score, and I know immediately that I'm sitting in . . . 117th place.

The next morning, thinking about nothing but how I'll advance from 117th place, I emerge from my room at the Red Roof Inn. Thanks to my son's nocturnal needs, it's my first contiguous night of sleep in a month—thanks to pinball excitement, it's only six hours of sleep.

Oh, right, I suddenly realize. *The weather is gorgeous, it's a Saturday, and I'm in the mountains.* Yet I'm going to spend the day indoors staring at electronics. That somehow feels wrong, but here we are.

Even more wrong is the feeling that, for the weekend, I've abandoned my family. Marina calls to say good morning, and she puts our daughter on the phone. Maya is effusive about most things, and today it's the pancakes that Marina's mother cooked.

"They had chocolate chips on top and chocolate chips on the bottom," Maya reports with glee, "and when I saw them, I said yum right away!" She's three. That's the age when every other sentence out of a child's mouth is surprising, cute, or quotable. Our dining room is littered with paper scraps of Maya's quotes. How many quotes will I miss today?

Seemingly just to enforce the feeling of choosing pinball over family, I've also removed my wedding ring. I'm not trying to pick up love-starved pinball singles; I'm eliminating any barriers to an effective slap-save with my left hand. Still, yeah, pinball over family.

Pulling back into the PAPA parking lot, I reach for my cup of tokens.

Oh, right. To keep it from tipping in the car, I've placed it in my daughter's car seat. *No, Maya, it's not what you're thinking. You and your baby brother are my top priority. I've only physically replaced you with a cup of tokens.*

• • •

It's time for my second entry. If I can pull off a few good games, maybe I can supplant the cruddy entry that earned me 117th place.

But on *The Addams Family* (1992) it's drain, drain, drain. That's one drain per ball, for those keeping score—which, unfortunately, the Addams Family was. This entry includes a brilliant game of *Jack*Bot*—twentieth highest overall!—but paired with *The Addams Family* and three other lousy games, it's a fat lot of nothing. Another ten dollars spent on an entry, and I've moved from 117th place to . . . 115th place.

The problem is, I'm flailing too much. Good players know that, as much fun as it is to manically shoot everything at once, the way to win is to focus on *catching* the ball, then deploy it in a more controlled way. Catch, aim, shoot. Catch, aim, shoot. But catching is an amazingly difficult task to accomplish using flipper buttons rather than fingers, so my pattern is more like shoot, kind of aim, shoot again.

My third entry is not as good as my second, but somehow in the shuffle of other players, I've climbed to seventieth place. The victory feels as unexciting as it sounds.

I notice I'm flagging, missing some easy saves. My wrists have started to hurt, like in the carpal tunnel area. It's a strange feeling, because it's a muscle group I rarely use anymore—are there even muscles inside the wrist?—and now I'm making it work repeatedly. Every time I flip, a tiny nerve ending requests that I please not do that again. I'm thinking of taking Extra Strength Tylenol so that the pain doesn't deter me from flipping. Yes, I'm considering doping.

Entry four. I freaking dominate *Johnny Mnemonic*, not even touching the super spinner yet scoring just shy of two billion points—the sixth-highest score on the machine. And it's my first game of this entry. Unfortunately, yet again, it will be the only game I'll play well during this entry, and my domination of *Johnny* turns out to be meaningless.

I should point out that two billion is a great score on *Johnny*, but unless you know the machine, you wouldn't automatically be able to figure that out. Each machine has its own scoring framework, and as with foreign currencies, a high score on one machine may be worthless on another. Ten million on *Mousin' Around!* (1989) is a champion-level score. Ten million on *Attack from Mars*? You practically get that just for launching the ball.

Some of the scoring disparity can be attributed to a gradual point inflation over time—presumably players in the 1950s felt satisfied with scores in the thousands, but half a century later, only a score in the billions would do. A notable exception is the 1997 game *NBA Fastbreak*, which, for good or ill, adopted a basketball-style scoring system of two- and three-pointers. A great game of *NBA Fastbreak* may end with a score of 150.

Pinball is an inherently frustrating activity, because *every* game—even the ones you achieve the supersecret wizard mode on—ends in a drain, as that little ball trickles into that hole twelve inches from your hands. It's *right there*. I *just* lost it.

Better play again.

As the daylight dims through the few skylights, I feel mighty once more. Despite my aching wrists, I decisively churn out entry five.

Feeling mighty is different from being mighty, and entry five is another dud.

Before I can consider a sixth entry, I run into Joe, Julie, and Scott, three competitors from the Free State Pinball Association (FSPA), the Maryland-based pinball league where I played in my pre-offspring days. Joe and Julie, who are probably one of the only married couples competing at PAPA, have a custom-built basement in their suburban Virginia home with more than a dozen pinball machines. I don't know how many machines Scott has, but he frequently wears a soldering iron on his belt, so he's pretty badass already.

Joe, Julie, and Scott gather the FSPA players and alumni, and we carpool to dinner.

"*World Cup Soccer*," says Dave Hubbard, reading from his phone in the back seat, starting an impromptu guessing game to name the bottom score achieved so far on each machine. Hubbard is a Maryland-based web developer who used to kick my ass in pinball league.

"A hundred and fifty million," someone speculates.

"In A Division? Really?"

"All right, a hundred million."

"Can you even get that low if you try?" someone else muses.

"Seventy-three million," reads Hubbard, to sounds of amazement. No one in this car is anywhere near the top of their division tonight, so it's reassuring to hear about how poorly others have done.

We claim a large table at faux-tropical chain restaurant Bahama Breeze, the concept of which feels all the more ridiculous because we're outside Pittsburgh. The playful psyche that generally defines a pinball player combines with the euphoria of dinner with friends, and a lot of straw paper is shot across the table.

"Julie," Joe asks his wife, handing her a plastic coffee stirrer, "can you put this in your hair?" Julie is one of the top female pinball players in the world. She complies without looking up from the menu. I feel like I'm at the Mad Hatter's tea party, or maybe the eighth grade cafeteria.

There's something wonderful about competitive pinball players, people who regard as a serious pursuit what the rest of the world considers a diversion. I still remember the first time I went out to dinner with the FSPA. I had never seen so many adults order milk shakes, and I realized that they—like me—were just a bunch of big kids.

I never order alcohol, but what the hell? I get a drink called a Painkiller. It tastes nearly as good as the feeling of pressing its chilled glass against the underside of my damaged wrists. Seriously, body? You can't play pinball anymore without agony? Did my wrists and tendons used to be stronger?

Hubbard tells a story about pinball celebrity Lyman Sheats Jr., who designed and programmed some of the best games over the past two decades and ranks among the world's top players. The man is so revered that the concession stand outside PAPA sells a beverage called Lyman-ade.

Today Lyman was playing *Black Hole*, a 1981 game with a lower playfield, a secondary scoring area embedded under the main play-field that has its own flippers and targets, visible through Plexiglas. Hubbard apparently knows *Black Hole* better than Lyman, so in the middle of his game, Lyman, the pinball luminary, asked Hubbard what he should shoot for.

"Lyman Sheats," Hubbard recalls loudly, beaming as he finishes his story and his drink, "is asking *me* for advice!"

Lyman Sheats also happens to be sitting at the Bahama Breeze bar.

I've spent an inordinate amount of time trying to figure out who Lyman Sheats looks like—the closest I can get is a cross between actors Noah Taylor and Karl Urban, author Neil Gaiman, and, in his younger days, comedian Eric Idle. Hearing his name, Sheats raises his drink and gives our table a friendly nod.

"That's what I love about pinball," announces Hubbard. "All of the pinball legends, all the people who made the game what it is, they're all alive *right now*, and you can *talk* to them."

● ● ●

Back from dinner, it's time for entry six. This one kicks off with a lackluster game on *Johnny* and never improves. Number six may be my most miserable ticket yet, not a bright spot in the bunch. Another wasted entry.

The lines for the tournament games are longer than ever, as every-one not in the top twenty-four is hurrying to play entries that might qualify them. Even those above the cut are continuing to play, lest they get knocked off the roster by all of the Saturday night madness. The result is that an entry now takes more than an hour to play, most of which is spent waiting for an open machine.

It's late. I'm tired. My forearms hurt when I use a pen. My contacts are dry, and true to its biochemical nature, alcohol is a depressant. I can't just be out of practice, because I have no certainty that I could have done any better when I was playing regularly. It's one of those "I'm just not as good as these people, and I never will be" moments.

There's time for only one more entry before qualifying ends. Should I throw away another ten dollars on a seventh entry, or should I just have fun and play pinball? It's always the last attempt that leads to victory, isn't it? It's only when you've given up entirely that miraculous things start to happen.

So I begin entry seven. I put up three terrible games right away and assume I'm done. But my terrible game on *Johnny* turns out to be twenty-sixth best, so I still have a chance if I can slaughter the last two games.

I choose *Corvette*, a game I know nothing about and thus have been largely avoiding. Now I'm hoping that the novelty and my thorough unfamiliarity with *Corvette*'s rules will somehow magically translate to an awesome game.

They do not.

After PAPA shuts down at midnight, I drive back to the hotel and run numbers while brushing my teeth. My best entry was still my second out of the seven, which I played last night, and I've finished the tournament in . . . eighty-second place. In the lowest division. Granted, it's 82nd out of 169 players in that division, but still.

If I could collect my highest scores from each game and put them all on the same ticket, I would have finished in fourteenth place, and I'd return tomorrow for the finals. Instead, I'm left with just a miserable ranking, a plastic cup of tokens, and, as I soon discover while my wrists continue to throb, a complete inability to unbutton my pants.

● ● ●

While most attendees spend Sunday ambling around playing pinball for fun, the top twenty-four players in each division begin the playoffs. At least the pressure is off for the rest of us. Between games, I check the results on the real-time-updated website—this guy beat that guy, so this guy advances.

I say "guy" because, despite plenty of female competitors, those who qualify for the playoffs are almost exclusively men—in all three divisions. By my count, A Division has ninety-five players, and only four are female—the most successful of whom has finished in seventy-sixth place. This isn't a new phenomenon. For years, PAPA players and organizers have debated the uncomfortable problem, with the most vociferous opinions emerging over one question: Should PAPA have a separate Women's Division?* PAPA already offers a Juniors Division (under sixteen) and a Seniors Division (over fifty). So why not a Women's Division?

If you've ever read discussions on Internet message boards, you can guess the diversity and vociferousness of the responses.

"Yes! We need to attract more women to pinball!"

"No! Creating a Women's Division implies that women are unequal to men!"

"Yes! Dozens of screaming men in a small, roped-off area can be intimidating to women!"

"No! If you're going to segregate women, why not have an Asian Division? A Transgender Division?"

Inevitably the debate takes a predictable turn when someone points out that all of the arguers so far have been (surprise!) men.

Tournament organizers often wonder why there aren't more female pinball players: Is it a matter of inherent discrepancy in interests? Less free time? Inadvertent but legitimate bullying? There's no easy answer. I can't imagine, however, that the artwork helps.

---

* I propose calling it MAMA.

Pinball machines are beautiful. The sheer complexity contained within each one is staggering—if you ever get a chance to peer underneath the playfield, you'll see a landscape of solenoids, a spaghettilike network of wires, the machine's own circulatory system.

Then there's the artwork.

I have to wonder about the men who provided the art for pinball machines. I say "men" again, because it's hard to imagine that a woman would have felt comfortable drawing the clownishly large-boobed maidens that leer down from backglasses. They're practically a requirement in older games, even when these balloon-breasted adolescent fantasy temptresses have zero to do with the machine's theme.

Even just looking at the machines in a single section of PAPA, that aspect of the art is unavoidable:

- *Pinball Pool* (1979): A billiards-shooting robot impresses two barely dressed women.
- *Car Hop* (1991): Sexy roller-skating waitress.
- *Rollergames* (1990): Sexy roller-skating everyone.
- *Robot* (1985): A nearly naked woman in the clutches of a giant robot. Shoot some billiards, robot! Women like that!
- *Band Wagon* (1965): Three underdressed women, two clowns.
- *Star Race* (1980): Three women in winged helmets wearing dangerously incomplete space suits and flying space scooters.
- *Jumping Jack* (1973): No fewer than six women, each with a waist narrower than a typical ankle, surround a jack-in-the-box. (Woe be to the sexually hungry women when they discover he has no legs or torso.)

The litany of casual sexism in pinball art goes on and on. And while you could call 1978's *Playboy* pinball machine a product of a bygone era, you'd have to forget about the 2002 *Playboy* pinball machine—which allowed the operator to decorate the game with their choice of clothed, topless, or nude decals.* Not to mention a 2015 game, announced amid a flurry of controversy, called—subtly—*Whoa Nellie! Big Juicy Melons*, whose cabinet art is exactly what you're picturing.

It's Comic-Con fantasy women, it's Lara Croft, and it's the Black Widow, but it's worse. It's gratuitous beyond gratuitous. There are drawings that would make Barbie's physical proportions look reasonable by comparison.

Many players—male and female—insist that the sexy caricatures of impossibly proportioned women are simply a part of pinball's beauty and history, or at least that their prevalence and irrelevance to gameplay makes them blend into the background. But every now and then, such as at PAPA, I'll look around and wonder why I'm being leered at, from every angle, by lascivious fake women.

One day, visiting my parents, I told them I was writing a section of this book about why more women don't play pinball, when I realized I happened to be speaking to an actual woman.

"So, Mom," I asked, "why don't you play pinball?"

Her answer was straightforward, logical, and doesn't speak for all women, but I think I can say it certainly represents some: "Probably because there are so many other things to do instead." Thanks, Mom.

* * *

You've probably heard the explanation, "Well, it was a different time," as a means of excusing politically incorrect missteps that wouldn't pass muster as easily today. It's dismissive, but it's not false. Many games reflect the attitudes of their eras. And sometimes that attitude was, frankly, a little racist.

---

* Paul Faris, who created the artwork for the 1978 *Playboy*, has said that Hugh Hefner disliked the machine's backglass because it prominently featured Playboy models and not Hef. Because let's be real: people don't read *Playboy* for the articles, they read it for Hef.

You won't find most of these at PAPA, but thanks to the Internet Pinball Database (IPDB), which contains photos and information about nearly every pinball machine ever made, it's possible to ask an interesting question with a horrifying answer: What were the most racist pinball machines ever?

For the purpose of this query, I'm going to go ahead and exclude a special class of pinball machines, specifically the bizarre and horribly jingoistic slate of conversion kits produced by Victory Games between 1942 and 1947. Conversion kits are like makeovers for existing games. You could take a 1941 *Star Attraction*, for example, a pinball machine whose theme appears to be "some numbers and also some stars"—and, for a mere $9.50, purchase a conversion kit that included a backglass, bumper caps, and a scorecard, which you'd use to convert the game to a shiny new 1943 *Bomb the Axis Rats*. An ad in a 1943 issue of *Coin Machine Journal* boasts "Only five minutes required to make this STARTLING CHANGEOVER." Startling indeed.

Other Victory Games changeover kits whose names speak unapologetically for themselves include *Girls Ahoy* (1944), *Artists and Models* (1945), *Tail Gunner* (1944), and an array of games that involved doing not-nice things to Japanese people: *Hit the Japs* (1942), *Slap-the-Japs* (1942), *Smack the Japs* (1943), *Sink the Japs* (1942), and the 1942 classic *Knock out the Japs*. It's as though the Victory Games executives sat around a conference table to discuss their next pinball theme:

Executive 1: Well, we've hit them, slapped them, sunk them, and knocked them out. Let's see, Japs, Japs, Japs . . . what could we do to Japs . . .

Executive 2: Kick them?

Executive 1: Seriously, Johnson? That's racist.

Moving on from conversion kits, here are some more racially cringe-worthy pieces of pinball's past:

Diner (1990): You're the waiter. Can you serve food to all of these ethnically stereotypical customers in time? There's Haji, the nonspecific Muslim/Sikh ("Could you please give to me a hot dog and a root beer?"), drawn to look a little like Dwight Schrute with Barack Obama's complexion, plus a turban; Pepe the curly-mustached Mexican; and good old Soviet Boris.

Big Indian (1974): Loincloths, headdresses, war paint—not a detail is missing from Gottlieb's attempt to have a little fun with the tribes. But you know who didn't think it was fun? The actual Native Americans working in Gottlieb's wiring and assembly plant in South Dakota. In fact, the title of *Big Indian* is the concession the workers won after protesting its previous name, *Big Injun*.

Poker Face (1953): Not to be confused with the 1963 J. H. Keeney game of the same title set in a gunslingin' saloon, Gottlieb's *Poker Face* included squaws, teepees, smoke signals, and . . . is that . . . someone being burned at the stake? Oh dear God.*

Minstrel Man (1951): The theme of this game is those happy-go-lucky white performers who painted their faces black and danced and sang, all for the amusement of more white people. The backglass features a minstrel man and minstrel woman, supported by a nightclub band of at least seven more minstrel musicians, with an additional nine minstrel faces adorning the scoring lights, and they even found a way to fit eight more minstrel men on the playfield—four with full bodies, one as a giant face, and three above stand-up targets.

Black Fever (1980): The Spain-based pinball manufacturer Play-matic must have sympathized with the injustice of white women being the center of sexist pinball art and made *Black Fever* as their attempt

---

* And the list of Native American–themed games goes on. O. D. Jennings and Company made *Red Man* (1934). Lindstrom Tool and Toy produced *Indian Chief* (1934). Italian manufacturer AMI did *Navajo* (1976). Williams made *Arrow Head* (1952), *Thunderbird* (1954), *Tom Tom* (1963), and, not to be confused with either of Gottlieb's *Big Indian* or its two-player version *Big Brave*, the 1965 game *Big Chief*. Gottlieb itself also made *Golden Arrow* (1977) and *Sweet Sioux* (1959), the latter of which semi-ironically hosted one of the company's standard slogans on its backglass: "Amusement Pinball, as American as Baseball and Hot Dogs!" And, you know, Native Americans.

to even the score. Three black women adorn the backglass, and you know they're black because you can see about 95 percent of the surface area of their skin.

And the award for the most ethnically prejudiced pinball machine goes to *Happy Gang* (1932). *Happy Gang*'s implicit assumption clarifies a dimension to racism that may not have been obvious to those, like myself, born after 1932. Not only were other races and nationalities stereotyped in offensive ways, but they were basically told to be pleased about it. Billed as "The Game of Nationalities," *Happy Gang*'s advertisement tells you everything you need to know, so I'll just step back and let this sentence sink in: "Cheer up the Masses—The Goldberg's, the O'Reilly's, The Sambos, The Scotch, The Chinese—The Drys, The Wets—Cheer 'em all with THE HAPPY GANG." Wow. That's the melting pot right there, folks. And there they all are, painted on the playfield along with their names: O'Reilly is the Irish cop. Mac Burnie, the Scotsman, plays bagpipes. Señor Bulls, a Spaniard, serenades a woman on a balcony with his guitar—not to be confused with Wet Pancho, the Mexican singing next to a cactus. Chief Standing Bear makes the Washington Redskins logo look culturally sensitive by comparison—he's naked, with a bow and tomahawk. Goldberg, the white-bearded Jew, for some reason pushes a wagon of fish. The Chinese man with a Fu Manchu mustache is named Wun Lung. And black Sambo—unlike the other characters, who simply stand above holes the pinball can fall into—catches balls in his mouth. Paradoxically, it's quite possible that the designer of *Happy Gang* felt he was *promoting* tolerance, as if declaring, "Yep, that's us in America in 1932! We may have our differences, but we're all a part of one big happy gang. Ain't this country grand? Oh, nice, here comes Goldberg with my fish."

* * *

Today, on the final day of PAPA17, pinball is enjoying one more addition to validate it as a sport: spectators. Against the wall behind A Division, a small set of actual metal bleachers has been arranged, and lots of people are watching pinball.

Watching pinball is not only interesting but also realistic, thanks to one of PAPA's own innovations, PAPA TV. Each pinball machine has a camera mounted overhead broadcasting the game in high definition to a portrait-oriented flat-screen television. Spectators are watching multiple games at once, some even following the overall scoring on laptops. Elsewhere in the world, pinball fans who couldn't make it to PAPA are logged in to PAPA TV, monitoring multiple games from their computers. Remember, to each his own: while watching pinball may sound to you like watching paint dry, to me it sounds about a thousand times more interesting than watching golf.

Right now, everyone has gathered to watch one player who's no stranger to televised contests: Bowen Kerins, a Stanford graduate and math textbook writer with a side job as a mathematical consultant for game shows who once won $32,000 on *Who Wants to Be a Millionaire?* He also happens to be the A Division champion of PAPAs 4, 8, and 16, the first of which he won at age eighteen.

When not winning PAPA, Bowen uses PAPA TV to host a series of how-to videos, including episodes titled "Pinball Flipper Skills— Flick Pass" and "*Lord of the Rings* Pinball: The Valinor Strategy." The channel has more than two million views.

At the moment, Kerins is struggling—on *Johnny Mnemonic*, no less—having lost his first two balls almost immediately. As he approaches the machine for his third ball, I find I'm rooting for him, because even though he's a pinball celebrity and guru, he seems like such an underdog. Maybe it's because he's such a friendly, well-intentioned fellow, or maybe it's because he's friends with my friends.

Kerins starts multiball, a mode that gives him three balls on the playfield at once to shoot for high-value jackpots. "Let's go, baby!"

he yells to himself as spectators applaud. "Come on! Get some points back!" Then he pauses and adds, "You sound like a dumbass!"

That's Bowen Kerins—smart and skilled, with an encyclopedic knowledge of pinball and a self-deprecating sense of humor. After he drains his final ball, resurrecting his game from a certain loss to a reasonable 523 million, he sits in the bleachers, where he's greeted with compliments—not on his final score but on his skill in general. "Those live catches were insane," Joe tells him. "They looked beautiful."

Maybe so. But Kerins's final score on *Johnny* is, I note with some pleasure and some spite, lower than most of mine. And it's significantly lower than that of his competitor on *Johnny*, Cayle George. George is a tall, young Seattle-based software designer with longish blond hair, dressed in all black with a backward black hat and lime-green sneakers. Everything about him, combined with the fact that he's never won PAPA, screams dark horse. Once George's *Johnny* score hits 1.3 billion, he's easily overtopped all of his competitors, and so—why rub it in?—he voluntarily drains the ball. And just like that, Kerins is out. Sixth place.

In the finals, I watch Josh Sharpe, son of Roger, put up more than one million on ball two of *Alien Star*, a space-themed 1984 game on which one million is pretty darn spectacular. The crowd has swelled to more than a hundred on the bleachers. Sharpe is, and there's no other way to put this, in the zone. He's so in rhythm with the machine that he can catch any shot, shoot any target, save any near drain. It's like watching someone with secret magnetic influence over the ball. The thirty-five-year-old whose dad saved pinball in 1976 is not draining anytime soon, and he knows it.

And I know something, too. I'm also thirty-five. And I'll never, ever be that good.

On ball three, Sharpe drains the ball down the middle—*and recovers it*. Through a lucky bounce and a sudden, precise double flip, he somehow propels the ball back up between the flippers.

This is allowed, but it requires artistry. There are, incidentally, several other methods for recovering a ball from certain doom that are so risky and effective that they appear on PAPA's "Illegal Techniques" web page, listing the machine manipulations that can immediately disqualify you. A "death save," for example, involves thrusting the entire machine against an already drained ball, nudging it via a series of clever angles back into play. Even more severe is the "bangback," a well-timed smack on the front of the cabinet to bounce the ball off the metal bracket near the drain and up through the flippers. The latter includes an instructional video with a warning that a bangback could damage the machine and you, possibly breaking your wrist; yes, you can break your wrist playing pinball. (Maybe that's why Tommy's were supple.) The player demonstrating the bangback in the video—"*for informational purposes only*," stresses the web page—sums it up well when he says, "I'm not hitting it pretty hard, but I'm hitting it hard enough to—actually, it kind of hurts."

The spectators watching Sharpe's save go as nuts as I've seen them go, with one collective gasp followed by applause, like they've witnessed a near fall from a trapeze. We're all viewing this on the flat-screen, so it feels like sitting at a sports bar watching your favorite football team on TV.

Josh Sharpe ends up taking second place in A Division, with his younger brother, Zach, finishing third. The dark horse wins the day as Cayle George earns his first ever PAPA championship.

I start the drive home after PAPA has officially closed, though that's apparently when the real fun begins. With the pressure of the contest gone for the players—and for the scorekeeping staff—the lights dim, the music blasts, and the best pinball players in the world combine ramp shots with alcohol shots. It's basically an all-night pinball rave.

Not for me, though. Not this time. My wife and kids are waiting, and I can't justify making them wait any longer. I do, however, make a quick stop at a service plaza in Breezewood, Pennsylvania, a town that exists only to sell gas and food at the junction of I-70 and the Pennsylvania Turnpike. It's 11:00 PM, I'm drowsy, and my wrists are numb. Still, I find myself wandering past the minimart and toward a sign labeled "ARCADE"—just, you know, to see if they have pinball. They don't.

It's kind of amazing when you think about it. People have traveled to PAPA from all over the world. They've flown, driven, abandoned their families for a weekend, rented hotel rooms, rented cars, bought tokens, bought entries, flicked their wrists for hours upon hours—all to obsess over the control of an eighty-gram steel sphere.

To an outsider walking into PAPA, poking his head into a boardwalk arcade, or just sitting at a bar and watching some folks in the corner play pinball, the game looks like a cacophonous mess of strobing lights, fast action, and sound effects. One might assume a pinball player's job is to make sense of the chaos, to chart an elegant path through the clamor by directing the ball to go this way, that way, this way. Not so. The best pinball players try to maintain control as they complicate the situation even more—playing multiball, stacking scoring modes, building additional complexity, all while focusing on keeping the game going.

When I get home, after a long drive on dark roads, Maya and Benjamin are asleep. They are my complications, my multiball, the extra factors I've happily added to bounce around my life—while I try, every day, to keep the game going.

4

"It's More Fun to Compete"

PRETTY MUCH EVERY ARTICLE, documentary, or informative list about pinball includes one particular machine, a game-changing game produced by Gottlieb in 1947. The machine, still technically illegal in many places at the time it was manufactured, featured a new invention that proved critical for setting pinball on a path to reacceptance: flippers.

The game was *Humpty Dumpty*, and it had *six* flippers, three on each side, up and down the playfield, flapping like the stubby legs of a dancing insect. "With a little practice," reads a 1947 *Billboard* article, "the game's manufacturers believe that players can become accustomed to the principles of flipper button action and attain high scores." It's not clear exactly where designer Harry Mabs, who invented the flippers, intended for them to direct the ball—the important element was that the ball *could* be directed, that players could do more than simply plunge, stare, nudge, and cheer or curse.

Again the caveats are necessary: *Humpty Dumpty* had the first electromechanical flippers, meaning that they operated by pressing buttons that used electricity to move mechanical pieces, as opposed to purely mechanical flippers or tiny baseball bats, which had already been on games for fifteen years—one early machine was even named *Flipper* (1932). (The difference between a mechanical and an electromechanical flipper is that the former is operable the same way you'd control a miniature soccer player in foosball—the actual physical spin you put on the handle dictated how hard the bat hit the ball.)

Yet another case of ambiguity and scandal surrounds the electromechanical flipper, as Chicago Coin Machine Manufacturing Company designer Jerry Koci claimed to have beaten Mabs to the invention, though Chicago Coin didn't adopt it before Gottlieb could. Koci finally did get electromechanical flippers, albeit in a weird configuration, on a 1948 game called *Bermuda*, just a few months after *Humpty Dumpty* made history. For what it's worth, if anything, Mabs took the credit, but Koci ended up with the patent, number 2,520,283, "Pivotal Ball Return Means for Pin Games."

And pivotal it was, in both senses of the word, because flippers gave players something to do after launching the ball. Mabs called the buttons that operated his flippers "control buttons," a deliberate name choice meant to underscore the element of skill. This was no game of chance. How could it be? Players used control buttons. They had control.

Some control, at least. The six flippers on *Humpty Dumpty* faced outward at unnatural angles near the game's sides, in contrast to the central, V-shaped, two-flipper configuration we know and love today, which almost feels like an extension of the player's own hands.

"I've seen so many changes in pin games," designer Steve Kordek says in the 2009 pinball documentary *Special When Lit*. Indeed, at the time the documentary aired, Kordek was ninety-seven years old and had led teams responsible for designing over one hundred pinball machines. "But when those six flippers came out on *Humpty Dumpty*, I said, 'I've gotta do something like that.'" So he did—and since every flipper increased production costs, Kordek compromised and gave his next game, *Triple Action* (1948), just two flippers, both at the bottom, though they still pointed outward in the pigeon-toed direction. *Triple Action*, whose theme is one of those "Well, it was a different time" motifs, shows three women in bathing suits labeled (with no further explanation) "single," "double," and "triple."

He also gave those flippers direct-current power, making them much stronger than *Humpty Dumpty*'s—which meant, as Roger Sharpe told the *New York Times* for Kordek's 2012 obituary, that "a ball skillfully flipped from the bottom of the playfield could actually get to the top, and anywhere in between, with some semblance of accuracy."

Unlike mechanical flippers, the electromechanical flipper button kept the action under the player's control, but it made that action harder, a little less one-to-one, allowing a lot of "Oh, almost!" and "I *flipped*, you stupid machine!" Sentiments like those kept players pumping in the coins, convinced that the outcome of the game was in their hands, and neither completely right nor completely wrong about that.

Suddenly pinball was a different game. In a way, it now bore a stronger resemblance to racquetball than to slots. But even with the element of skill placed front and center, pinball was still a physical game of solitaire, not exactly a sport, nor really capable of becoming one.

Then in 1954, Gottlieb invented a new motivation for people to play. Since gambling was illegal and high scores were not always sufficient amusement for adults, the manufacturer introduced a circus-elephant-themed game called *Super Jumbo*, the first flipper pinball game that allowed multiple players to compete against each other.

Gottlieb saw multiplayer games as the wave of the future. With several competing on each machine, the cash dropped in the coin box with each game would be doubled, tripled, or quadrupled. Technically it was possible to compete before *Super Jumbo*, but only by playing a complete game beginning to end, then remembering your score and waiting while your friend played a complete game. *Super Jumbo* required players to switch after each ball, not after each game, and it displayed four different scores at once on the backbox.

"The earnings of this machine increase when more than one player use it at the same time," explained Gottlieb in an instructional letter sent to pinball operators. "Therefore you and your serviceman, as well as the location owner, should tell the players that it is more fun playing in competition. Four players can choose partners for team play. Have the location owner play with them until they become thoroughly familiar with the machine."

Whether or not location owners actually attempted a disingenuous "Hey, Mac, let's you and me and your buddies all play a game of *Super Jumbo* together!" attitude, Gottlieb started using the slogan "It's more fun to compete," a five-word catchphrase that would appear on dozens of games over the next few decades.

But as some sought to distance pinball from its gambling-oriented past, a significant part of the industry was perfectly happy to explore the possibilities for its gambling-oriented future.

In 1951, Bally Manufacturing had doubled down, so to speak, on the wagering aspect, introducing a line of bingo pinball machines that visually resembled regular pinball, including steel balls, a wooden playfield, and a spring-loaded plunger—but the game itself was essentially regular bingo, with a five-by-five grid and payouts awarded for filling rows, columns, or diagonals.

Bally released its first bingo pinball machine, *A-B-C*, in 1951. I saw one at Pinball Perfection, the museum where I played *Jig-Saw*: it was essentially a self-serve roulette wheel, and it seemed to count as pinball only insofar as it involved launching a steel ball onto a play-field. What happened after the launch? On the playfield, a spinning wheel captured the ball in a numbered hole. The end.

Well, not quite the end. On the backglass was a bingo card with the numbers one through twenty-five, and dropping the ball in one of the holes lit the corresponding number on the bingo card. At that point, it was no longer self-serve roulette but self-serve bingo; players tried to light lines of numbers, and the game awarded (wink-wink) "credits."

Aside from *A-B-C*, with its wheel, most of these machines had the exact same layout: twenty-five holes spread over the playfield and a rubber bumper here or there. According to Jeffrey Lawton's book *The Bingo Pinball War*, Bally and another company, the thrillingly named United Manufacturing, spent the better part of the '50s battling to dominate the bingo pinball market, each one-upping the other with new features. Most of these features were not physical gadgets, but ways players could potentially fill their bingo cards. A bonus for all four corners! Diagonal scoring! Play six cards at once!

In other words, the bingo pinball market—thriving though it was—consisted of the exact same game manufactured over and over again with different rules and art. None had flippers, even though they had been invented. And for some reason, many of the machines were named after geographic locations, a list of which sounds like a where's where of destinations considered exotic to the working stiffs of the '50s: *Tahiti* (1953), *Rio* (1953), *Palm Springs* (1953), *Havana* (1954), *Mexico* (1954), *Hawaii* (1954), *Nevada* (1954), *Singapore* (1954), *Manhattan* (1955), *Miami Beach* (1955), *Monaco* (1956), *Key West* (1956), and *Brazil* (1956).

As bingo pinball rose, fell, and became a footnote in pinball history, the trunk of pinball's phylogenetic tree continued its growth to evolve into the game that ensnared me.

The 1960s and early '70s saw the invention of a few more playfield staples, like spinners, thin targets that flip around like pinwheels when the ball passes under them. Drop targets. Multiball. Manufacturers started experimenting with toys and gimmicks, many of which became the centerpieces of the machines they adorned. A 1970 Chicago Coin game, for example, used extralong flippers. It was called—will ingenuity never cease?—*Big Flipper*.

I had the opportunity to play a game of *Big Flipper* at PAPA. Swinging the five-inch flippers at the regular-sized ball felt like trying to hit a softball using a roll of industrial carpet.

Of course, not all of pinball's novelties during this experimental period were keepers. There were two-player head-to-head pinball machines with two full playfields facing each other. There were miniature pinball games built into cocktail tables, underneath a flat piece of glass, which were probably played during either the most awkward or the most awesome first dates. In 1979, a new game called *Hercules* made *Big Flipper* look tiny. Marketed as "18 square feet of excitement," *Hercules* had flippers the size of chicken drumsticks, a playfield so massive it was hard to reach both flipper buttons simultaneously, and, instead of a small steel ball, a billiard ball.

Many of pinball's oddities are the stuff of eBay clamor, as bidders overtop one another to enhance their collections. But for those without the time, money, or basement space to accumulate vintage machines, there are other places to enjoy the output of an industry struggling to find direction in a nation struggling to do the same: pinball museums.

* * *

Pinball museums aren't as rare as you might think. If Google can be believed, as of this writing, at least twenty thriving pinball museums can be found in Alameda, Banning, and El Cerrito, California; Seattle; Las Vegas; Roanoke, Virginia; Asheville, North Carolina; Ann Arbor,

Michigan; Pittsburgh; the Wisconsin Dells; Tarpon Springs and Delray, Florida; Portland, Oregon; and Hockley, Texas—not to mention Paris, Budapest, Krakow, and Rotterdam.

That amazes the hell out of me. It means that twenty people, at a minimum, independently thought it would be a terrific idea to open a museum, an actual educational museum, solely on the subject of pinball.

They weren't all correct.

In December 2010, David Silverman invested $300,000 into building the National Pinball Museum in Washington, DC. The idea made sense at the time—after all, DC is flooded with tourists seeking every other type of museum. Silverman housed his inside a former FAO Schwartz toy store, using two leftover dinosaur legs to dictate the motif of a floor-to-ceiling dinosaur pinball mural. He re-created a French ship—complete with rocking floor—to illustrate bagatelle sailing across the Atlantic, and he filled the space with dozens of machines from his personal collection of over nine hundred.

It was a beautiful museum. I attended its opening-night party—the place was ten minutes down the road from me, for goodness sake—and I even got a membership card. I knew I'd come back often.

Unfortunately, I never got the chance. Silverman, dreaming big, had built the museum inside a swanky mall in upscale Georgetown, where after only six months, the mall's owners sent him a rather unwelcome letter.

"In that letter it basically says we're taking your lease . . . and we're throwing you out in 60 days," Silverman told the *Georgetowner*. The owners cited renovations, but there were murmurs that the museum's general incompatibility with Georgetown's swanky Georgetown-ness also didn't help. Even Perez Hilton's website eulogized the museum, calling its fate "a bunch of bullshizz."

Rather than recount the entire sad story of the homeless National Pinball Museum, I'll let news headlines do the job:

- June 30, 2010, *Washington Business Journal*: "Pinball Museum Heading for Georgetown."
- May 23, 2011, *Washington Post*: "National Pinball Museum to Close."
- May 27, 2011, *Arcade Heroes*: "National Pinball Museum Looking for a New Place to Stay After Lease Revoked."
- September 21, 2011, Reuters: "Nation's Largest Pinball Museum to Open in Baltimore."
- February 20, 2013, *HuffPost DC*: "National Pinball Museum Closing in Baltimore After Moving from DC One Year Ago."
- August 8, 2013, *Baltimore Sun*: "National Pinball Museum in Search of Home Again."
- April 21, 2014, WTOP-FM: "Former Pinball Museum Owner Selling Off Collection."

Silverman, who truly loved collecting pinball machines—his very first purchase filled an apartment so tiny that he slept, every night, underneath the game—began auctioning off his prized machines, one by one, to recoup his losses from having opened and closed two museums in two years.

It seemed a cautionary tale, with much to caution against, particularly the choice to stake one's financial future on the success of a pinball museum. But as I learned from a slideshow depicting Clay Harrell's misadventures founding the Ann Arbor Pinball Museum, sometimes that success can be as accidental as the museum's existence in the first place.

In 2006, Harrell was already renowned in the pinball community as the star of a pinball repair DVD series and podcast called *This Old Pinball*. He began bouncing his collection of games through a series of initially friendly venues—an empty Rite Aid, a video store called Crazy Carl's, a warehouse he named Tilt Town—in an effort to find a roof to keep them under without having to pay too much. He had no intention of building a museum, only the classic hoarder's dilemma.

But at Tilt Town, Harrell genuinely tried to turn his collection into something for all to enjoy, charging a yearly membership fee to play the games. Which worked fine, Harrell says, until his ads on Craigslist attracted the nut jobs.

"Look around the room," he explains, gesturing to the crowd of pinball enthusiasts I joined to watch Harrell's public presentation on the tribulations of founding a pinball museum. "We're all pinball people. We're all fucking weird. But this set a whole new standard for what was weird."

As Tilt Town deteriorated toward what Harrell calls "a drunkard's paradise," a city manager showed up for a surprise inspection.

"I basically told them to fuck off," Harrell says. "You never want to do that to a city manager. They get really mad." The inspection had been triggered, it turns out, by an online ad—not one of his but one posted by some joker advertising "pinball, booze, and hookers."

"This kind of gave a negative presentation to the whole event," deadpans Harrell.

So he moved his 130 games to a new warehouse, which he called Flipper City, but this time with much tighter secrecy.

"The first rule of pinball club," he says, and you can guess what comes next, but here it is anyway, "is don't talk about pinball club."

Harrell had now occupied four different venues in six years. He wasn't a small businessman; he wasn't building an arcade. He was simply looking for an affordable place to drink beer with friends and play pinball without running afoul of city ordinances.

When a rent hike ousted him from Flipper City, Harrell knew he needed a new tactic. So when the opportunity arose to purchase a defunct VFW hall in Ann Arbor, he discovered a clause in its residential zoning laws that offered business exemptions for day care centers or museums.

"We were just a club that I wanted to put all my crappy pinball machines in," says Harrell, shrugging, "but now we're a museum."

Kind of. The city voted to approve the Ann Arbor Pinball Museum, but for whatever reason—maybe "not in my backyard," maybe general bureaucracy—it would only allow the museum to operate four weekends a year. It's an attitude that Harrell summarized as, "We like that you're a museum, but we don't want you to ever be open."

At this point, you may be wondering, do people actually *go* to pinball museums? Isn't it only a subset of a subset of the general public that would even set foot in such a place? To find out, I spent an evening inside one of the world's most successful pinball museums, one that prides itself on its appeal to the masses.

If you've heard of Asbury Park, New Jersey, you may be thinking of its connection to Bruce Springsteen—the Boss titled his first album *Greetings from Asbury Park, N.J.* and kicked off his career there at the famous Stone Pony. But the seaside town, with its wide boardwalk and Victorian architecture, is also home to a place named New Jersey's "Top Museum Worth Traveling For" by TripAdvisor's *FlipKey* blog, granting it the honor of sharing a web page with the Strataca Kansas Underground Salt Museum, the Idaho Potato Museum, and the National Mustard Museum in Middleton, Wisconsin (where, seriously, they offer continuing education through a faux college called Poupon U and whose Mustardpiece Theatre has hosted such musicals as *The Sound of Mustard*, *The Full Mustard*, and *Annie Get Your Bun*).

It's the Silver Ball Museum, and like many of the world's pinball museums, it was founded by accident. Rob Ilvento, who had previously risen to prominence by founding the Cluck-U chain of college-focused chicken restaurants while a sophomore at Rutgers, decided to indulge his daughter's love for his Gottlieb *Melody* (1967) by purchasing additional games until they overflowed his home. In 2009, Ilvento moved his machines to the basement of a record and clothing store, then six months later, to the Asbury Park boardwalk. The museum now holds over two hundred games, representing about a third of Ilvento's collection.

Much like the PAPA facility's 2004 flood, the Silver Ball Museum had a fun time in 2012 with Hurricane Sandy, which knocked the seaside attraction out of commission for two months.* The difference between PAPA's crisis and the Silver Ball Museum's crisis was, according to a 2016 *Washington Post* article, a mere five inches—that's how close the water level came to the bellies of the machines after Sandy. Let's have a moment of silence, however, for the shorter video games that did not survive the flood.

"Today's arcades," laments general manager Dan Toskaner, "everything is prizes. Kids win the tickets, and that's all they want to do." At the Silver Ball Museum, he's seen what happens when a child, used to the neon lights and quarter pushers that constitute the de facto gambling of redemption games, presses START on a pinball machine for the first time.

Sometimes, apparently, not much. Toskaner says he's watched in frustration more than once as a child starts a game, presses the big flashing button or pulls the knob to launch the ball, then does *nothing*, unaware that flipper buttons exist. The child watches the ball roll down between the flippers, thinks, *Well, that wasn't thrilling*, and loses interest immediately. They can figure out classic video games—at home, they play video games—but short of buying an actual, full-size pinball machine there's no true way to duplicate the pinball experience in the living room.

It's a lament I've heard from more than one source. "Jersey Jack" Guarnieri, the CEO of Jersey Jack Pinball, told *Pinball Magazine* that in arcades and at trade shows without pinball fans, "the game is on free play and they have no clue what to do. They push the coin return button. It's so sad."

At practically every pinball museum and arcade I've visited, it's a given that the owner has to brag about the diversity of attendees—all

---

* Interestingly, as I discovered, the Silver Ball Museum doesn't post "OUT OF ORDER" signs on nonfunctional machines. Instead, the signs say "UNDER RESTORATION." Neat trick.

ages, all skill levels, more than one gender. Sometimes, upon hearing the almost cliché declaration of "We get everyone in here! Even kids! All types!" one gets the sense that they may be exaggerating pinball's diverse appeal just a bit.

"Sure," they say, "tonight it's all pudgy middle-aged white men, but *last month*, you should have been here this one Tuesday . . ." However, on the Saturday evening in August when I visit the Silver Ball Museum in Asbury Park, this is no lip service. It's a legitimately popular hangout, just like arcades in the '80s, only not unscrupulous. Just electromechanical family fun.

There really are all types here. Grandparents and toddlers. Black kids and Orthodox Jews (it's after sundown). Swimmers in flip-flops and packs of teenagers. Those who read the informational placards above every game detailing its role in pinball history and those who aren't quite sure what this place is.

Someone named Patrick is having an awesome eleventh birthday party.

There are even guys playing pinball with their girlfriends. That means two things: One, couples are finding pinball to be a good date-night activity. And two, guys who play pinball on Saturday nights actually do have girlfriends.

Even Springsteen himself has visited the museum, as have celebrity chef Anthony Bourdain and the marginally less fun Governor Chris Christie.

This is not an amusement park. There are no rides. No tickets, no prizes. Just vintage pinball, plus a few older arcade games, and everyone is having a blast.

"People's eyes light up," says Toskaner. "'Wow, that's the machine I played thirty years ago when I was a teenager!' People come happy, and they leave even happier."

The three primary ingredients for a pinball museum, then, might be delight, nostalgia, and general financial insolvency. "Thankfully the owner is not using this to make his living," he admits, "and as long as it's not losing money, he continues it."

And here's why I think pinball has a future. I watch Patrick and his birthday party friends, between games of air hockey and Skee-Ball (the Silver Ball Museum has Skee-Ball machines from three different eras, none of them modern), go to town on a Gottlieb *Knockout*. That's right: in 2015, I'm watching a pinball game made in 1950 being thoroughly enjoyed by a kid made in 2004.

* * *

Running a pinball museum is a labor of love. It freaking has to be, because it's sure not a way to make money.

Tim Arnold, who owns the Pinball Hall of Fame in Las Vegas, where I once dragged an entire bachelor party (not mine) for a few hours, readily confesses his massive facility is anything but profitable—not that it matters, since he donates the museum's proceeds to the Salvation Army. Right on the Hall of Fame's main web page, Arnold declares, "There's no real economic reason for this to exist, or capitalism would've already built it."

He's right. Based on standard business principles, there's no reason pinball museums should exist. Then again, there's no reason pinball itself should exist. It's inefficient, unnecessary, complex, and breakable. That's what makes it so charming.

And thankfully, after decades of hiding in shadows, the kind of family fun I witnessed at the Silver Ball Museum is finally legal again. For this, we can thank the man who played a particularly crucial game of pinball, a game that undid everything Mayor La Guardia did to rid New York City, and the world, of the scourge of pinball: Roger Sharpe.

5

How Josh and Zach's Dad
Saved Pinball

O N MAY 13, 1976, Roger Sharpe, a young writer with a drooping
black mustache the size of a kielbasa, sat in a meeting of the
New York City Council. He was preparing to play what has become
the single most important game of pinball in history.

"I grew up pinball ignorant," says Sharpe, who has since become
one of the most revered figures in the pinball world. "I can't even
call it pinball deprived. I just didn't know that the games existed."

That all changed when he attended the University of Wisconsin,
where he triple majored in business, English, and journalism. Because
a triple major apparently leaves gobs of free time in one's schedule to
hang out at bowling alleys, Sharpe hung out at bowling alleys, which
often had pinball machines.

Burgers, bowling, beer, and pinball. It all fit together. "And I,"
says Sharpe, "was just absolutely terrible."

He describes a day he watched a fraternity brother playing *Buck-
aroo* (1965), miming each prop that contributed to his character:

"Hamburger. French fries. Soft drink. Cigarette." Sharpe waxes rhap-
sodic about how the man embodied coolness, cradling the ball on
one flipper while using his free hand to eat or smoke, bobbing his
head as I imagine hepcats did in the '60s. "It was like a light turning
on," he says.

"It became something of an obsession, rather than a compulsion,"
Sharpe clarifies. He chooses his words carefully, and why not? Sharpe
is a former managing editor of *GQ*. "It was just glorious. I mean, I
was *good*. It was something that just kind of came to me."

After college, Sharpe moved to New York City. "Lo and behold,
there's no pinball," he says. "I go from feast to famine." He eventually
found where all of the pinball machines were hiding, because hiding
is exactly what they were doing: pinball was illegal in the city, so the
only places to play were inside, for example, peep shows.

Sharpe is not a peep show qua peep show kind of guy. He's the
sort of person who probably legitimately read *Playboy* for the articles—and attended peep shows for the pinball. Yet he found himself
stopping by houses of—let's not say ill repute but mixed repute—three
times a day.

The problem with having an illegal hobby is that your obsession
(sorry, compulsion) can be withdrawn at any time, and you have no
recourse. One day Sharpe walked into his usual source of games and
gams only to find the pinball machines disabled. "They came in and
busted us," the owner told him.

I find all of this odd. Not just because pinball is, you know, *pinball*,
a challenging but ultimately frivolous game. But also because it's hard
to reconcile the idea of something being illegal—and enforcedly so—
yet standing so gigantic and prominent and unmissable. You know
what I mean? You can sneak candy bars into movies because you can
slip them in your coat pocket. But if the verboten snack was, say, a
washing machine, how could anyone commit such an obvious violation for any length of time without getting busted?

Yet that was the situation in New York City and, indeed, in much of the country. Pinball had, in 1976, been illegal in the city for thirty-five years; games of luck counted as illegal gambling, and games of skill were exempt. Pinball combines both, hence widespread confusion and disagreement.

The November 20, 1965, issue of *Billboard* gives a good sample of the landscape of pinball-related hostilities across America at that time: In Kentucky, Governor Edward T. Breathitt clashed with pinball operators he claimed were running de facto gambling operations. In Alaska, the Third District Superior Court disagreed with the Fourth District Superior Court about pinball. In Snohomish County, Washington, a judge ordered five games pulled from a bowling alley, but downstate in Clark County, an attorney deemed a pinball machine no more a gambling device "than a deck of cards that is used for a game of fun."

"I've always viewed my relationship with pinball as being totally and completely different than anybody else's," says Sharpe. "I don't want this to come off as being vain or egotistical, because it's not meant to be, but there is no one else that has had the life of pinball that I have had."

He's right for two reasons. First, every aficionado has a distinct relationship with pinball that no one else can replicate, whether it conjures fond memories of a beach arcade or a Fonzie wannabe at a college bar.* But second, unlike everyone else, Roger Sharpe can boast that without his influence, pinball might still be outlawed.

---

* Arthur "the Fonz" Fonzarelli, Henry Winkler's leather-jacket-wearing, motorcycle-riding rebel character on *Happy Days*, was often seen playing pinball—which, in both the 1950s (when the show was set) and the 1970s (when it was filmed), was a low-grade act of insurrection, tantamount to his ability to score free music on the jukebox with a well-placed fist pound. In 1977, Coleco released a stripped-down Fonzie-themed pinball machine, the wonderful commercial for which has been uploaded to YouTube by the Museum of Chicago Classic Television. "Aaay! It's me talkin'! The Fonz Pinball! Wanna play me?" the game yells at a faux-surprised boy in bellbottoms, who, as you may guess, ends the commercial giving the

In 1975, Sharpe volunteered to write an article on pinball for the winter 1975 issue of *GQ*, both as a means of sharing his passion with a wider audience, and as an excuse to perform the necessary research to figure out how to buy a pinball machine for his own apartment. Only that research turned out to be more difficult than he'd imagined, as he soon discovered when a trip to the New York Public Library to research pinball uncovered a 1972 *Playboy* article about pinball*—and no other information.

For a writer, it was both a good problem and a bad problem to have. It meant that Sharpe would have to do a lot of research from scratch, but it also meant that the amount of from-scratch research might overflow a *GQ* article, and, thus, he should write a book.

That book became the colorful 1977 volume *Pinball!*, whose simple title and exclamation point accurately encompass its comprehensiveness and loving enthusiasm. "I'm standing in the center of Paris, City of Light, scene of a thousand separate pleasures," Sharpe gushes in the first chapter, "and all I want to do is duck into a dark bar, cozy up to a *Spirit of '76* and whip it into a frenzy of flashing lights, ringing bells, and rapidly whirling scoring drums."

Sharpe was nothing if not committed. "Playing pinball is like making love," he wrote. "It demands the complete concentration and total emotional involvement of the player." It's a description that may make some pinball players nod in understanding, but it might also make his sons, Josh and Zach—who I watched earn second and third place at PAPA17—say, "Eww, Dad."

---

camera a big double thumbs-up. It was a home model of a pinball machine, a cheap minigame with folding legs that kinda sorta brought the excitement of pinball into the rumpus room. The game lit up and even used legitimate flippers, but it had the sturdiness of a card table, so it wouldn't last if a player decided to, as Fonzie would say, sit on it. Incidentally, an interview request I sent to Winkler's agent, on a whim, was met with a polite but decisive reply that "Henry's schedule is swamped and he is unavailable," even though I had attempted to get my foot in the door by revealing that I attended Hebrew school with his cousin's daughter.
* See, he does read it for the articles.

So in May of 1976, Sharpe was a semipublic figure with a couple of pinball articles under his belt, a book in progress, industry contacts but no industry affiliation, and an exhaustive knowledge of the past forty years of pinball. All of these qualifications, plus his abilities as a player—to this day, he's still ranked in or near the top one thousand players worldwide—made Sharpe a perfect choice to represent a hobby in dire need of a champion.*

I had always pictured the relegalization of pinball as a formality. The outlawing of the game may have been prudent in the days of Bonnie and Clyde, but these were modern times, the mid-'70s, and surely all thoughtful New Yorkers could agree that the pop bumper and the playfield multiplier posed no real threat. In fact, I had always thought of it as one of those "wacky law factoids," the kind you read about on a website of weird but real laws: "In New York City, it is illegal to play pinball! In Billings, Montana, it is illegal to raise pet rats!"†

Yet when Sharpe showed up to testify as the star witness for the Music and Amusement Association, he found the New York City Council just as surly and suspicious as they must have been a generation previous. "The first question asked of me after I was sworn in was,

---

* Sharpe, carrying a pistol and wearing a sheriff's star on his Wild West vest, would later appear on the backglass of the 1979 game *Sharpshooter*, a buxom maiden hanging from each pant leg—one of whom was, and still is, his wife, Ellen. Sharpe designed the game, and he's hardly the only pinball designer to sneak his own likeness into a game's artwork. Thanks to the "Hidden Artwork on Pinball Machines" page on the Belgian website Flippers.be, we know that artist Python Anghelo drew his head on a snake on *Bad Cats* (1989), John Youssi and his young son can be seen on *Funhouse*, Greg Kmiec is a pilot on the *Supersonic* (1979) playfield, and John Popadiuk appears as an acrobat on *Cirqus Voltaire* (1997). Popadiuk, not content to limit the Easter eggs in his art to homo sapiens, even drew his cat on three different machines—*Cirqus Voltaire*, *Theatre of Magic*, and *World Cup Soccer* (1994). Cat people, am I right?

† According to Section 4-304 of a very large legal document, this is true, unless the rats are used for research purposes. Whether rats can be trained to play pinball may never be determined, at least not in Billings—but you'll be thrilled, if unsurprised, to learn that the Internet has no shortage of videos of perplexed cats trying to swat pinballs beneath the playfield glass. Again with the cat people.

'We understand you're doing a book. So who's paying for that?'" he says, mimicking a skeptical councilman. "I mean, this *anger*."

Sharpe respectfully answered their questions, but testifying in the verbal sense is the less significant part of what Sharpe had come to the City Council meeting to do. He was there as a pinball advocate, but he was also there to do something in front of the council curmudgeons that would prove, once and for all, that pinball was a game of skill.

Sharpe was going to play pinball.

Positioned prominently by the door sat *El Dorado* (1975), a cowboy-themed pinball machine Sharpe knew well. He had planned to walk the council through the various ways a player could truly control the game—catching the ball, knocking down specific drop targets, aiming at the rollover that changed which drop target was lit and therefore worth more. However, since this was an important moment for the pinball industry, manufacturer D. Gottlieb and Company had supplied not one machine but two. The second, *Bank Shot* (1976), hid in a corner in case *El Dorado* suffered a last-minute mechanical failure.

In the fall of 2015, a much older Roger Sharpe, sitting on the floor of an unused hotel conference room outside Chicago, tells me the story of the shot heard round the pinball world. He's still every bit as passionate about pinball as he was forty years ago, and as is evidenced by his willingness to sit for an hour on a dirty hotel carpet at midnight, he's retained some of his old stamina.

Sharpe wears a turtleneck under a collared flannel shirt—Chicago casual, let's call it—and his thick mustache and sideburns are just as prominent as, though a few shades lighter than, they were during the Ford administration. He's now not only a father but also a grandfather, to Josh's children, and I can tell he's at the point where he's been asked more than once to tell this story. He's one of pinball's biggest celebrities, if such creatures can be said to exist; a 2014 *Wired* article called him "somewhere between the Michael Jordan and Santa Claus of pinball."

"The cameras are all set up around the game, because everybody knows that this person who's testifying is going to play to show that pinball's a game of skill," Sharpe says. He took two steps toward *El Dorado*, and then a mistrustful councilman shouted, "Not that game! *That* game." He wanted Sharpe to play *Bank Shot*, the backup game, because he assumed *El Dorado* had been rigged.

It was meant to be a gotcha moment. What the councilman didn't realize, Sharpe explains, was that "*Bank Shot* lent itself much more to the information that I wanted to provide in terms of geometry, objectives, and game rules. The science of really laying out a pinball playfield. As opposed to *El Dorado*, which is a spell-out game."

Looking at the *El Dorado* playfield, one can see that its designer, Ed Krynski, basically bet the ranch on drop targets. The game has no fewer than fifteen drop targets, those little plastic rectangles that poke out of the playfield like teeth and retract when hit, which is practically a record for one machine. (Practically, but not quite—the 1971 game *2001* holds the record with an amazing tally of twenty drop targets.) So on *El Dorado*, the bulk of Sharpe's game would have been a demonstration of how to shoot at, and knock down, drop targets.

The number of drop targets in *Bank Shot*? Zero. What the billiards-themed game—also, incidentally, designed by Krynski—did have, however, were five parallel lanes at the top of the playfield, numbered one through five. And after a player launched the ball with the spring-loaded plunger, it had to roll through one of the lanes on its way to the rest of the playfield. Remember those lanes. They will become very important.

Sharpe casually narrated his strategy as he played, describing the game's objective and showing off his ability to hit whichever stand-up target he aimed for. (Unlike a drop target, which drops after it's hit, a stand-up target stays standing up. Some pinball jargon is self-explanatory.)

Then the time came to launch his third and final ball. Before pulling the plunger, Sharpe remembered games he'd played in a bowling alley in Skokie, Illinois—games with no plunger that could be pulled back. Instead, the games in the bowling alley had automatic plungers—you'd press a button, and the game would launch the ball onto the playfield for you. Many modern games have those, and most players don't think much of them one way or another. But in Skokie, at least to Sharpe, automatic plungers were damned annoying. With scarcely sufficient power to launch the ball onto the playfield, automatic plungers stole one more bit of player-controlled finesse from the game and replaced it with blind chance. Sharpe calls it "pseudopinball."

Ironically, the reason the bowling alley's games in Skokie only had automatic plungers was their mandatory compliance with local gambling laws, specifically the ones that somehow identified the plunger as the element of chance. Maybe it looked too much like the arm on a slot machine. Regardless, Sharpe thought about those Skokie machines, crippled by a nonsensical and unnecessary law, and he made a decision.

"See these lines?" he asked the council, indicating the tiny tick marks painted around the plunger spring. "These are gradient lines, and there's skill even to the plunger." The gradient lines, like lines on a ruler, help a player pull the plunger back to the same spot each time, giving the ball a more repeatable amount of momentum. Sharpe knew that if Skokie, Illinois, and other towns restricted to automatic plungers were ever going to lose *their* restrictive laws, he would have to show not just that he could make shots from the flippers but also that *every* part of a pinball machine could be manipulated with skill.

In the grand scheme of a pinball game, pulling the plunger is a minor task. In a single game, a player may press the flipper buttons hundreds of times each but only plunge three times. If pinball were basketball, flipping would be like dribbling and shooting combined, and plunging would be the tip-off. The tip-off is important, and it takes skill, but one probably shouldn't spend a majority of basketball practice on winning the tip-off.

Because it's practiced less, and because a spring of unknown springiness gives a player much less time to acclimate to its quirks than a flipper of unknown flippy-ness, calling your shot from a plunge— declaring that the launched ball will roll through lane one, and not lanes two through five—is hardly guaranteed. But if Sharpe could pull it off, he would drive home his point that even the chanciest components of the machine could be mastered.

"I tend to speak, 90 percent of the time, before I really think about what I'm saying," Sharpe laughs. "Center lane happened to be lit."

Like Babe Ruth had done in game three of the 1932 World Series, Sharpe called his shot.

The story of what happened next is one that fans of pinball know and know well, almost to the point of cliché. Any Buzzfeed-style listicle about interesting tales in the history of pinball is practically legally required to include this anecdote. It was even depicted in an episode of Comedy Central's *Drunk History*, in which a mullet-wigged actor with a massive black handlebar mustache (not too dissimilar from Sharpe's in 1976) reenacts the event as described by drunk comedians.*

Carefully he drew back the plunger, feeling the tension of the spring and gauging, to the best of his ability, what might happen when he released it. Sharpe let go. The ball zipped onto the play-field, bounced briefly on a rubber rebound bumper—then fell cleanly through the center lane, exactly where he said it would.

In interviews, Sharpe has credited luck. He's entertained the influence of divine intervention, presumably by either a pinball-loving God

---

* *Drunk History* also implied that Sharpe had never previously played the machine the council put before him, adding to his mystique as a profoundly talented pinball sight-reader. "Yeah, right," Sharpe told me. "I played all the games, and I've actually played every production game made since 1966. I take a lot of pride in that." I guess, contrary to common sense, you just can't entrust faithful communication of historical facts to drunk comedians.

or a God who left the celestial electromagnet on. These should be taken as signs not of Sharpe's fortunate bumbling but of his general humility. "Obviously I had some notion as to how far back to pull that plunger," he confides, now too far removed from the event to keep shrugging and saying, "Got lucky, I guess!" And besides, he admits, if the ball fell just right or left of center, he could have bumped the machine around a bit and argued that, with his influence, it at least came close.

"I knew that I could get it somewhere in the middle, absolutely," he says. "Did I think it could be dead middle, without a touch? No."

Lest anyone forget, Sharpe's plunge has been immortalized in an oil painting titled *He Called the Shot*, prints of which are sometimes auctioned off at pinball fundraisers. I love the sheer obscurity of the reference: imagine mounting that painting above your mantle, subtly edging houseguests over toward it for years until one finally says, "Wait—is that . . ."

The moment the ball passed through the center lane, Sharpe says, the gruff councilman interrupted. "That's it," he muttered. "We've seen enough."

And with that, by a six-to-zero vote, pinball became legal once more in New York City on June 1, 1976. Sharpe, and everyone else, could once again play their favorite game in public. It was, appropriately, the same strategy that had zinged Jacob Mirowsky, the Bronx-based proprietor hauled into court in 1935 whose experts failed to outperform their counterparts at bagatelle—but when Sharpe did it, it worked.

Sharpe's game of *Bank Shot* did not instantly legalize pinball around the country. American anti-pinball laws were so hodgepodge that relegalization in each municipality was its own separate project, which is why so many articles on the subject are content to say that after Sharpe convinced the New York City Council, "the rest of the country followed suit." In fact, when Sharpe dazzled the council room in New York, pinball had already been legal in Los Angeles for almost two years. But Sharpe's episode was so dramatic, such a triumph of sense over stodginess, that it has become the moment renowned as a turning point in pinball history.

Many write-ups of the event oversimplify Sharpe's contribution, making it sound like he haplessly yanked the plunger on *Bank Shot*, crossed his fingers, and hey presto, pinball became decriminalized as arbitrarily as it had been outlawed. Nothing could be further from the truth. His plunge was a deliberate act of showmanship, an over-the-top(-of-the-playfield) demonstration in response to the reluctance he perceived in the council. And, lucky for all of us, it worked.

What did Sharpe do after he changed the world? Right there in the council chamber, with everyone walking away and his hands still on the flipper buttons of *Bank Shot*, he kept playing. After all, it was ball three, and he was having a pretty good game.

● ● ●

Josh and Zach Sharpe grew up in a house saturated in pinball. "There's never been a point in my life where pinball wasn't around," Zach wrote to me. In 1998, at PAPA6, Zach won the Juniors Division, which led to a father-son television appearance on the Nickelodeon gameshow *Figure It Out*, where they were billed as "past and present pinball wizards."

To the Sharpe brothers, pinball not only was an interesting hobby but also gave them an opportunity to spend time with their dad. It reminds me of my dad's attempt to interest me in his own hobby, the card game bridge. He'd been playing since high school, traveling to tournaments and reading a monthly magazine called *The Bridge World*. My first paying job, at age ten, was as a bridge caddy at one of those tournaments, moving cards between tables, collecting score tickets, refilling water pitchers, and probably violating child labor laws.

Sometimes I wonder if he hoped his son would one day adopt his passion, and we'd play bridge as partners. Or maybe that was not his hope but his fear, and bridge was a way to spend a night away from the kids. Regardless, bridge never interested me the way pinball snared Josh and Zach.

Today Zach is a senior producer at a creative and marketing agency, and Josh is chief financial officer of an arcade game manufacturer. They also run the International Flipper Pinball Association (IFPA), the umbrella organization that oversees worldwide player rankings, sanctions leagues, and runs competitions. During the decade with Josh as president and Zach as vice president, the number of IFPA-endorsed tournaments around the world has exploded from fifty in 2006 to more than twenty-five hundred, and the number of registered competitive pinball players has grown from five hundred to over forty thousand. Both are usually ranked among the top players worldwide; at the time of this writing, Josh is fifteenth and Zach is second. Forty years later, Sharpe's plunge has achieved mythical status. His sons own T-shirts reading "MY DAD SAVED PINBALL," and when they wear them to pinball events, everyone knows what that means.

* * *

"To help insure that pinball will hold its place in history," Roger Sharpe wrote nearly forty years ago in *Pinball!*, "I have proposed that pinball leagues be established, similar in style to bowling leagues." It's a seminal bit of text buried at the end of his seminal book, and it goes even further: "We already have pinball tournaments, but why stop there? A Pinball Olympiad is the next logical step toward determining just which of the millions of players is really the World Pinball Champion."

Today, the abundance of leagues predicted by—and partially brought about by—Roger Sharpe has come to pass. And with league victories worth world pinball player ranking (WPPR) points that con-tribute to a player's worldwide ranking, success in pinball leagues can actually place one within flipping distance of earning the World Pinball Champion title.

"Pretty much anything competitive pinball related didn't exist before my dad and Steve Epstein invented it," Josh Sharpe wrote to me. It began with a recognition that bowling leagues brought play-ers into bowling alleys on otherwise slow nights—maybe, Roger and Epstein thought, the same could happen to arcades.

In early 1978, Roger started asking himself how exactly a pinball league would work. It would be more complicated than bowling, for example, where a lane is basically a lane, whether you play in a league in Cleveland or El Paso. A score of two hundred on one bowling lane is as impressive as a score of two hundred on another lane. But pinball machines—even different copies of the same machine—can handle quite differently. One could be set with a tighter tilt or a shallower incline or a malfunctioning gizmo or a weak flipper that makes a certain ramp shot impossible.

So Sharpe, along with Broadway Arcade owner Steve Epstein and their friend Lionel Martinez, began gathering data to help design their new league scoring system. And by "gathering data," I mean playing tons of pinball.

For the next three years, the founders of what they called MES (Martinez, Epstein, and Sharpe) International played thousands of games, meticulously recording their scores. They then used those numbers to lay the foundations of a league scoring system, the heart of which is that players compete against their groupmates on a given machine, not against everyone who's ever played that game in any location. In 1980, MES International was ready to begin testing and tweaking their scoring system in a Sunday-morning league at a New Jersey arcade called Game Town.

Today some pinball leagues still play in arcades. Others can be found in restaurants, bars, or even private homes. Anyplace with a few pinball machines can host a league, provided it can recruit sufficient players. One goal of the original leagues, Sharpe says, was to feed players to the various larger competitions, and it's still working: WPPR points accumulated for league play increase a player's overall ranking, and every New Year's Day, sixty-four of the top-ranked players are asked to compete in the IFPA World Pinball Championship (not to be confused with the PAPA World Pinball Championships), an invitation-only tournament reserved for the best of the best.

That's not me.

It's been more than four years since I played in a weekly pinball league, having retired my flipper fingers shortly before Maya was born. I even remember panicking about whether she might arrive early and prevent me from competing in that season's finals.

With Marina's full (but tenuous) permission, I have now signed up to play an eight-week season, partly to practice for the next World Pinball Championships and partly to learn why pinball leagues have recently become so popular. As of my first week back, IFPA registers a whopping 237 independent pinball leagues around the world, with a collective population of over six thousand players, from the Alley Pass Pinball League in Flint, Michigan, to the WNY Pinball League in Rochester, New York. There's a London Pinball League in England and a London Pinball League in Ontario. There's the Space City Pinball League in Houston, the Magic City Pinball League in Birmingham, Alabama, the Liga de Pinball de Madrid, and the Osnabrücker Flipperliga in Osnabrück, Germany. Even in my local area, there are two separately operating pinball leagues, the Free State Pinball Association and the DC-Maryland-Virginia (DMV) Pinball League, with nearly two hundred players between them.

I join the DMV League, since it allows players to compete once per week at any league location—this Mexican restaurant in Baltimore on

Wednesday nights, this bar in Glen Burnie, Maryland, on Tuesdays. For my first week, on a frigid Sunday night in January, I walk into the Black Cat, one of the hippest venues in DC. It's hip in the earned, legitimate sense, not in the quinoa sense—for more than two decades, the Black Cat has hosted indie bands that cool people have heard of in a checker-tiled, brick-walled, standing-room-only theater with room for seven hundred people. And now, somehow, in the maroon-walled bar at the front of the venue, someone has convinced them to plug in a bunch of pinball machines.

A sign on the door reads, "NO CROWD SURFING OR STAGE DIVING OR YOU WILL BE REMOVED WITHOUT REFUND," presumably a warning for concertgoers, not for pinball players. Fair enough, Black Cat.

Many of my fellow league members look like the nonpinball patrons of the Black Cat, who on this night have gathered in a different part of the club to hear a Southern politipop performer called the Grey A covering Depeche Mode's "Personal Jesus." Maybe that's how pinball leagues are filling their ranks—with the sort of modern urbanites choosing between this, dodgeball, and darts.

Pierce McLain, an early thirties tattooed Black Cat employee with his head partly shaved in a manner inscrutably yet casually cooler than anything I'll ever achieve fashion-wise, welcomes the new players and divides us into groups of three. I crush my opponents that night on all four games we play, and as the weeks pass, I develop a habit of hitting the reload button while on the DMV Pinball Standings web page at least twice a day, watching the new scores come in. I'm scoring high and fist-pumping my way home each night, describing every victory to Marina, who cares very little.

One week, I can't get into the Black Cat. There's a line of people down the block, some of whom have camped there in the cold for hours. I'd later learn that they've all turned out to hear Australian singer-songwriter Matt Corby, who I've never heard of, and frankly, his fans are blocking the pinball machines.

Corby's presence makes league night a little more interesting; we get to witness multiple concertgoers yelling at the Black Cat's management ("We waited for *three hours* in the cold, and now you're telling me that because I don't have my ID . . ."), each crisis effectively diffused by a Black Cat worker with a firm, "You don't want to go to fucking jail."

Corby probably isn't a pinball fanatic, but there's one musician who definitely is. It's Ed Robertson, lead singer of Barenaked Ladies. A self-described "pinball freak," Robertson has a personal game room filled with pinball machines. In 2015, Barenaked Ladies even released a pinball-centric album, *Silverball*, with pinball not only appearing in the album's title and art but also featuring prominently in music videos for the songs "Silverball"* and "Say What You Want." The former was filmed in Robertson's game room; in the latter, the band performs the song inside a giant pinball machine. Robertson even once injured his hand—the one he needs for the guitar—by playing too much pinball.

I'm no Ed Robertson, but in the league, I'm playing surprisingly well. I almost feel like I know what I'm doing. It helps that many of my randomly assigned opponents are new to pinball—I'm even playing against people who flip both flippers at once. In pinball, that's kind of *the* mark of an amateur, someone so unused to the game's geometry that they flail with every possible resource whenever the ball comes near.†

---

* The lyrics to "Silverball" are wholeheartedly, unapologetically laden with pinball references, including lines like "The multiball was on track again / But I watched it fall through the center drain" and "I'll change your mind if I nudge you oh so carefully." The chorus is probably the finest example of combining pinball with sexual desire: "Light me up, and knock me down / I'm free game whenever you're around. / So lock me in; we're special bound, / 'Cause you're my silverball." It's a far cry from a much older song about pinball, Red Foley's 1954 "Pinball Boogie," whose protagonist eschews sexual desire in favor of pinball: "One night I had a chance to date a lovely girl. / I went into a joint to watch the pinball whirl. / I shook it and I shook it for a few free games. / It wasn't long till I forgot about that dame."

† The unnecessary double-button press is also sometimes frowned upon. At Pinball Perfection, the museum of pinball antiquity, I saw a warning sign that looked like a free-verse poem:

The double-flippers remind me of an incident involving a kid named Herb I used to play chess with at summer camp. Herb was some kind of chess champion, and he almost always beat me, but I learned a lot from him—and as you may be picturing, neither of us had an overabundance of conflicting social obligations.

One day, one of the jocks in our bunk asked to play. As was often the case throughout childhood, we couldn't be certain if he was making fun of us, though he probably was.

"No," Herb told the jock. "You're not good enough." Though not the kindest reply, this was a great moment in nerddom, the ability to exclude a popular kid, who looked genuinely hurt that someone told him no. The jock begged, and finally Herb reluctantly let him sit down to play.

The jock opened by advancing his rook's pawn, a completely useless move. Herb never touched his own pieces. He just said, "See. You're not good enough." And he took his board away.

The double flip is the rook's pawn opening of pinball. In my attempt to avoid acting like Herb, I'm becoming self-conscious, congratulating the newbies when they do well, cursing myself when I drain, and pretty much staying silent otherwise.

To avoid playing in pinball league on Valentine's Day (the correct choice, I'm told), I switch to a venue that meets on Thursday nights, Lyman's Tavern—named after owner Kevin Perone's grandfather, not pinball designer Lyman Sheats. It's a narrow bar in DC that serves drinks in mason jars, features a giant mural of chimerical jackalopes clutching cans of Pabst, and embraces pinball down to the painted flippers on the marquis.

"Gift of the gods!" yells my groupmate Francis, a short, jocular fellow with a shaved head, as he drains his ball on *Star Trek*. He explains

---

FLAPPING FLIPPERS / LIKE BIRD WINGS / AND REPEATED DRUMMING WILL NOT BE / ALLOWED AND IS CAUSE FOR / EJECTION FROM THE MUSEUM / THIS IS NOT AN ARCADE / TAKE CARE OF THESE MACHINES / WAIT FOR THE BALL / ONE FLIPPER AT A TIME / THANK YOU.

that his unique expletive came from a shot on *Gilligan's Island* (1991) during an intense tournament. When "Gift of the Gods" is lit in the left outlane, draining the ball that way awards one million points—to all of your opponents. This shot cost Francis the tournament, so when he loses a ball in a manner he deems unfair, he yells, "Gift of the gods!"

Even at Lyman's, playing against more experienced opponents, I'm still winning most games. I don't get it. Maybe it's luck. Maybe I'm actually learning how to play well. Or maybe it's a gift of the gods.

The next week at Lyman's, I notice that two machines have been changed out since my previous visit—*Flight 2000* (1980) and *Genie* (1979) have now become *James Cameron's Avatar* (2010) and *Red and Ted's Road Show* (1992).* Switching machines around is no small task. Moving a pinball machine requires a special dolly and, depending on how far one is moving it, a van. Most games on location will sit in their designated spots for years; rotating in the other members of one's collection shows unusual dedication on the part of the operator. In other words, to swap out two games, you have to feel confident that the increased profit will offset the amount of hassle—or you just have to do it for the love of variety in pinball. Perone, who owns both the bar and the machines inside, clearly loves pinball.

One day after a league night, I find myself opening a secret browser window and Googling "tingling left arm." In movies, this is a precursor to a heart attack. My entire left arm has been tingling all morning, as though it's fallen asleep but just won't recover.

Various legitimate-sounding websites confirm my fears, but it also may be one of a dozen other things. Did I recently put unusual strain on my arms or fingers? Well . . . I did score ten billion on *Attack from Mars*. So I guess there's that. Luckily the tingling subsides after a day,

---

* On *Road Show*, a construction-themed game featuring hard-hatted workers Red and Ted, someone has written on a beer coaster they've placed on top of the glass: "Congress has voted against funding our infrastructure. Red and Ted are unemployed. VOTE BERNIE!" Sometimes it's easy to forget that I live in our nation's capital. Sometimes it's not.

but now I can add "made me think I was dying" to the list of things pinball has done for me.

Despite the generally cheery environment of pinball league, I get to see a few heated disputes over rules, particularly regarding unplanned misfortunes at the hands of physics. The official ruling for these occurrences, adopted from rules outlined by PAPA and IFPA, sounds like a good description of life in general: "Unusual events and outright malfunctions cannot be prevented, nor can they be perfectly compensated for."

Pinball's fast-paced unpredictability, in fact, has led PAPA and IFPA to categorize no fewer than *seven* different types of malfunctions and their consequences: minor malfunctions, major malfunctions (breaking a flipper), known malfunctions (a broken flipper everyone knows about in advance), catastrophic malfunctions (power outage), beneficial malfunctions (a broken tilt bob), stuck balls (problematic during normal play but beneficial during multiball), and player errors (bashing the machine around so severely that you tilt not only your own ball, but the next player's).

The DMV League's specific rule set is a delightful combination of strict and casual. Other rules include "Please have clean hands" and "Reserve trash talking for members you know are cool with it."

I don't know anyone well enough to know if they're cool with it, so I do my trash talking gleefully out loud alone on the ride home. By the time the eight-week season ends and the finals begin, I'm somehow in *first place* out of the 108 players in the league, just above former FSPA player Dave Hubbard.

The IFPA website says Hubbard ranks in the top one hundred worldwide, even once rising as high as fourteenth. Like a cartoon character on a tightrope only becoming scared when he sees how high up he's balanced, learning Hubbard's international ranking induces a crisis of confidence. Suddenly I'm picturing every opponent as Dave Hubbard, a tall, sandy-haired man in his early forties with a goatee and a seemingly endless pinball T-shirt collection who sometimes engages in vociferous online debates about rules and policies. In my imagination, he's racking up a world-class score on some game, which I've certainly seen him do before, and I'm flailing at air. He plays in A Division at PAPA, for goodness sake. He gave advice to Lyman Sheats. When he sees my name as an opponent, he must be relieved.

To prepare for the finals, I surf PAPA's massive collection of pinball tutorial videos starring the one-and-only self-deprecating pinball champion Bowen Kerins. "Hey, it's Bowen, and we're here at PAPA to play some *Walking Dead* pinball, one of the newest machines from Stern," he narrates in a much-watched YouTube clip as the camera pans over the *Walking Dead* (2014) playfield.

Next comes a wide-angle shot showing Kerins lingering by the machine like a trespasser in the otherwise empty PAPA facility. "I tend to have difficulty with this game," he lies, "but let's give it a shot and see how far we can get."

Kerins's gameplay is amazing. If the ball approaches his flipper, he rarely bats it back onto the playfield—he catches it. His game is all about control, and he regularly makes the shots he's aiming for, partially because he's just that accurate and partially because, with a caught ball, he can take his time with each shot. It's not a fun and fast-paced way to play the game, but it works. Kerins calmly narrates the whole game, describing his strategy and often disparaging his mistakes. His games frequently run over an hour.

There are several ways to catch the ball on a flipper, many of them demonstrated by Kerins in a separate set of tutorial video clips on the PAPA website. I can do the "dead bounce," in which one refuses to flip when the ball falls toward the flippers from a certain angle, letting it bounce easily from the still flipper onto the other flipper. Then there's the "drop catch," which I can't do—hold the flipper up and release it the moment the ball touches it, thus killing its momentum.

The "live catch" is harder to describe. The ball rolls toward a flipper, and then there's a subtle and perfectly timed slap, and then . . . the player is cradling the ball. It looks for all the world like the ball is under a magic spell, or like there's an electromagnet in the flipper. It's a crucial part of Kerins's strategy: Catch everything. Mitigate risk. "If you don't have a reason to shoot something," he told the *Pavlov Pinball* blog in 2014, "then it is a bad idea because you are putting the ball in danger with no purpose."

I read recently about the phenomenon of people watching other people play video games on YouTube. The practice was presented semimockingly, implying that we've discovered new depths of laziness—not just stagnating in our living rooms with Xbox controllers in our hands but stagnating in our bedrooms, staring at laptops, watching *other people* play Xbox.

But I'm not like them, I think as I watch another hour of Kerins playing pinball. *This is not the same thing at all.*

Not that his techniques help me in the finals. Inspired by Kerins, I start the first round of the finals by choosing *The Walking Dead* against a player who—oops—has the same machine in his basement.

Still, somehow I survive the various eliminations throughout the day to make it to the very last round. I shake hands with the other three finalists, wishing everyone good luck. Per the conclusions of the New York City Council, it may be more appropriate to wish them all good skill, but these guys already have it. Somehow my premonitions have come true, and here I am, about to start the finals, proud and amazed to have made it this far but knowing that I'm about to lose to Dave Hubbard.

Yet . . . I don't. By the last ball of the last game, *Medieval Madness*, I'm feeling different. I'm feeling sweaty. It's a good sweat, an adrenaline sweat, a sweat born of tuned focus. I'm going medieval on *Medieval Madness*. I'm live catching, actually *live catching* like Kerins in his videos, and when I finally drain and release my fingers from the flipper buttons, there's applause. I look around to see who the applause is for, but it's for me. What the fuck? It's for *me*. In this bar, in this city, on this day, I'm the A Division finalist whose game people are watching, the same way I watched Kerins and Elwin and Cayle George from the bleachers at PAPA. I'm the slap-saving, live catching whirlwind of pinball magic who might have squeaked into the finals, sure, but I belong here. I *belong* here.

Clutching my envelope of $100 cash—local league prizes aren't quite at the level of PAPA's—I smile and pose with Dave Hubbard in a photo for the DMV Pinball League's Facebook page. Hubbard holds up two fingers, and I hold up one.

I still don't know how the hell I did it. Nor do I know whether I could ever do it again, or whether Marina would even let me try. But I guess that's all it takes, right? One good ball. One good game. One good day.

6

Space Invaders

THE MID- TO LATE '70s were a wonderful time for pinball. Games could be found at Laundromats, in drugstores, even capping the ends of aisles at supermarkets. Sharpe had done his song and dance for the New York City Council, and it worked: at one point, the largest manufacturers—Bally, Williams, Gottlieb, and Chicago Coin—were designing and producing eight to twelve new titles a year—*each*. That's about forty different games per year. (By contrast, nowadays, there are around three to five titles a year across the entire industry.) And, unlikely as it must have seemed at the time, pinball found fame as the subject of a certain rock opera by the Who.

If pinball owes its resurgence partially to *Tommy*, it's reasonable to ask why a band like the Who even decided to write an entire rock opera about pinball. The answer, according to British author Richard Barnes—who had suggested in 1963 that the band change its name from the Detours to the Who—is that Pete Townshend wrote a rock opera about pinball to impress a rock journalist named Nik Cohn who liked pinball. Townshend wanted a favorable review from Cohn, so while kicking around ideas one day, the musician floated the possibility that Tommy might play pinball. Cohn replied, "It'll be a masterpiece."*

Townshend hurriedly dashed off the song "Pinball Wizard," pausing to marvel at what he called "awful, the most clumsy piece of writing I've ever done."† Cohn, however, loved it, and thus the famous deaf, dumb, and blind kid became a pinball prodigy.

Imagine how different the world would be if Nik Cohn liked backgammon.

Pinball turned out to be the right choice for the rock opera, the perfect selection of a campy, semirebellious pastime to lionize and partially mellow the album's otherwise seriously spiritual overtones. In doing so, Barnes wrote in the liner notes of a reissue of *Tommy*, "it captures part of the magic, or whatever, of the sixties." I missed the '60s—the time period when the title character displays his pinball wizardry—mainly due to my parents not conceiving me during their adolescence, but from what I've heard, there's hardly a more apt description of the era than "magic, or whatever."

The *Tommy* album had been available for listeners to see it, feel it, touch it, heal it since 1969. But it was the star- and musician-studded 1975 film, which gave screen time to Roger Daltrey, Ann-Margret, Elton John, Tina Turner, Jack Nicholson, Eric Clapton, Keith Moon, and Pete Townshend himself, that really got the world once more buzzing about pinball.

The machines themselves also reached a new plateau in their evolution, using microprocessors and circuit boards to give the games

---

* Cohn was not easy to please. He would go on to negatively review *Abbey Road* in 1969, writing in the *New York Times* that the Beatles' iconic album was an "unmitigated disaster" and calling individual songs "mediocrity incarnate" and "purest Mickey Mouse." Yet the man was swayed by pinball. Go figure.

† The phrase "pinball wizard" has also become so much of a cliché in the pinball community that I would like to hereby formally apologize for the title of this book. Every time an article about pinball appears in the mainstream press that uses the phrase "pinball wizard," somewhere, each in their separate basements, thousands of pinball enthusiasts groan. So, I'm sorry.

brain power. (Some terminology: before this transition, the games were called "electromechanical," or "EM," since those were the primary ingredients—electricity and machinery. The new games were called "solid-state.")

For example, the introduction of semiconductors meant the introduction of memory, and memory meant that a player could score in more complex ways—earning an award on the playfield, for example, and having that award stay lit on the same player's next turn. And now games could make noises beyond the sounds associated with one metal part hitting another.

One of the most important advantages of solid-state electronics was the ability to keep score electronically. As Marco Rossignoli reminds readers of *The Complete Pinball Book*, underneath its gameplay, a pinball machine is essentially an adding machine.

Pinball machines weren't always adding machines. While the games of the early '30s forced players to perform mental math, they soon gave way to light-up scoring—various numbers to various powers of ten would be displayed, and if lights shone behind, for example, "500,000," "10,000," and "2,000," then you knew your score was 512,000.

Then the '50s brought the invention of the drum score reel, a series of rotating circles with painted numbers, like in an older car's odometer, which gave backglass artists more space for decoration without having to somehow incorporate thirty different numbers into their artwork.

Those mechanical scoring reels had one major deficiency: you could have the ball zinging and slinging between high-scoring targets, and the machine's tally of your score couldn't keep up simply because the reels couldn't turn fast enough. Microchips allowed pinball machines to register every target hit, and more accurate scoring allowed for more targets, which meant that playfields, and rules, could now become more complicated and interesting.

Another plus for digital scoring: the new games could accommodate multiple players much more easily than earlier ones, for which one-player, two-player, and four-player versions had to be manufactured separately.

Of course, solid-state electronics benefited more than pinball. And one of the technologies made possible, while it would partially complement and promote pinball, would ultimately smash it to bits like a barrel thrown by an angry monkey.

If you were born in such an epoch as to have missed the 1980s, you may find it hard to believe how nuts people went over the most rudimentary, monochrome, detail-free video games. Seriously, go look at *Pong* on YouTube. That's Atari's first video game, circa 1972, and that's what people were lining up to play—a black-and-white Ping-Pong game in which the ball was a square, the paddles were rectangles, the net was a dotted line, *and that's it*. "Black-and-white" didn't even mean gray—it meant black, and white. You know what was way too futuristic for *Pong*? A circle.

Old stalwart pinball faced a challenge when confronted with the fresh, exciting, and addictive allure of video games. For a generation raised on television, Roger Sharpe says in his interview in *Pleasure Machines*, "the idea of controlling something on a TV screen was incredibly compelling." (The closest my parents' generation had come to interacting with a television, from what I understand, was a show called *Winky Dink and You* that aired from 1953 to 1957. Kids whose parents purchased a Winky Dink kit would stick a piece of clear vinyl to their television screen, then trace a connect-the-dots puzzle at the behest of a cartoon boy named Winky Dink. Kids whose parents *didn't* purchase the kit, or who simply forgot to affix the clear vinyl to the screen, ended up drawing directly on their televisions.)

Now the television, the appliance that imported entertainment and information to their living rooms, became something much more interesting: a competitive public pastime. With video games like *Space Invaders, Asteroids, Pac-Man,** *Donkey Kong,* and *Pole Position* (released in that order) driving their rampant popularity, the *New York Times* reported that the number of arcades doubled between 1980 and 1982.

Not that everyone loved arcades. As they grew and blossomed, so did a sort of arcade culture that made adults nervous. In the documentary *Special When Lit,* Dr. John Broughton of Columbia University describes them as places of "downward mobility, wasting time, [and] developing highly refined skills in an area that was going to be relatively useless in adult life."

It was yet another moral (or, rather, moralizing) battle between the excited youth and the cautious adults in pinball's history. Roger Sharpe described the dominant fear at the time among adults: "We don't want an arcade in our area because children are going to congregate, and when children get together, bad things happen."

As I recall from avoiding the Time Out arcade in my local mall, arcades in the '80s weren't seedy per se, but they weren't exactly wholesome either. They were places the kids with the rattails spent their Saturdays, chugging Mountain Dew and joking about stealing sneakers.

Occupying those arcades were two main activities, pinball and video games, sharing space and customers. Of all the pinball fans I've met, probably half love arcade games just as much as pinball, and half, like me, have no interest in video games whatsoever. In the short documentary *One Quarter at a Time,* multiple people talk about how conquering a video game is tantamount to memorizing patterns—but pinball is, pardon the expression, a whole different ball game, with its literal mechanical physics that simply can't be replicated on a screen.

---

* *Pac-Man* is the highest grossing arcade game in history, selling more than four hundred thousand cabinets and earning more than $1 billion in its first year alone. That's *billion,* and it's all in quarters. The name Pac-Man was coined (another arcade pun!) when the game moved from Japan to the United States because its previous moniker, Puck Man, was deemed too easy to vandalize into obscenity.

For a while, both pinball and video games enjoyed the arcade boom together, though each was fully aware that it had to vie with the other for quarters—both the spatial and monetary kind. So pinball designers now concentrated heavily on operator profitability. The goal became creating games on which players would average about half a minute per ball—so a standard five-ball game for the average player should last about two and a half minutes. If that sounds stingy, remember that most game buyers weren't youth seekers finding pinball machines for the rec rooms of McMansions, which would not start to gobble the landscape for another two decades. They were pub owners, grocery store owners, arcade owners—and the shorter the game, the sooner another quarter entered the slot.*

In case you're wondering, yes, a five-ball game really was the standard. What a time to be alive! The default arsenal would later shrink to three balls in order to bring playing times more in line with those of video games. Actually, in many ways, video games forced pinball to up its game—literally. Suddenly pinball machines had multiple levels: upper miniplayfields reachable via ramps or VUKs, lower miniplayfields underneath a transparent window. Some had additional flippers, windier ramps, prettier backglasses, weirder toys.

Pinball even added speech for the first time, starting with a game set in a fantastical hellscape, called *Gorgar* (1979). The ad for *Gorgar* bragged that "GORGAR SPEAKS," and indeed, *Gorgar* was capable of saying seven different words, two of which were "Gorgar" and "speaks." (The other five were "beat," "you," "hurt," "me," and "got," and *Gorgar* could shuffle them into any order to form more complex sentences, such as "Me got you" and "Me hurt," which sound like lyrics to a love ballad sung by Cookie Monster.)

---

* According to arcade machine distributor BMI Gaming, in 1990, less than 5 percent of new pinball machines were sold directly to consumers. By 2007, the number had risen to 45 percent.

Depicting pinball's innovations as a struggle to keep pace with video games almost makes it sound like pinball rode into success on the coattails of the newcomer. But Sharpe claims the opposite. "Without pinball, video games would not have emerged," he asserts. "There would have been no place to put them." It's a good point: arcades existed long before *Pac-Man* munched his first ghost. Video games just made them insanely profitable.

For a while.

If pinball machines enabled video arcade games, they soon ironically became burdensome in their own realm. Arcade owners saw where the quarters ended up; they also saw which type of machine required the most repairs. Dan Toskaner, of the Silver Ball Museum, summed up the industry-wide snubbing of pinball in the early '80s: "Video games made a lot more money, required a lot less maintenance, and they took up less space." It was like inviting your younger, cooler friend to stay in your basement, then one day learning your wife prefers him to you.

The uneasy peace between video games and pinball machines ended, unceremoniously, with pinball as the clear loser. According to a 1989 article in *Crain's Chicago Business*, in 1980, Williams Electronic Games—which was one of twenty-three pinball manufacturers at the time—produced fifty thousand pinball machines. In 1983, they only produced twenty-three hundred. Video games, meanwhile, according to a 2013 *Slate* article, consumed $1 billion in quarters in 1979, and three years later that number had ballooned to $8 billion.

Or consider this: according to the Internet Pinball Database (IPDB), Williams sold over seventeen thousand *Firepower* pinball machines in 1980. Just two years later, they manufactured a new game called *Defender*. They sold 369.

But arcade games didn't last much longer either. Continuing its celebrated history of declaring things dead, the *New York Times* tolled the chime for video games on October 17, 1983, writing that "the electronic centipedes, outer space invaders and spooky goblins that only a year ago seemed to have an extraterrestrial grip on the play hours of America's children are consuming each other like so many Pac-Men." The *Times* cited boredom ("You kill the invaders and that's it," lamented an unimpressed 12-year-old) for the massive loss in revenue that had already begun to shutter arcades by the hundreds.

Those who predicted the end of all video games in 1983 could not have been more wrong, of course; they could not have imagined the thorough cultural saturation video games would one day enjoy. How could they have foreseen a family in a restaurant booth waiting for dinner to arrive, children tapping away at Minecraft on iPhones to give the adults a moment's peace—so that the adults can play Fruit Ninja on their Samsung Galaxies?

Pinpointing (again with the puns) what killed arcades can't be as simple as the fact that kids were enthralled in 1982 but jaded in 1983. Yes, children are fickle, but the bursting of the arcade *Bubble Bobble* had less to do with the whims of youth and more to do with what was happening in the children's living rooms.

In 1983, home video game consoles were nothing new. My parents, for example, owned a 1978 video game system called the Magnavox Odyssey². It was an inconvenient dinosaur of a toy—when we wanted to play, we had to take the parts out of its cardboard box and attach the wires, using a screwdriver, to inputs on the back of our television. Playing video games became an event, and not an event the kids could undertake on their own. Now video games fill the two minutes in the bank line or the ten minutes on the subway, and this time it's the kids who aren't necessary.

The games themselves, by nearly any standards, sucked. For example, we had a game called *Computer Golf!* that featured a little blue golfer with about as much physical detail as a Tetris piece. Players would maddeningly direct him around a green rectangle and try to "swing" a "golf club" at a "golf ball." All of those terms are in quotes because none of those items or activities resembled anything but moving rectangles and squares from one place to another.

This is why everyone went to the arcade: like miniature World's Fairs, arcades showcased the newest, zippiest technologies that simply couldn't appear on a home television set. But soon they could. Graphics improved, game cartridges improved, and by 1982, the Atari 2600 had already sold ten million units. Who needs to waste quarters on a few minutes' worth of an experience that can be enjoyed limitlessly at home?

Game designers attempted to win kids back to the arcades with even more advanced technology—which, at the time, meant laser discs. Remember those? Designers knew they needed to offer an experience that dwarfed the home games, so they pinned their hopes on larger and more immersive—and expensive—machines.

In modern arcades, which rely on the same bigger-is-better strategy, that machine can be a redemption game on which you *nearly*, but not quite, win a pair of Beats headphones. It can be a six-passenger motion simulator ride, a massive air hockey table, or a side-by-side racing game with two full-size motorbikes. Or it can be the one quality that home video games can never re-create, a feeling one can only find at brick-and-mortar arcades, a sensation younger players may not want and older players may not know they want: nostalgia.

• • •

That arcades exist today must strike kids as odd. Arcades feel so arcane, so much a part of someone else's past, that it's hard to imagine children wandering into one unless they're playing *Pokémon Go* and spot a Jigglypuff near the change machine.

Let the kids think what they want. Not only are there arcades today, there are arcades that aren't always meant for kids. It's been a good ten to fifteen years since the last arcade generation reached legal drinking age, which means they now have both a wistful recollection of days gone by and enough money to occasionally chase that feeling. Hence the barcade.

Barcades represent a new form of interactive theme bar, and they've been popping up across the nation like mushrooms from Mario's question block. They promise a night in which you can relive the adolescence you *wish* you had—i.e., an adolescence with no bedtime and abundant alcohol—and have names like Insert Coins (Minneapolis), HiScores (Las Vegas), 16-Bit Bar+Arcade (Columbus, Ohio), and The 1-Up (Denver), which features a custom-built game cabinet that dispenses craft beer.

The name Barcade itself is now a registered trademark of one of the first barcades, in (of course) Brooklyn, a venture so successful it has expanded to six locations.

Beercade, on the other hand, is a bar/arcade in Benson, Nebraska, a far cry from Brooklyn both geographically and culturally. General manager Ash Preheim sits across from me at a booth after pouring me some kind of draft beer with "peach" in the name. Preheim is in his late thirties, with a dark mustache, short shirtsleeves, and a brown Odell Brewing cap, and he's come equipped with two packs of Camels. He looks like many of our dads did in grainy photos from the '70s.

Even though it's late on a Monday night, the vintage arcade games and pinball machines at Beercade are popular with—okay, let's just say it: I think these are all grad students. But Preheim assures me that the place is full of families on Saturdays, which semicopy the conditions that attracted many kids to pinball a generation ago: Dad gets a whiskey and a beer, and junior plays the games.

Preheim developed an affinity for arcade games in a gas station game room, where he'd spend his junior high days smoking cigarettes and playing *Rollergames*. Today pinball is an integral part of Beercade, and just like in the halcyon arcade days, it's the part that's the biggest pain in the ass. Not only do the stresses of constant play break his games on a daily basis, but since the pinball machines have a steeper learning curve than the video games, Preheim reports that sometimes patrons will demand a refund "because they don't know where the START button is."

So here's the plight of today's pinball operator: it's the operator's job to bring pinball machines to locations, hope patrons know how to play them, cringe while the machines withstand abuse, and fix them a lot more frequently than the quarters in the cash box make worthwhile—only, unlike during the arcade craze, without the volume of patrons required to justify the headaches. It's not that pinball machines are poorly quality controlled or especially fragile. They just have so many moving parts that can fall out of harmony when they're smacked repeatedly.

They're also huge, requiring a trailer to lug them around, and expensive—Preheim estimates that about $33,000 of the bar's assets are tied up in their eight pinball machines.

"Everything always breaks on a Friday night," he says, "usually right when I'm about to walk out the door."

Preheim tells me, not looking too pleased, he has $1,000 worth of pinball machine parts in the back. Pinball machines are money pits, and it would be different if their earnings offset their cost and annoyance. But that's not the case: bar sales, not quarters, keep Preheim solvent. At Beercade, the beer subsidizes the cade.

Beercade's most important mission, with its exposed ductwork, brick mural, and massive tile mosaic of Mario, is fighting back against the basement arcades that swallow pinball machines and video games, never again releasing them into public hands. Preheim considers home-use-only enthusiasts as deplorable as private art collectors, as they selfishly hoard assets meant for all to enjoy. It is Preheim's hope that pinball can still exist as a social activity—not an antisocial activity.

He's not alone in that mission.

Without a doubt, the hippest, freshest-looking pinball venue I've visited is a club in downtown Los Angeles called EightyTwo. The place is half pinball machines, half classic arcade games, with *Mortal Kombat* live-streamed over the bar and a rotating cadre of food trucks.* Kids in their twenties (they're kids to me) pull up in Ubers, then wait behind the velvet rope—an actual velvet rope—to show their IDs and come in. Multiple times at EightyTwo, amid the loud club music, I've had to elbow my way past couples making out.

On the other side of the country, in a back room filled with electronics, Bill Disney—no relation to Walt—stares at a circuit board illuminated by a headlamp; his wife, Linda, shuffles papers nearby. He works on software for Unisys, and she's a kindergarten teacher, but together, the couple in their late fifties operates Pinball Gallery, a pinball arcade in Malvern, Pennsylvania, where they sell ice cream instead of alcohol.

"Ten years ago," he says, poking around with a screwdriver, "I couldn't even name a place where you could buy a pinball machine." In those ten years, during which he presumably figured out where to buy them, he's purchased more than a hundred.

Like Preheim, the Disneys built their collection with the intention not of hoarding the fun but of sharing it. When his first purchase, a 1978 *Sinbad*, broke, he learned to fix it.

"I like to buy them when they're not working," he says. Machines are plucked from the dust heap, restored, and, best of all, made public. The couple recently purchased their third *Sinbad*. But it's their day jobs, Disney says, not an influx of quarters, that keep their labor of love financially feasible.

If pinball doesn't pay the bills, how—and why—do so many modern pinball arcades stay afloat? Maybe answering that question is a matter of wandering through a neighborhood in yet another corner

---

* I ordered grilled cheese stuffed with filet mignon. How very L.A.

of the country. I chatted with Constance Negley, one of the owners of D&D Pinball in Tucson, Arizona, which at the time was the second-largest pinball arcade in the American Southwest (after the Pinball Hall of Fame in Las Vegas). And a stroll through the community revealed the secret of Negley's success.

I know nothing about neighborhoods in Tucson. In fact, I ended up outside D&D Pinball accidentally while in town for a conference. But here's what I saw when I walked up and down the street.

There's a bar advertising thirty-four taps. There are at least three specialty bookstores in five blocks. There are tattoo parlors; a food co-op; an improvisational theater; two smoke shops *and* two hookah lounges; a pizza parlor with a built-in bocce court; a medical marijuana dispensary called 420 Social Club; stores called Generation Cool, Tucson Herb Store, Wooden Tooth Records, Surly Wench Pub, Chocolate Iguana, and Mr. Head's Gallery and Bar; and a brand-new streetcar that only runs up and down these few blocks, presumably because lots of customers patronize the locally owned businesses— and also because after 10:00 PM, many of those people are probably drunk or high.

I see a neck-tattooed woman in a long dress greet her friend's young son: "Hi, Balthasar!"

When one store becomes retro-chic, it's gauche. It's obnoxious. It's trying too hard. But when entire sections of cities make themselves over this way, clearly a real demand exists. And pinball can be part of that demand.

It's like Greenwich Village in New York; Hampden in Baltimore; Adams Morgan in DC; South Street in Philadelphia; Dolores Park in San Francisco; the Old Fourth Ward in Atlanta; Christiania in Copenhagen; Benson, Nebraska; or pretty much all of Boulder, Colorado. I've found hipster enclaves in nearly every city I've visited, from Chicago's West Loop to the Design District in Los Angeles. And they're not *Portlandia*, a wild caricature of pretention masquerading as refined grittiness. They're laid-back neighborhoods with bike lanes, farmer's markets, and coffee that's not Starbucks.

Now they have pinball.

. . .

From the glass display case stuffed with Nintendo Power Gloves and Tiger Electronics games to the 1988 Bangles ballad "Eternal Flame" blasting through the speakers to the name of the arcade itself, Yestercades in Red Bank, New Jersey, is unashamed to capitalize on nostalgia. But Yestercades is not just another modern retro arcade: it may hold the key to success for arcades to come.

Ken Kalada is not someone you'd peg as a retro-arcade owner. For starters, like Preheim, he's in his thirties—which means that for him, nostalgia ends in the first Reagan administration. Consequently, Yestercades has no 1950s baseball pitch-and-bats, no woodrails, no *Pong*. Though his customers include young kids and old-timers, Ken's primary clientele appears to be young professionals who want to relive their youth, not by sipping malts by the jukebox but by snarfing Fun Fruits and Hi-C Ecto Cooler while waiting for a turn at *Double Dragon*. It's possible that this demographic seems to dominate because I've chosen to visit Yestercades at midnight on a Saturday.

Growing up watching his father run his own business—a pharmacy that I assume was much less fun than Yestercades—Kalada decided that he would someday own a toy store, ski resort, or arcade. Thus, Yestercades is less a business venture and more the product of a big kid finally designing an ideal arcade for himself, filling it with the machines he loves, and finding to his delight that others happen to enjoy it, too.

Kalada has always had an entrepreneurial spirit. As a kid, he bought and resold old Atari games on Usenet, a sort of proto-Internet discussion board that thrived more than a decade before anyone would type the letters "www." At age thirteen, he proudly told his parents that he had earned more than $1,000 this way, and Kalada's father—who, now in his seventies, plays at Yestercades every weekend—replied gleefully that he'd never have to buy his son a video game again.

At Yestercades, the pinball machines are in the back, like the unruly kids who commandeer the last row of the school bus. Kalada is more a video game fan than a pinhead, and he's never heard of events like PAPA, but the pinball machines are an essential part of the experience.

And, just like at every other arcade, nothing is as infuriating for Kalada as maintaining the pinball machines. There are sixteen, and they demand more of Kalada's time than his eighty video games.

When someone visits Yestercades and asks Kalada how he's able to stay in business, he responds the same way as Clay Harrell at the Ann Arbor Pinball Museum. "We get people coming in here all the time," he says. "'What are your start-up costs? How many bracelets do you sell?' I'm like, 'Fuck off!'"

It's a funny but ultimately insufficient answer. Throughout my tour of modern arcades, I had the feeling of a lingering unanswered question, one that undid arcades thirty years ago. It's this: With today's cheap and abundant entertainment options—you can binge-watch any television show in your underwear for a few dollars a month—isn't there *less* motivation than in 1983, or ever, to visit an arcade?

For Kalada, the answer lies not just in nostalgia but also in something else that we lost when arcades closed, something we all need even when we think we don't: a sense of community. Perhaps, he says, that's the reason arcades haven't vanished entirely. You can buy beer, he points out, and drink it in your kitchen, or you can go to a bar and pay five times as much. Yet people go to bars all the time because life is just better when there are other people, even strangers, enjoying the same pursuit in the same room.

"I love it," Kalada says. "People are coming in here to remember a simpler time in their lives. So even if it's just for an hour, it allows them to escape. We'll see people come in here in the worst mood, but they're grinning when they leave."

It's nearly 1:00 AM at Yestercades, and a woman with an iced coffee and eight rubber bands spaced every few inches down her long ponytail plays a *Q*bert* console. A kid on a stool, probably in his early teens, is kicking ass at *Donkey Kong*. Two guys on beanbag chairs trash-talk each other over a game of the original *Pokémon* on a large flat-screen television while two more guys on the adjacent leather couch play *Madden*. It's like a magical living room where no one ever has to put away the Xbox and go to bed.

Back on the darkened streets of Red Bank, New Jersey, it's 2015 again, a year when there seems to be little reason an arcade can survive. But in Red Bank's neighborhood—in which Yestercades thrives despite looking nothing like Benson's or Tucson's—during the one-block walk to my car, I pass Lacrosse Unlimited, which sells sticks with nets, and a paint-your-own-pottery store called A Time to Kiln. If a need for those stores truly exists, why the hell not an arcade?

Pinball owed its near death when arcades closed, Roger Sharpe explains, to the same doom and gloom that nearly took out other forms of entertainment. The phonograph will spell the end of live concerts, everyone feared; television will kill theater; cable TV will destroy the cinema. In each epoch, it's a general question of "Now that we can re-create the experience of leaving the house, why leave the house?" Yet we continue to leave the house.

I'm typing this in a tea shop. I can make tea at home. Today I choose not to. All around me are people who made the same choice.

I've often watched stand-up comedy open mics in which the performer closes by reminding their audience, "Tip your bartenders, drive safely, and thank you for supporting live comedy."

So thank you for supporting live pinball. Thank you for supporting live anything.

. . .

In the late '80s and early '90s, after *Pac-Man* and *Space Invaders* had become relics and kids couldn't be pried from their home Nintendo controllers, something weird happened. Pinball suddenly found itself enjoying a new renaissance; when video arcade games lost their novelty, the good old wood-and-steel beasts were still standing.

And stand they did. By 1989, according to *Crain's Chicago Business*, two large pinball manufacturers, Williams (which had acquired Bally) and Midway Manufacturing, ran a combined facility in Chicago that had over one thousand employees and produced about half of the sixty thousand machines that would be sold that year.

It was a far cry from *Pac-Man*'s four hundred thousand units, to be sure. But sixty thousand pinball machines are sixty thousand pinball machines. The industry had weathered the crash and, according to Roger Sharpe, emerged "a little bit better, a little bit less young."

Throughout my childhood, the pinball machine that seemed most ubiquitous was *Funhouse*. If the name doesn't ring a bell, it may help to think of it as the game with a giant, obnoxious talking puppet head on the playfield.*

"I'm not sure where the idea came from," says Pat Lawlor, who designed the game. He pauses. "I mean, it was my idea." The head's name was Rudy, and though he taunted players throughout the game, he was more than a distraction—part of *Funhouse*'s goal was

---

* If the game you're picturing has two obnoxious talking puppet heads on the playfield instead of one, then you're remembering *Red and Ted's Road Show*, Pat Lawlor's 1992 creation that would later sport a "VOTE BERNIE!" beer coaster.

to advance the clock to midnight, lull Rudy to sleep, then use an upper flipper to shoot pinballs into Rudy's open, snoring mouth.

"The way I ended up designing it," Lawlor tells me in the lobby of a hotel outside Chicago, "it can be a target that's hard to get to, the head can be somewhat annoying, and you can want to hit it." That's exactly the kind of well-thought-out whimsy that characterized pinball machines in that era, the era when I fell in love with them.

Pinball had risen in the '30s, fallen in the '40s, surged in arcades in the late '70s, and fallen again by 1983. But then it was about to come back in a big way.

Ask any pinball player to identify the game's modern zenith, and they'll inevitably point to one machine made in 1992, another of Lawlor's designs, renowned for being the best-selling pinball machine before or, unfortunately, since: *The Addams Family.*

"In 1989, we were selling maybe 2,500 of a game at Williams," reminisces Lawlor. (Recall that in 1983, post-crash, game sales were measured in the hundreds, not thousands.) "By the time we got to *Whirlwind* (1990), we were selling seven thousand of a game. By the time we got to *Funhouse*, we were selling twelve thousand of a game. And by the time we hit *Addams Family*, we did twenty-one thousand games."* Thanks to the success of machines like *The Addams Family,* the industry produced nearly twice as many pinball machines in 1992 as it had in 1989—and with its sixty-thousand total machines, 1989 had been a terrific year.

The reasons for the runaway success of *The Addams Family,* as opposed to any other machine, are not obvious. The game was fun, easy to play yet hard to master, but so were many others. The game's

---

* Initially, 20,270, according to IPDB. The 20,232nd game produced broke the official record, and it appeared, along with the humans who designed and manufactured it, on the cover of *RePlay Magazine.* The game was so successful that Williams churned out another thousand in 1994 as a "Special Collector's Edition" with gold-trimmed accents and numbered certificates of authenticity. Lawlor himself owns #1.

big toy—a giant plastic Thing hand that emerged from a box and stole the pinball—was neat, but other games had cool toys as well. The best I can conclude is that *The Addams Family* sold well because 1992 was a good year for pinball, and 1992 was a good year for pinball because *The Addams Family* sold well.

I remember 1992. I celebrated my bar mitzvah, grew four inches taller, and played *The Addams Family* at Funland at Rehoboth Beach. The sounds of that game—Raul Julia as Gomez Addams declaring, "Keep the ball! I have a whole bucketful!"—are mingled in my memory with the sounds of the carnival rides and with the sights and smells of that idyllic shore town. And somehow I've ended up, twenty-three years later, talking to the man who dreamed it up.

"We touched a nerve not only in the normal pinball community, but we touched a nerve in the community of people who don't normally play those games," says Lawlor.

The problem with a record-breaking game is that it sets the bar even higher for the next game, and with binoculars from the present, we can identify 1992 as the year pinball peaked. In 1993, high on the success of *Addams* but watching sales start to slip, Lawlor embarked on an even more ambitious game, one that included a working gumball machine that dispensed pinballs onto the playfield, invisible interactive magnets that could move the ball like ghost flippers, a special ceramic pinball that triggered its own mode, and more—so many toys, in fact, that they widened the playfield by more than six inches and called it a "SuperPin." The theme was Rod Serling's cult classic sci-fi television series *The Twilight Zone*.

Lawlor was the driving force behind *The Twilight Zone*'s innovations. "I went to the management at WMS," he tells me, referring to the Williams Manufacturing Company,* "and I said, 'Look, we know

---

* You may have noticed that the acronym for the Williams Manufacturing Company ought to be WMC, not WMS. You're very observant! The name WMS actually isn't an acronym—it's short for WilliaMS.

that we can't keep doing the same thing over and over. We're going to have to change the candy bar.'"

According to the Internet Pinball Database, *The Twilight Zone* sold a respectable 15,235 units, which today would blow any pinball machine out of the water—but following *The Addams Family*'s record, it should have been cause for concern. Lawlor would never sell more than ten thousand of a single game again.

"In the modern history of pinball machines, anything above ten thousand is rarified air," he reflects. "You can count those games on your hands. I've been lucky enough that I've had three of them."

It's a unique sort of legacy. When Saint Peter greets Lawlor at the pearly gates and demands an accounting of his accomplishments—his three blockbusters that shaped the world—Lawlor will be able to list two machines based on television shows from the 1960s and one with a creepy jabbering doll head.*

More than twenty years later, *The Twilight Zone* has probably become the most modified, or "modded," pinball machine in existence. Collectors delight in buying custom toys to sprinkle on the playfield—one website lists light-up robots, a functional mini-TV, and even a launch knob shaped disturbingly like Rod Serling's head. The extra gizmos don't affect gameplay; they just light up or decorate an empty area or . . . whatever Rod Serling's head does.

The extrawide SuperPin was meant to be the new standard in pinball machines (i.e., a game layout with more room so that more fun gadgets could be packed onto the playfield). But by the end of 1994, though seven different SuperPins were manufactured, cost savings

---

* IPDB reports that, in the modern history of pinball machines—in other words, the part that doesn't include tabletop games like what they'll play in '32 (*Ball-y-hoo!*)—the number of games sharing that rarified air is forty-one. Twenty-eight of these were made during the arcade renaissance of 1975–1982, and the other thirteen all fall between 1986 and 1993. That's how peak-y and trough-y pinball's peaks and troughs are: no game selling more than ten thousand units was made during any other period.

became more important than toys, and SuperPins would become plain old Pins again.

Technologically, pinball was flourishing. Dot matrix displays could play videos and give instructions. Shaker motors, introduced on *Earthshaker* (1989), could vibrate the game to complement gameplay. Timed ball savers resurrected many prematurely drained balls, and electronic plungers—now much swifter than the ones at the Skokie bowling alley that annoyed Roger Sharpe—launched balls into play. It seemed each new game had its own featured gadget, often with patents obtained expressly for using that gadget on that game.

I've always viewed increased complexity in pinball as a good thing; it was the reason I found the game so appealing to begin with. The toys represent cleverness in design within a context of restrictions, an opportunity to watch designers' imaginations run wild in the few hundred cubic inches under the glass, and complexity is the enemy of boredom.

But as technology improved and the limits of ingenuity stretched and the rules for each game became ever more elaborate, fans of the late '70s games soon found themselves staring at the games of the '90s, carping that there's just too damn much going on.

"They've made the game so complicated that 5 percent of the people that play 'em understand the rules," complains Gene Cunningham, the former CEO of parts supplier Illinois Pinball, in the documentary *Special When Lit*. To me, the crazy-deep rule sets are part of pinball's appeal—juggling priorities and making split-second decisions, using as much information as is available, knowing that there are cool things I still haven't seen. It never occurred to me that for other pinball fanatics, this intricacy destroyed pinball. The rules, they said, aren't worth learning—and the toys aren't fun, they're distracting.

It is a truth universally acknowledged that unnecessary convolution is part of pinball's gestalt. At least, that's what I thought before talking to a lot of older pinball players. Even Roger Sharpe, who's

played every game, only disdainfully tolerates the over-the-top complications of the newer games. *Apollo 13* (1995), for example, includes
a wacky-ass thirteen-ball multiball that's either incredibly fun or not
all that fun depending on who you are.

"Great. I'm gonna get thirteen pinballs spun at me, all at once.
Wow, that's exciting as heck," says Sharpe unenthusiastically. "Seriously, really? And without a ball save? For what purpose?"

Pinball designers started taking their cues from players, and players wanted harder games; they wanted the machines in their basements
to challenge them for years. *The Simpsons Pinball Party*, for example,
features a Super Duper Mega Extreme Wizard Mode requiring so
many subtasks to be accomplished first that few players in the world
have reached it. To some, that's awesome; to others, why bother?

"It became this albatross of designers needing to get affirmation
from their audience," says Sharpe. "In the late '90s, the fact that you
would go up [to a new machine] and be totally lost as a player wasn't
fun. What do I do first? I mean, the old way of playing pinball was,
you shoot for the flashing light."

After its peak around 1992, pinball would nearly disappear *again*
by the end of the millennium. Unlike the postarcade crash in 1983, this
time it was more of a slow, painful process, like the way my daughter
removes a Band-Aid over the course of half an hour. Searching for a
cause, I had always assumed that the Internet killed pinball this time
around; after all, the timing made sense. But this time the cause of
death, like pinball itself, was complicated.

In *One Quarter at a Time*, Tim Arnold, owner of the Pinball Hall
of Fame, described how the mid-'90s evaporation of "the little mom-
and-pop stores and the little corner beer-and-shot joints" reduced the
number of possible locations for pinball machines. As an operator
himself at the time, Arnold had more and more trouble finding locations amenable to hosting machines, "and with no locations, there's
no pinball."

"Where pinball had its greatest strength was in street locations," agrees Sharpe, referring particularly to bars. "The DUI laws and getting rid of happy hours basically killed that. Bars really died." The result was, in a way, the extinction of the bar crowd's middle class—not middle class in terms of income, necessarily, but in terms of casualness. Corner taverns continued to dispense beer to regulars, and going-out spots continued to host late-night parties, but that middle slice of the bar's business—those stopping by for a quick game of pool or darts or pinball—started finding their entertainment elsewhere.

That's certainly part of the reason pinball began drifting toward its third near demise, a ruin that would come closer than ever to eliminating the game forever. But many people in the industry I've talked to cite another antagonist that killed pinball in the late '90s: pinball.

The strange fact is that pinball's success in the early '90s was responsible for pinball's decline in the mid-'90s. Because *The Addams Family* and its contemporaries sold so well, arcades were starting to get full.

"The pinball market is like any other marketplace," explains Lawlor. "The market was saturated with pinball machines. And it can only absorb so much."

Pinball became a victim of its own success; if everyone loved *The Addams Family* and continued to feed it quarters, operators had less reason to replace it with a new game. Even worse—or better, depending on the year one wants to consider—*The Addams Family* and its Bally-Williams contemporaries were running new, very reliable software, which was easier to operate and repair. The games simply became too appealing, and too reliable, for operators to want new ones.

This fact didn't stop new manufacturers from trying, ultimately unsuccessfully, to join the game. Alvin G. and Company entered the race in 1991 with their first machine, *A. G. Soccer-Ball*, marketed under the slogan "For years everybody has asked for something different."

It was certainly different, a weirdly configured head-to-head soccer-themed pinball with no backbox and on which either two players could compete, standing at opposite ends of the cabinet and facing each other, or one player could battle the machine flipping its own flipper. Alvin G. was out of business by 1994. Capcom suffered a similar fate, manufacturing games in 1995, 1996, and that's it. Data East, which had been selling pinball machines since 1987, sold all assets in 1994 to Sega Pinball (yes, the makers of *Sonic the Hedgehog* had a pinball company)—which itself hopped off the bandwagon in 1999, selling all assets to Stern. Even Gottlieb, which had been purchased in 1984 by Premier Technology but continued to sell games under the Gottlieb trademark, closed its doors after a sixty-five-year run, bookended by the popular *Baffle Ball* in 1931 and, ignominiously, *Barb Wire* in 1996, based on the insipid postapocalyptic thriller starring Pamela Anderson Lee.

The truth is pinball had been in a precarious position to begin with. Unlike a video game, for which maintenance generally means "spray it with Windex," a pinball machine requires skilled technical care. After a while, the abundance of pinball machines outran the efforts of the technicians, and machines fell into disrepair. Disrepair meant less interest from players, which meant fewer locations sinking their cash into pinball, which meant fewer technicians employed, which meant more disrepair.

One by one, the manufacturers fell. Call it a correction, call it oversaturation, or blame the extinction of simplicity. No matter where you point the flipper finger, just as a pinball launched up the playfield inevitably finds its way back to the drain, pinball would nearly disappear again before the year 2000. Only this time it almost didn't come back.

7

Come (Back) to PAPA

IT'S MY SECOND TRIP to the World Pinball Championships, PAPA18, and as I yet again motor over the Appalachians to Carnegie, Pennsylvania, and its adjacent brown brick warehouses that seem to have fewer intact windowpanes and a smaller percentage of existing roof each time I visit, I'm ranked 12,799th in the world. This makes me eligible for the new division PAPA has added, D Division, which is only for players ranked somewhere between 7,500th and infinity.* It's meant for novices, for people who find C Division too competitive, but I want to finish in the top twenty-four in *some* division and qualify for the playoffs.

Not that I'm required to play in D Division. I could play in A Division if I wanted, especially if my primary interest is in donating entry money to the winners. But I like my chances in D Division.

---

* Not to get too technical, but it's worth explaining that WPPR points (sometimes called "whoppers" when speaking aloud) are the pinball expertise ranking system that survived a protracted battle. Whoppers are awarded like prizes when you win a tournament, which explains my dismal ranking, since I haven't played many tournaments. For a few years, WPPR existed alongside a parallel ranking system called the PAPA Advanced Rating System (PARS). Full disclosure: when I said in the introduction that I peaked at eightieth in the world, it was according to PARS. At that time, WPPR had me at 232nd. I'm glad I got that off my chest.

As of the live standings posted online at the beginning of the competition, A, B, and C Divisions each have over thirty entries played, while D Division only has only eight—from just three people. Man, I like those odds. (In retrospect, the difference was probably due to D players being less likely to begin their PAPA experience on the less popular Thursday.)

One of the first people I see is Dave Stewart, a former FSPA league player and electrical engineering professor at the University of Maryland who once had his students build a rudimentary pinball machine over the course of a semester.

Stewart and I catch up while waiting in line for tokens. I casually mention that the new rules have placed me in D, and that feels a bit wrong. Seeking confirmation that I'm not a bully stomping around the kiddie pool, I ask, "I'm not sandbagging, am I?"

His reaction is decisive and uncompromising. "You're definitely sandbagging if you do D," he says. When I reach the front of the line, Stewart gleefully declares to the volunteer at the desk, "He's sandbagging if he does D!"

Thanks a lot, Dave.

So it's C Division again after all, and there's just enough time to begin my first entry, including a great score on *24* (2009), a machine themed after the action-adventure television drama. PAPA closes for the night (Jack Bauer: "The following takes place between 11:00 PM and 12:00 AM"), so I drive to a cheap hotel and pass out.

I'm eager to finish my entry the next morning, but I have to wait, because on a whim I've decided to do something weird just to see what happens—I've signed up to work at PAPA18 as a volunteer. For all of Saturday morning, instead of muttering about draining my ball down the stupid left outlane while approving my terrible score on some volunteer's tablet, I'll listen as players mutter about the stupid left outlane to me.

My first job, since the facility is open but not yet available for qualifying, is to shoo players away from the games until 10:00 AM.

Wearing a gray T-shirt with "STAFF" in huge white letters on the back, I gather yesterday's discarded Mountain Dew bottles while Rich Achterberg and Rob Wintler-Cox, two FSPA players volunteering with me, discuss their chances in the Seniors Division (age fifty and older). That's where I've been assigned to work—it's a bank of games designated for both the Seniors Division and the Split Flipper Division.

Oh yes. Split Flipper. That warrants some explaining.

Most of the time, a player stands at a pinball machine with his or her right hand on the right flipper button and left hand on the left flipper button.* In Split Flipper, two players stand at the machine, each in charge of one button, each allowed to only use one hand. It's a silly-looking way to play the game, and it's a lot harder than it looks to coordinate flipping with a second person. It helps if the flipper splitters are mentally in sync, and it helps even more if the flipper splitters are Josh and Zach Sharpe.

Split Flipper is one of a few minitournaments, sideline competitions with an element of whimsy, as if regular pinball was somehow deficient in whimsy. Another popular minitourney is the frosted glass tournament, in which players compete on a standard machine with the playfield glass made partially opaque, either using cardboard, that Christmas snow window decorating spray, or, in PAPA's case, a custom-machined semifrosty PAPA logo.

There are minitourneys that restrict players to one hand only or one ball only or one minute only. The Swedish Pinball Open even offers a delirium pinball tournament in which players compete on a bizarre Franken-game made from pieces of other games.†

---

* A notable exception is *The Simpsons Pinball Party*, which includes a Springfield Mystery Spot mode that reverses the action of each flipper—the left button controls the right flipper and vice versa. Many players find it easier to cross their arms and grab the opposite button rather than mentally cope with the change.

† The 2008 delirium pinball winner, Reidar Spets, scored eighty million points on a *Fish Tales* machine with a *Theatre of Magic* backglass, sounds from *Terminator 2* (1991), and two reversed-button flippers—one an upside-down curvy "banana" flipper that

I'm nervous about scorekeeping. I've seen what happens when impatient players can't flag down a volunteer to record their score fast enough—especially if that volunteer isn't doing anything else important but just happens not to see the player's waving hand. It's brutal: even the best-intentioned players will roll their eyes at the line forming behind themselves, as if to say, "Yeah, now we're all just waiting for no great reason. *These people.*" And may Montague Redgrave Himself help you if you mis-enter someone's score.

Some of these competitors look intense. I don't see any golf gloves this time, but more players seem to be wearing headphones, as though they're saying, "I will choose my own level of sensory input and social interaction, thanks."

Achterberg hands me a Nexus tablet to input scores, then issues a quick series of instructions—too quick. "And don't hit refresh," he says while walking away. "It just does random shit. Oh, and there's a glitch with voiding scores, so just do the green screen thing."

The what?

And he's gone.

The next two hours are a blur of typing scores on the tablet, asking players to approve and press the ok button, and reporting glitches. Every division has a car door remote nailed to a block of wood, and pressing the remote button somehow summons a higher-level volunteer to emerge from the token booth to make repairs or settle disputes. It's like pressing the flight attendant button or the "It's saying I didn't weigh my grapes, but I weighed my grapes" button on a supermarket self-scan machine. In the event of a catastrophic malfunction, PAPA has supplied a stack of signs reading "omg it's broken" that one can place on any defective machine. I notice later that someone has taped one to a bathroom stall.

Williams Electronics introduced and immediately abandoned in the late '70s and one a tiny *Addams Family* miniflipper. Oh those crazy Swedes.

Echoing the volunteers who've recorded my own scores, I cheerily say "Good luck!" to each new person. It's hard to keep cheerful, though, because every single person who calls me over is pissed off at the world, having drained their ball just a second ago.

I hear a woman tell her husband, with a measure of urgency in her voice, "Have fun. *Have. Fun.*" She says this before leaving him in the C Division area. He has a tropical shirt, a ponytail, and a big, fluffy, red beard. What she doesn't realize is, when he drains and curses and realizes he needs to buy another ten-dollar entry to have any shot at feeling like a worthwhile human being, he *is* having fun.

About an hour in, just when I'm getting the hang of the tablet, I become *that volunteer*. I enter someone's score for the wrong player, delaying the whole crowd while I run back and forth between the tournament game bank and the main desk, trying to undo my mistake. Then I get called in to mediate a dispute over the rules of Split Flipper—there's a kerfuffle over whether each player's unused hand is allowed to touch the machine at all, as long as it's not pressing the flipper button. I can't solve it. Then I enter someone else's score incorrectly.

But hey, free T-shirt.

I can see why no one knows where to put their extra hand—there's no way two dudes can share a pinball table without invading each other's personal space. Nearly every split flipper team appears 100 percent unsure where to place that unnecessary arm, like a first-time stand-up comic obsessing over how to use the hand not holding the mic.

It's with no small measure of relief that I turn over my Nexus tablet to the next volunteer and go finish off my first entry in C Division. Drain three balls, tap OK on the volunteer's tablet, take out my phone, refresh refresh refresh, and . . . I'm in fifty-third place in C Division. (Remember that my ranking within the tournament, where I'm angling for twenty-fourth place or higher among my hundred or so cocompetitors, is different from my overall WPPR ranking of 12,799th.)

So, entry two. For the first time, three out of my five games on the entry are halfway decent! I blow it on *The Shadow* and *24*, but now I'm up to thirtieth place in C Division.

Inhaling a hoagie for lunch, I start to feel the strain on my wrists, but less so than during PAPA17. I don't think I've developed better wrist muscles—I think I've just taxed my tendons less by playing games that count as entries rather than playing random machines for fun. I eat while staring at a *Popeye* video game with a Post-it announcing its repair status covering the "ye" and spend way too long imagining an arcade game called *Pope.**

Entry three isn't bad, but two is still my best. I've dropped to thirty-first, but now I'm getting two or three good games per entry to balance the clunkers. *I can do this.*

So I drop another ten dollars right away on entry four, which starts with a disappointing game of *NBA Fastbreak*. This machine was supposed to be my secret weapon this time, the same way I relied on *Johnny Mnemonic* at PAPA17. Years ago, I was a member of my university's grad student government. The administration gave us a bunch of money to use for such grad student extras as wine mixers and conference travel grants and coffee hours—but if we didn't spend it all by the end of the year, they gave us less money the following year.

Toward the end of one academic year, we were discussing what to do with a surplus of a few thousand dollars. "Hey," I suggested, "how about buying a pinball machine?" It's one of those offhand proposals you offer in a jokey, long-shot kind of way, like saying, "Hey, how about we get a daycare at work?" But because the grad student government was run by grad students, instead of debating the practicalities of the suggestion, they basically said, "Sure, why not?"

---

* The game would offer Infallible Mode. The buttons on the console would be A, B, and HOLY SEE. When your score is announced, white smoke rises from the machine. And so on.

That's how *The Twilight Zone* ended up in the student union; I later exchanged it for two machines, a video *Ms. Pac-Man* and a pinball *NBA Fastbreak*. It's also how I ended up with a key in my pocket that opened both. (It may also be why my PhD ended up taking seven years.)

The point is, I know *NBA Fastbreak* very well, almost as well as *Johnny*. The machine in the student union had my initials all over the high score list, with several scores over two hundred. (Recall that *NBA Fastbreak* uses a basketball-style scoring system, on which double- and triple-digit scores are the norm.) And here, at PAPA, on my fourth entry, I've scored a damn seventeen.

The next entry, entry five, does a good job of showing my inconsistency; it includes the absolute best game anyone has yet played on *The Shadow* and the third-worst game anyone has played on *High Speed* (1986), a game based on a moving violation. The story goes that pinball designer Steve Ritchie evaded the police on a California highway at 146 miles per hour in his 1979 Porsche 928, then essentially said, "Hey, my disregard for authority and willingness to risk human life would make a kick-ass pinball theme!"

While I'm waiting in line, Marina calls to remind me that it's my grandmother's birthday. Benjamin, now eight months old, says "la la la" on the phone, and it's adorable, but my mind is elsewhere. I don't remember exactly how the conversation went, but probably something like this:

Marina: The kids are doing okay—Maya, hold on a minute, I'm talking to Daddy—we just got back from the grocery store—Maya, please wait—can you leave that there? Can you just leave that there until I'm off the phone?

Benjamin: La la la!

Marina: So—oh, hold on, Benjamin, what's in your mouth? Maya, did you see him put something in his mouth?

Maya: Can I have a Popsicle?

Marina: Benjamin, I'm sorry to reach into your mouth—is that paper? Where did you get paper?

Me: I freaking dominated *Shadow*! It was awesome! I was playing Vengeance Mode, and I shot all four ramps, and I even played Khan Multiball three times, and . . .

It's a wonder I'm still married.

Having precalculated some likely outcomes, I tell Marina that I can easily lock in a spot in the playoffs with this entry—I think—with a score of about forty million on *Indiana Jones* (1993).

There's a pause, and Marina says, deadpan, "We'll pray for you."

I don't hit forty million on *Indy*, but I'm close, about thirty-five million, which puts entry five in twenty-third place. If it were midnight, I'd make the playoffs for sure—unfortunately, there are still several hours for the other C Division players to keep topping my scores, so I need to keep playing.

Entries six and seven include an *NBA Fastbreak* game with a total score of . . . eight. Yes, eight points. I'm never playing *NBA Fastbreak* again.

As midnight approaches, bringing with it the end of qualifying, I have time for only one more entry, so it's all riding on number eight. Miraculously, it's a good entry—four decent scores, including an okay score on *NBA Fastbreak*, which I had previously promised never to play again. This puts me in striking distance of the finals, provided my fifth game is good.

I run some numbers, compare the remaining games, and determine that I can feel confident about qualifying if I score 1.5 million on *High Speed* or 700,000 on *Centaur* (1981). I need some expert advice, so I find Scott and Sergio, two FSPA players who know the games well.

The question is which task do they think is harder—scoring 1.5 million on *High Speed* or 700,000 on *Centaur*? The answer, Scott and Sergio agree, is meh, either one.

I realize I'm disappointed, not just because they didn't reach a clear conclusion but also because it doesn't appear I've posed an interesting question. I guess I had envisioned a lively debate about the merits of each strategy, but instead I found two tired players who didn't really care all that much what game I chose for my fifth game of my eighth entry in C Division.

Many obsessive hobbyists know this sense of pointlessness. It's one of those moments when it hits you that the thing you've been focusing on all day, the goal for which you've striven, the path whose details you've analyzed to death, is something that no one else really cares about. Trust me, I know that feeling well—I used to be a grad student.

"The beauty of pinball—different from video games, by and large, and a lot of other endeavors—is that there's no single right way to play," Roger Sharpe once told me. "Any approach, depending on the level of effectiveness and risk and reward, can be just as good—and get you the same results." So I close my eyes and choose *High Speed*.

A million and a half points, and then I'm in the playoffs. A million and a half points, and then I'm in the playoffs. Shoot the highway loops, Scott said, and the ramp if it's convenient. Here we go.

Aaaaand . . . here we do not go. Here we hit no freaking loops at all. Here we end the game with 366,000. Here we yet again fumble what should have been a doable attempt to make the playoffs. As I can hear Jack Bauer say repeatedly on the adjacent *24* machine, "*Damn it.*"

It's 11:16 PM. I rush to the front desk to buy a ninth entry, an entry I'll barely have time to play, but screw it. As the poker players would say if asked to make pinball puns, I'm on tilt.

"And you're the last one," says the woman at the front desk. That would be a relief to hear, except she's said it to the man in front of me.

Decorum, if it had existed in the first place, is gone now. I'm in Carnegie, Pennsylvania, on a Saturday night, my armpits are wet, my contact lenses are dry, and I still smell like the hoagie I ate twelve hours ago. Guess what time it is, boys and girls! It's begging time!

Somehow my begging works, and the woman sells me entry nine. I run back to the games, not stopping to second-guess whether I've just debased myself in front of strangers, and I have no time to spare, so I can only choose short-playing games, and I've gotta finish gotta finish, and I quickly zip through three good games and two bad ones, and then—

"Hey," booms a voice over the loudspeaker, "you know what time it is. Aww yeah."

That "aww yeah" marks midnight,* the end, done, and after some last-minute shuffling, with the top twenty-four advancing to the play-offs tomorrow, I'm in twenty-eighth place.

"So you don't need to play tomorrow?" Marina asks on the phone.

"Uh, no."

"What time will you be home?"

"Well, I'm still going to watch the A Division finals, and those end around 5:00—"

"So you'll be back after we're all asleep."

"Yeah. I guess so. It's a five-hour drive."

"Okay," she says, and because I'm male, I have absolutely no ability to gauge from her tone whether it's really okay.

"And . . . after the finals . . . there's kind of like a big party, where they turn down the lights, and everyone plays pinball and gets drunk," I continue, then pause to assess the silence. I can't, so I err on the side of good judgment, finishing the sentence with, "but I don't need to stay for that."

"Okay," she says.

I've abandoned my kids for the weekend, left my wife on solo childcare duty, and—oh, shoot—forgot to call my grandmother to

---

* Sometimes midnight is a good time to play pinball. If you're playing *Johnny Mnemonic* and the game's internal clock hits midnight, everything suddenly goes nuts for a rare mode called Midnight Madness. I've, um, played *Johnny Mnemonic* at midnight a few times.

wish her a happy birthday, all so that I can shove a little ball around. Seriously, it sounds like I should be confessing this to a therapist: "First I started leaving my kids on the weekends. Then I missed my grandmother's birthday. Then I converted Maya's college fund into tokens."

I'm going to go out on a limb here and guess that most of this is not okay.

8

The Day Pinball Died

—————

PINBALL HAD ONE LAST SHOT. The industry had been on life support for much of the late '90s, selling about tenfold fewer machines in 1999 than in 1992. If pinball was to have a future, manufacturers would need to do something drastic.

"Management said we need to make it profitable," said designer George Gomez in a now-famous seminar at the annual public Pinball Expo, later transcribed verbatim in *Pinball Player*, the magazine of the Pinball Owners Association. It was Saturday, October 23, 1999, and Gomez had arrived to triumphantly boast how he and his dedicated coworkers had just saved the industry with their new invention. WMS, Gomez's employer, told him and his fellow designers that "the world has changed. Nobody wants what you guys are doing. You're boring everybody. Invent something new."

To Gomez's colleagues, it must have seemed like a "What more do you *want* from me?" moment. All they'd done for the past several years was innovate; each new game was cleverer than the last, and still pinball was going down the toilet.

So Gomez, with the help of Pat Lawlor, Lyman Sheats, and dozens of others, devised something innovative. Something no one had created before, something fantastic and fun, something that, according to game designer Duncan Brown, "actually turned a profit for the first time in a long time."

Perhaps you've seen Pinball 2000, the mashup of pinball and video games that WMS produced as its Hail Mary pass. It was essentially a regular pinball machine, slightly smaller, but with a holographic video display somehow magically projected perpendicular to the playfield. Playing Pinball 2000, a.k.a. PB2K, was like playing real, physical pinball from inside a video game. The first machine using Pinball 2000 technology was called *Revenge from Mars* (1999), and among other neat holographic tricks, for example, the game could project a little green Martian at the bottom of a ramp—and sending the pinball up that ramp "squashed" the Martian, which vanished after a brief animated death.

No two ways about it, PB2K was awesome. For a while, it looked like the geniuses at WMS had done it again, inventing not just a new gadget but rather a whole new revolutionary platform for pinball machines, devised from the ground up, amazing, beloved, lucrative.

But not lucrative enough. And when Gomez gave his seminar at Pinball Expo, he must have felt the winds of change starting to blow. "My spider sense has been on fire this last month," Gomez cautiously concluded his talk. "Pinball will survive . . . [but] I fear that our company may have lost the ability to make it make economic sense. If that's the case, being as it's a business, they might choose not to be in the pinball business."

Unfortunately, Gomez's spider sense was excellent. On the very next working day after Gomez's seminar, Monday, October 25, 1999, WMS—the only publicly traded pinball company, which at the time had a 70–75 percent market share in the pinball industry (the rest belonged to Stern Pinball, which had recently bought Sega)—stopped producing pinball machines forever.

CEO Kevin Verner told the *Chicago Tribune* that he didn't want "to continue losing money." Ironically, Williams redoubled its efforts as a manufacturer of slot machines—apparently Verner had no problem helping lots of *other* people lose money.

I've always found the decision to ditch pinball for slots ironically appropriate for historical reasons: from gambling devices came pinball, and to gambling devices pinball manufacturers returned.

"They handled that all really badly," writes Brown, who was one of the employees on the WMS chopping block on October 25. He and his colleagues, who had just spent a cautious but gratifying weekend at Pinball Expo, where Gomez gave his seminar, "had a very strange morning, with rumors swirling around and weird card access and computer network things coming and going." Finally, at an all-company meeting in the cafeteria, Brown, Gomez, Lawlor, and everyone else was asked to leave.

The wheels of industry ground to a halt over the span of a few weeks, with the grand layoff followed by the shuttering of factories. In November, Williams made its last pinball game in Waukegan, Wisconsin. After *Revenge from Mars*, they had begun selling their second PB2K title, *Star Wars: Episode I* (1999). The Day Pinball Died is immortalized within the game's code; shooting the right ramp to spell "JAR JAR" awards 19,992,510 points—a reference to October 25, 1999.

I ask Brown, who jumped on the sinking Williams ship in 1997 and helped program *Episode I*, why WMS would request something like Pinball 2000, and then, when Gomez and his team produced exactly what they wanted, kill pinball anyway.

Part of the answer, he says, lies in a management decision to raise the prices of both PB2K machines to recoup costs. Distributors balked at the new price, which WMS refused to change, and suddenly the momentum from Pinball 2000's sales started to slow.

Another reason was *South Park* (1999). At the same time WMS debuted the magical Pinball 2000, Sega—not yet sold to Stern—made a *South Park* pinball machine based on the irreverent cartoon series. The *South Park* game had no innovation, no triumphs of engineering prowess. But it did have a large toilet and a toy Kenny you could kill and talking feces. It was *South Park*.

Brown explains that WMS had gone all in on the narrative that Pinball 2000 was the wave of the future, convincing operators that the added expense "would pay off in the cashbox." Yet perhaps because players simply enjoyed the theme, *South Park* earned just as much for operators as either Pinball 2000 game.

In December, just a few weeks before the Y2K bug that would wreak nothing upon no one, the *Chicago Tribune* declared "Pinball Runs Out of Wizardry." The *Economist* later agreed, in a depressing article called "The Last Pinball Machine," making a "game over" joke and announcing that "nobody much cares anymore" about pinball.

Toward the end of his 1999 Pinball Expo talk, the one Gomez gave just before losing his job, the soon-to-be-unemployed pinball designer had made one more prescient comment, this time about his competitor.

"Gary Stern might just be the last man standing," said Gomez.

And then, he was.

* * *

"For dedicated pinball players, there is only one ball left in play," wrote Bruce Headlam in the *New York Times* on October 28, 1999, three days after WMS closed its pinball division. Headlam quoted pinball historian Russ Jensen, who feared that "with one company left, there's the possibility that pinball may not live into the next millennium." And the current millennium only had two months left in it.

Gary Stern, the last man standing, grew up in a culture of pinball manufacturing. In the 1930s, when pin games were starting to appear on every bar counter, a young Sam Stern, Gary's father, decided to get in on the action. He bought a few games, installed them in drugstores, and stopped by to empty the coin trays before dates, hopefully with women who didn't question why he bought their drinks with pennies. One night, Sam discovered that one of his games had a jammed coin acceptor—those readers of a certain age will recall when coin acceptors, like those at the laundromat, were long, flat pieces of metal you had to physically slide into a machine to deposit money.

Dismantling the machine, Sam Stern immediately discovered what was jamming the coin acceptor: many, many coins.

He decided to become a full-time pinball operator, naming his new company Scott Cross—a name that meant absolutely nothing but that his friend in advertising thought sounded snappy. (To me, it sounds like the protagonist of a Christian graphic novel in which groups of teenagers learn the evils of binge drinking, but I'm not in the 1930s.)

Sam Stern eventually graduated from operator to distributor, growing his business and selling coin-operated machines in Philadelphia. In 1947, he met with one of his suppliers, pinball mogul Harry Williams. Semijoking, Sam Stern put his feet up on Williams's desk and asked, "Why don't you sell me the company?"

"Harry said, 'I have to think about that,' went up in his airplane, flew around Chicago for three hours, came down, and sold my father half of Williams,"* Gary Stern told me. Gary, who was two years old at the time, is now the seventy-year-old CEO of Stern Pinball, which was—until very recently—the last participant in a dying industry.

With his open-collared white Oxford shirt and long fringe of swept-back white hair, Gary Stern looks every bit like an ex-lawyer with membership in a yacht club, which makes sense, since he's an ex-lawyer with membership in a yacht club. His thick-rimmed white eyeglasses look like an Apple product. You can tell just from his

---

* It was actually 49 percent, but still. Must have been some plane ride.

appearance that he's an iconic figure, a personality, a CEO. He can often be found carrying a glass of what he calls "adult water" (i.e., vodka—Russian, he says, not Latvian).

"Gary, please," I hear him correct someone who calls him Mister Stern. "Mister Stern was my father, or, when I was a kid, the dog's name was Mister. So Mister Stern was a schnauzer."

At age sixteen, young Gary Stern began a summer job in the stockroom at Williams. The position gave Stern a direct sight line into what he now considers the most important part of pinball manufacturing: inventory control. He immediately noticed how a product with thousands of parts could see its profits evaporate if the manufacturer overordered—or, worse, how manufacturing halted if they underordered. You can have the best game in the world, but if your flipper bat supplier is two months late delivering the flipper bats, you can't make games. The secret sauce then—and this is probably the least spicy secret sauce imaginable—is a well-maintained material requirements planning, or MRP, program.

"The most important thing that the Engineering Design Department does is not the playfield layout," says Stern. "It's the bill of materials, the parts list, that drives the MRP." Imagine the nightmare of building a pinball machine without one. The bill of materials can run up to twenty single-spaced pages, but each item on it is vital. "If they leave off a ball guide," Stern points out, "all of a sudden we've got a million, two million dollars' worth of parts with which you can build *nothing*." In today's Stern Pinball factory, six different games are in production at any given time, all with different lead times for parts.

From the 1960s through the 1990s, Sam Stern and his son ended up at the helm of several amusement companies—Chicago Coin, Data East Pinball, Sega Pinball, even jukebox manufacturer Seeburg Corporation—primarily under the umbrella of Stern Electronics. On the day in 1999 that WMS stopped making pinball machines, Gary Stern had been running competitor Sega Pinball for over a decade, and he had a choice: bail or commandeer a potentially doomed monopoly. Did he really want to remain, as he told the *Chicago Tribune*, "the last dinosaur"—the world's only manufacturer of a product the world seemed not to want?

He did. For the first decade of the new millennium, Stern Pinball turned out games on reliable licensed themes, like *Austin Powers* (2001), *Elvis* (2004), *CSI* (2008), and appropriately, given Stern's lack of competitors, *Monopoly* (2001). That was the general landscape when I first joined my pinball league in 2003: pinball had passed its heyday, but at least for now, Gary Stern was keeping it from vanishing completely.

In 2008, as anyone with money remembers, everything went to shit. The economy tanked, and one of the first things people stopped buying were expensive toys for their basements. In a down economy, Wal-Mart thrives. Pinball does not.

In my lifetime, I've now seen three deaths of pinball: in the mid-'80s, the late '90s, and 2008. Stern Pinball, like most businesses, simply couldn't function without customers. The only pinball manufacturer in the world was about to drain its last ball. But then along came a man named Dave Peterson.

Unlike Roger Sharpe or Gary Stern, Peterson was neither a pinball fanatic nor a manufacturer. He was the managing director of Hagerty Peterson, a firm described on its own home page in the following exciting terms: "a merchant bank and private equity investment and advisory firm that builds companies by providing strategic direction, active management, board representation, and supporting capital." In other words, they save dying companies. Stern Pinball was a dying company.

Peterson had worked as a lawyer, first for the SEC and then for Morgan Stanley. His expertise in management and marketing—along with actual cash money from Peterson's investors—kept Stern afloat during the economic downturn.

Tall and lean with close-cropped, military-style graying hair, Peterson is the sort of person who needs to only speak for one or two sentences before you know he's a business guy.

"We were just concerned that this was going to be another 'buggy whip' company and wasn't going to last long," Peterson told the Chicago *Daily Herald* in 2015. The old business school analogy goes that when Ford introduced cars, buggy whips became a dead-end product.*

The first problem Peterson noticed was that Stern Pinball had alienated part of its market. Gary Stern was unenthused about enthusiasts, and in a muzzle-the-CEO moment, he actually told them he didn't need their business. Many collectors recall Gary appearing at Pinball Expo, the annual gathering for people with dozens of machines in their home arcades, and telling them they're not his market—he was only interested in selling machines to operators who could place them in bars to gather quarters. The operator market is important, of course, but you don't want to tell your biggest fans to buzz off. (Jody Dankberg, Stern's director of marketing and licensing, maintains that his CEO was only trying to reinforce the necessity of supporting on-location pinball and has been repeatedly misquoted.)

Under Peterson's guidance, Stern laid out its three market segments: operators, collectors, and rec room buyers. Then, cleverly, the company began manufacturing a version of each new pinball machine targeted at each segment. For operators, Stern made a "Pro" version, a basic game with fewer bells and whistles—it might lack a gadget or two that would have only added to the price and the list of breakable parts. Operators wanted a relatively cheap yet appealing game, one that Dankberg said would be "fast, mean, [and] play quick." An extra

---

* As Peterson correctly told the *Daily Herald*, though, even buggy whips aren't extinct. If you want one, just take a trip to Westfield Whip, the last surviving whip manufacturer in Westfield, Massachusetts, nicknamed the Whip City. Seriously. If you've ever watched horse-drawn carriages around New York's Central Park, their fancy buggy whips had to come from somewhere.

ramp or miniplayfield probably wouldn't attract enough additional quarters to offset the cost of the upgrade.

At the other end of the spectrum were the collectors, for whom Stern made a limited-edition, or "LE," version. This had every bell, every whistle (often literal bells, but probably not literal whistles), and other bonuses for the true collector—a hand-signed serial number plaque, for example.

In the middle was Stern's third segment, the one they called "rec room buyers." These were people who wanted a pinball machine in their rec room alongside the bumper pool table and home theater. These people had a lot of money to spend but not a lot of knowledge about pinball, so there was no need for the custom plaque. Stern's "Premium" category was aimed at them, taking the fancy-schmancy stuff off the LE version but leaving in some upgrades over Pro.

Take, for example, *Game of Thrones* (2015). All three versions have a dragon toy, but on the LE and Premium models, it moves. LE and Premium have an additional miniplayfield with its own full-sized flippers. And at the top tier, LE includes a certificate of authenticity, designer Steve Ritchie's autograph on the playfield, and hand-painted cabinet art. The price difference is not insignificant: $6,000 for Pro, $7,600 for Premium, and $8,800 for LE. And especially with recent games, like *Game of Thrones*, each of the different versions has its own set of rules.*

Not only are the three market segments necessary for sales, but Stern now recognizes how all three must be appeased in order to keep the game going. The games that operators buy for twentysomethings to play in bars in 2015, for example, will be the games that rec room

---

* This doesn't please everyone. On an electromechanical machine from the 1970s, there's one rule set, and you can know it inside and out. On modern machines, not only have the rules become more complex, but there are even individual rules for each machine subtype and edition—*and* manufacturers issue software updates. So not only do *Metallica* (2013) Pro and *Metallica* Premium have different rules, so do *Metallica* Premium running software version 1.4 and *Metallica* Premium running software version 1.5.

buyers, during their respective midlife crises, will crave in 2035. It's a strategy he calls "keep the core player, broaden the base."

"If we don't bring people into pinball," Peterson told the crowd at Pinball Expo, "then pinball is obviously going to die a slow death." Again.

Stern likens it to selling a 1932 Ford Model A, the value of which has been on the decline, "because the guys who want to collect that car, who knew it when they were young, are dead." Nostalgia has a specific time window, and it seems to usually center around high school and college, those years when freedom is at its most novel and responsibility is low.

In a way, targeting different strata of buyers is akin to what pinball has done for years, targeting different strata of players. A novice can enjoy *Attack from Mars*, for example, because it has a huge UFO in the middle that needs to be bashed repeatedly. But actually progressing to the end of the game, performing a litany of other tasks during your three balls to begin a crazy wizard mode called Rule the Universe, is incredibly hard, which keeps serious players interested.

Breaking the customer base down even further shows why manufacturers would be foolish to disregard any of their market segments. Half of Stern's games are exported, and in Australia and northern Europe, like the United States, most of the customers are enthusiasts or rec room buyers. But elsewhere in Europe, people flock to low-stakes gambling halls and ale houses that include AWPs (amusement with prizes), so the operator market there is key. In Italy, nearly all of the business is to operators, both in bars and in traditional arcades. Stern even recalls shipping a pinball machine to Kuwait right before the start of the Gulf War. He later heard that the game had been spotted "in a truck going back to Iraq."

The size of the international market makes theme selection particularly important. You may think an NFL-themed game, like the one Stern made in 2001, would have universal appeal—but in Europe, what the hell is the NFL? *Game of Thrones*, Stern reminds me, is televised in 170 different countries and probably watched in a less than legal way in most of the others.

When Data East Pinball, under Gary Stern, made a *Simpsons* pinball machine in 1990, they were one of the first licensees permitted to use Springfield and its characters. It was still early in the cartoon's history, and Bart didn't have much of a following outside the United States, so the game's export market was small. When Stern released its follow-up *Simpsons* game, *The Simpsons Pinball Party*, in 2003, the new machine had much stronger international appeal.*

The Holy Grail would be a machine themed after a sport that humans in countries around the world all love; alas, there isn't one. Americans don't care for soccer. Basketball is popular in China but not most of Europe. "Baseball you can't do," Stern lists next. "We'd sell machines in Cuba and Japan, neither of which are really pinball markets."

So what does everyone like? "Movies, television, and rock and roll," says Stern. Take that, sports.

Another alternative is to simply release multiple versions of the same game. "When we made *NASCAR*," Stern tells me, "we re-arted it as *Grand Prix* for the export market." Not only was that a smart marketing choice, it's also the first time I've ever heard the word "art" used as a verb. Makes me want to walk into the Louvre and yell, "Hey, who arted?"

Even *NFL* was a re-theming of Stern Pinball's first newly designed machine, a soccer game called *Striker Xtreme* (2000). To make it

---

* Stronger, but even a show like *The Simpsons* has trouble finding universal acceptance. In September 2005, an Arabic satellite TV station aired what it deemed a culturally acceptable version of *The Simpsons* in which all potentially offensive material had been removed, thus introducing the show to a new audience. Homer Simpson became Omar Shamshoon, Bart was Badr, and Krusty the Klown was renamed Maarmish, which means "crunchy." Gone were all references to beer, bacon, homosexuality, Christianity, and Judaism. The resulting show was generally uninteresting, and it was cancelled after thirty-four episodes. *Worst Arabization ever.*

palatable to Americans, in addition to re-arting the graphics, Stern replaced the goalie with a linebacker and the soccer goal with a goalpost.

Today Stern has an active online presence, including a popular channel on gaming video platform Twitch.tv, hosted by the young, bearded, Raybanned minicelebrity "Jack Danger." For the release of *Game of Thrones*, Stern appeared in a billboard-sized publicity still, sitting on HBO's actual Iron Throne. The launch of the previous game, *KISS* (2015), featured Stern in full Gene Simmons makeup, posing next to the machine with his tongue sticking out.

Dankberg relates that, after the photo shoot, Stern elected to keep the makeup on and drive to the yacht club in his convertible to watch the Blackhawks game. What was meant to be a fun surprise for his friends nearly spoiled Stern Pinball's carefully crafted secrecy about upcoming themes—*KISS* had not been announced yet, and someone who recognized Gary took a photo of him at a gas station and sent it to his daughter, who posted it on her Facebook page. The Stern Pinball team had a hell of a time quickly undoing the picture's online footprint. I guess that's why it's sometimes safer to rock and roll all night than to party ev-er-y day.

That secrecy is all part of the marketing genius. Commenters on the Pinside forum—an online pinball discussion board—analyze photos on Stern's Facebook page with the scrutiny of crime scene investigators, drooling over each new detail that might allow them to guess Stern's next theme before it's officially announced.

As easily as he could claim credit for coming to the rescue on the Day Pinball Died, Stern insists repeatedly that he loves the game, but he didn't save pinball. Since the early '30s, however, when his dad joined the industry, the world had never gone more than a few months without a new pinball machine. If Stern had followed the pattern of business decisions in 1999, there wouldn't have been any new pinball machines, possibly to this day. You didn't save pinball, Gary? The hell you didn't.

While I'm talking to Stern, a middle-aged man in a pinball T-shirt interrupts to vigorously shake his hand and ask him to share a selfie.

"This is, like, surreal!" the guy says after his wife takes a picture. "This is kind of a dream!"

Shaking Stern's hand a second time, he's just so overcome with joy that he transforms into a kid in front of my eyes. "Mister Steeeern!" he says, suddenly sounding like a loud, gravelly-voiced teenager, "Woooooow! Huge fan! *Thank you.*"

I wonder if I should tell him Mister Stern was a schnauzer.

● ● ●

The radio has predicted "a dusting of snow" on the late March morning that I visit the Stern Pinball factory in Melrose Park, Illinois, a Chicago suburb about as attractive and vibrant as Carnegie, Pennsylvania. As it turns out, a Chicago "dusting" is the equivalent of a DC "holy hell I should just crash into a lamppost now and get it over with," and I slog through the parking lot to the front door an hour late, soaked to my ankles in gray slush. Somehow I've convinced Marina and the kids to join me on this trip, but instead of skipping gaily around Millennium Park, they're stuck in a hotel room with sleet battering the windows, Marina half knocked out from the flu, Benjamin restless, and Maya deciding to try out her new phrase "You're not in charge!"—all of them counting the seconds until we can go home.

I'm in wonderland.

Well, I'm in a factory. I blame Willy Wonka for distorting multiple generations' concepts of factories, casting them as magical places that make Pee-Wee's Playhouse look like the DMV. Some factories have spruced up for the sake of tourism—I'm thinking of Jelly Belly, Ben and Jerry's, Crayola, and Celestial Seasonings with its monstrous

Peppermint Room—but most put function and compliance first, aesthetics second. Even though a few corners of the Stern Pinball factory give way to whimsy, with hanging banners paying tribute to previous games and a small arcade in which employees are required to play fifteen minutes a day,* mostly it's a warehouse filled with shelves, boxes, and men in dark hoodies.

But inside the cardboard boxes labeled "Northern Precision Plastics, Inc." stacked by the loading dock is something unique: a pile of clear plastic ramps, all identical, all destined to become the frictionless highways for the silver ball, each one capable of sealing the difference between victory and heartbreak.

Colorful spools of cable line the workbenches, the wires waiting to be cut to the proper size and connected according to the appropriate wiring diagram.† Off to the side, two men spray and apply a long, trapezoidal *Star Trek* decal to a wooden cabinet, then squeegee out the bubbles—in this day and age, pinball cabinets aren't prettily painted, they're covered in UV-resistant, three-hundred-dots-per-inch stickers. A handful of quality testers meticulously assess each switch, lamp, and coil in the nearly finished machines, tapping areas of the playfield that the glass would normally cover.

This is not a factory that churns out a few million of the same simple widget. This is a factory that churns out a few thousand of the same very complicated widget, each one assembled from over 3,500 individual parts in multiple mediums—plastic, metal, wood, glass, electronics, paint, and half a mile of wire—each needing to be sanded, sculpted, melted, molded, soldered, or applied, sometimes by machine, sometimes by hand. In 2008, Stern told the *New York*

---

* This is a brilliant way of testing games still in the design phase, because among Stern's employees are some fabulous pinball players and some complete novices, so they can see how players of all levels respond to their games.

† Interestingly, the dozen or so workers doing the wiring—at least today—are all women. There's a clear gender divide between departments. Soldering: women. Packing and shipping: men. It's like a middle school dance.

Times that each machine takes thirty-two hours to build—longer than a Ford Taurus. Today the parts appear to include giant plastic Gene Simmons heads that dominate the new *KISS* machine, tongues outstretched to form miniramps.

The toys are probably the coolest parts (or "subassemblies") to see stacked on shelves or in bins. One shelf holds a stack of Starship Enterprises, rows of diamond-shaped wrestling rings from *WWE Wrestlemania* (2015), and a collection of medieval castles.

The castles themselves are an unambiguous tribute to the resurgence of pinball. While *Star Trek* and *WWE Wrestlemania* debuted in 2013 and 2015, respectively, the castles come from *Medieval Madness*, a WMS game from 1997. Stern recently purchased the rights to remanufacture *Medieval Madness*, and they've now begun making new machines essentially identical to the originals.

This is not normal. Pinball machines aren't often remanufactured—for the most part, once they're made, they're made. It's as though Ford decided yesterday to start producing, on a large scale, the 1955 Thunderbird—not a car that's this year's take on the '55 Thunderbird but the original '55 Thunderbird, made now.

Dankberg, who's leading my tour today, is just as excited about what's inside the games as what's on the playfield. "We make a unique set of wiring and cabling for every game," he explains, showing me their newest "node boards," essentially mini-computers that have helped Stern trim the half mile of wire in each game down to less than a quarter mile. He shows me digital power supplies that replace older-style transformers, trimming the game by thirty-five pounds.

Dankberg came to Stern Pinball in 2009, by way of the music industry. A self-described "*Star Wars* baby" with a black baseball cap, large glasses, and an easygoing, unshaven demeanor, Dankberg looks kind of like a roadie, but the roadie who reads Dostoyevsky during downtime.

When he was in his twenties, Dankberg thought he had a bright future as a guitarist. But he soon learned that "getting a record deal does not necessarily mean that you have a job." So instead of playing guitar, he sold guitar amps, eventually transitioning into jobs in artist relations and marketing. That's where he would have stayed, were it not for an overture from lawyer Dave Peterson, who knew Stern needed a marketer.

"I said, 'They still make pinball machines? Unbelievable!'" recalls Dankberg. "I never met [pinball designer] Steve Ritchie in my life. I just knew he was some jerk on the Internet." Little did he know he'd soon be deciding, for the majority of the world, exactly *which* pinball machines Steve Ritchie would design.

"My main mission," says Dankberg, "as the marketing guy of pinball, is to get people interested in pinball."

So far, it's working. If pinball is disappearing from the American landscape, it's sure as hell news to Stern's 250 employees, working in a 35,000-square-foot factory for a company whose revenue has quadrupled since 2008. (About a month after my initial visit, Stern relocated to a 110,000-square-foot facility down the road.)

Inside the factory's arcade, where everyone's mandatory fifteen minutes of daily pinball beta testing takes place, a handwritten sheet hangs from *WWE Wrestlemania*, where employees have written "Wrestler music still not loud enough" and "Shaker motor feels too violent." Wrestling fans rejoice: Body slamming your opponent and braining him with a metal folding chair is fine. But the shaker motor is too violent.

Another of the games in production during my tour is the infamous *Whoa Nellie! Big Juicy Melons*, a deliberate throwback to older-style games, both in terms of its mechanics (score is kept using electromechanical reels) and the unapologetic misogyny of its theme. This is not a remanufacture, as with *Medieval Madness*, it's a completely new game that looks like a completely old game. The machine was dreamed up by a company with the ability to design pinball machines but not manufacture them. That company is called WhizBang, which, perhaps not coincidentally, are two slang terms for things one can do with a penis.

Whoa Nellie! has some quirky features, like the fact that it sits on a faux fruit crate rather than metal legs, but there's no denying that the dominant double entendres about melons (thumping them; hand-picking them; their ripeness, juiciness, sweetness, and bigness) could—and here it's the *Pinball Aficionado* blog's inadvertent double entendre—"definitely rub some [people] the wrong way."

Deciding which titles to produce is no insignificant task, and Stern Pinball delights in announcing its upcoming machines with great fanfare and, increasingly, more than twenty simultaneous launch parties around the world, a practice Dankberg adopted from the music industry. As he walks me around the factory, I think I'm being coy when I casually say, "You know what would be a good theme? *Game of Thrones*." At the time of my visit, the game hasn't been announced yet, and when Dankberg smiles, I'm pretty sure he sees me as yet another pinball player providing unsolicited recommendations, like George Costanza on *Seinfeld* cornering George Wendt to suggest taking *Cheers* out of the bar.

As it turns out, Dankberg's smile meant something more like "Wait seven months." I'm still hoping for—no Iron Throne pun intended—royalties.

The tricky part of licensing, says Dankberg, is that the license holder won't necessarily give you carte blanche to go nuts with their theme. For example, if you bought the license to make and sell a *Frozen*-themed pinball machine, you could not depict Arendelle however you wanted. Disney would carefully choose and control the art, music, and sound bites that came with your license—lest you get overly creative and produce *Whoa Elsa! Big Juicy Snowballs*. Dankberg says the more your license grants you, the more immersive the game experience—*Game of Thrones*, for example, includes custom voice recordings made by Rory McCann, who plays Sandor "the Hound" Clegane. This means that at some point in his life, Rory McCann walked into a recording studio, script in hand, and said, "Ball one, locked."*

These days, Stern Pinball has found its rhythm. They produce three new games per year, with three versions of each, and they may even resurrect one or two "vault" games—a title from a previous year that was popular enough to produce again in a limited run. They make "studio" games, like *Whoa Nellie!*, designed by someone else but manufactured by Stern's powerhouse. And they've even begun making custom accessories, like a fist-shaped plunger knob for *WWE Wrestlemania* or a light-up KISS sign to mount on top of the *KISS* backbox.

When you're choosing only three themes a year, you have to be careful not to allow even one dud into the mix. A new blockbuster fantasy movie might sound like the ideal vehicle for a new pinball table, but Dankberg has to assess staying power as much as current popularity. As Dankberg told pop culture website *Inverse*, Gary Stern's standard cautionary tale is that he's the guy who licensed *Last Action Hero* (1993).

Roger Sharpe, who knows a lot about licensing, told the *Pavlov Pinball* blog that it's not always a strictly financial arrangement between pinball manufacturers and the companies whose licenses they seek. "Pinball is something of a speck on these companies' balance sheets," he said, so their decision to license a pinball machine is partially motivated by the uniqueness of the proposal. "[The TV show] *The Walking Dead* doesn't need to have a pinball machine," he continued, "but having a pinball machine as part of that is kind of neat." Yes,

---

* One of the holy grails of pinball licensing is *Harry Potter*, though rumors swirl (and Roger Sharpe has confirmed) that author J. K. Rowling is uninterested in a *Harry Potter* machine, even though it would give new meaning to the term "pinball wizard."

the multimillion-dollar pinball industry often relies on convincing executives that pinball machines are kind of neat.

Licensing may sound like some boring legal detail, but in pinball, it's everything. After all, pinball manufacturers can't just make any machine they want to—otherwise I'd be playing *Wallace and Gromit*, *Spinal Tap*, or *Pee-Wee's Big Adventure* right now. During interviews, I've heard people agitate for games based on the television shows *Big Bang Theory* and *Rick and Morty*. At my request, Dankberg lists some of the suggestions he's fielded: *Gwar*, *Reservoir Dogs*, and *Evil Dead*. In the documentary *Special When Lit*, Ron Shuster, a former youth pastor with a collection of over 150 games, envisions a Passion (as in, of the Christ) themed pinball machine. That would go nicely with the *Pope* video game.

Seven months pass (and the *Game of Thrones* game debuts) before I return to visit Stern's new, triple-sized factory, and this time I'm with a tour group of pinball enthusiasts, arriving on a yellow school bus. "It doesn't look that big," says the man in the seat behind me. There's no pleasing some people.

Since this is a public event, with hundreds in attendance, Gary Stern has upped the fun factor, hiring an oldies deejay in a Hawaiian shirt and displaying life-sized cardboard cutouts of himself and *Whoa Nellie*'s fictitious, fruitfully endowed trollop Melony to pose for selfies.

The new factory has an automatic zip-tie machine for bundling cables and a four-post press, an ancient gray behemoth that presses holes in playfields, originally purchased by Gary and Sam Stern together. Three men with calipers compare the exact measurements of steel parts to their drawings, picking a bracket from a bucket, measuring it, and grabbing the next bracket. A woman applies a heat gun to a plastic ramp next to balloons and flowers. (For me, visiting the Stern Pinball factory is like a birthday. For this woman, it's actually her birthday, hence the balloons and flowers.)

The factory has no fewer than twenty-two microwave ovens, since nearly three hundred workers need to eat their lunch simultaneously, literally at the blow of a whistle, to avoid slowing the production line.

Even the company's move itself barely slowed production. "We moved out of the old facility on a Friday," says designer George Gomez, who found a home at Stern Pinball after his downsizing from WMS, "and the following Monday we were building games here."

Today's games include *James* and *Politico*, if the labels on the metal guides through which workers drill holes into wooden play-fields can be believed. They can't be believed, though, because *James* and *Politico* are deliberate pseudonyms for *Metallica* and *Game of Thrones*. That's how closely guarded pinball machine themes are— just as the film *Return of the Jedi* was called *Blue Harvest* during production in order to keep *Star Wars* fans in suspense, new pinball machines have deliberately misleading working titles. (At this point, both games had already been revealed, but the metal guides had been labeled previously.)

At the end of the line, next to the loading dock, games sit upright in cardboard crates, protected by custom-shaped foam to keep them pristine until delivery. The crates are grouped by destinations stamped on the outside; I notice a handful of *Game of Thrones* games destined for New Zealand. (Take that, Frodo.)

Perhaps the coolest, and most secret, room is the model shop, a massive cage where workers tinker with prototypes of games in development. According to the photo frame on a desk in the cage, many of the models are made by the world's greatest grandpa.

But the most revered person in the room today, maybe even more so than Gary Stern (or Melony), is *Game of Thrones* designer Steve Ritchie. In a short documentary released by Stern, Ritchie says he spent more time working on *Game of Thrones* than on any other machine in his career.* That's saying quite a bit, considering Ritchie has designed more than two dozen pinball machines, first for Atari, then Williams, and now Stern. He's known as the King of Flow, meaning that it just kind of feels nice to flip a pinball up the ramps and loops on his machines. Ball goes up a ramp, ball swings over across the game, ball goes smoothly down to your flipper. It's a feeling that can be disrupted by a design-element shift of one-sixteenth of an inch, and Ritchie spends months futzing with a yardstick and repositioning ramps to optimize the movement aspects of his games.

"Steve's a pinball designer," says Dankberg. "That's what he is. That's why he wears the same clothes every day. The man is a genius." The clothes in question are a semi–Steve Jobs–esque black shirt and jeans, plus two hearing aids.†

A designer's dominion is the "whitewood," a blank, artless playfield that frankly doesn't look like much fun to play with. Designers experiment endlessly, balancing skill and luck, feeling for the first time the shots for which thousands of players will later develop muscle memory. It's a skill specific to a handful of people, but there may be a genetic component—Steve Ritchie's brother Mark also became a celebrated pinball designer, working on games for Williams and Capcom.

Perhaps the complexities of game design are best summed up by Alvin Gottlieb in Roger Sharpe's *Pinball!*: "How do you design a game? That's like asking a Jewish mother how to make chicken soup. You put in a little of this and a little of that until it's ready."

---

* Maybe it took so long because he read the books. According to Dankberg, when Ritchie was first approached about a *Game of Thrones* machine, he knew nothing about the fantasy novels or the television series—so he read all the books and watched every episode available. I've done the same, and the task occupied a full year.

† Because of the lead time required to design a pinball machine, Dankberg and Ritchie were two of the first civilians to hear the script of the 2013 film *Star Trek Into Darkness*. According to Dankberg, CBS couldn't send him the script for the sake of secrecy, but they arranged to read it to him, Ritchie, and designer Greg Freres, just one time, over the phone. This plan faltered when Ritchie couldn't hear the phone, and Dankberg spent over an hour hurriedly hand-transcribing the entire script on a legal pad for Ritchie to read.

In 2008, during Stern's darkest time, the *New York Times* had called the factory "the last of its kind in the world." It was a depressing, though accurate, way to frame Stern and indeed the whole of pinball in 2008—not only had all competitors gone out of business, but there was a general consensus that the end of this form of recreation was at last imminent.

At that point, not knowing that pinball would one day thrive again, who in their right mind would start a *new* pinball company?

9

Everything Nobody Needs

IT'S BEEN A LONG DAY for "Jersey Jack" Guarnieri. "I was here at four in the morning getting stuff set up," he tells me, slouching on a black leather couch in the late afternoon, "and I'm sure I'll be here at midnight putting shit away."

Midnight relocation of shit is not the most glamorous job for a CEO. But Jersey Jack, the namesake and public face of Jersey Jack Pinball, in his T-shirt, shorts, and sneakers—essential activewear for putting shit away—isn't just any CEO. Through toil, innovation, intuition, and a little braggadocio, he's done what no one else managed to do for an entire decade and a half after the Day Pinball Died: compete with Stern.

"I know if Gary Stern rings the doorbell, I'm going to welcome him with a hug and a kiss," says Guarnieri, though he's certain Stern wouldn't greet him so warmly. We may never know if that hug and kiss will take place (outside the context of some pretty obscure and unlikely fan fiction that I don't want to read), but we do know that, since 1999, Jersey Jack Pinball is the first company besides Stern to mass-produce and sell pinball machines.

They're not the first to try. In November 2005, a Melbourne-based company called The Pinball Factory announced its plans to make a Crocodile Hunter–themed game, but their timing couldn't have been worse: the Crocodile Hunter himself, Steve Irwin, was tragically killed by a stingray just ten months later. The Pinball Factory abandoned its project, and today it's nothing more than a footnote in pinball history and a cautionary tale about the best-laid plans of koalas and men.

Jersey Jack grew up repairing CB radios and televisions, then decided to take half a year off from high school to work as a pinball mechanic at colleges in and around New York. "I got to go to every college," he jokes. "I just didn't graduate with a degree from any of them."

In 1978, Guarnieri began his transition from repairman to operator. Thanks to the arcade craze, a few years later, Guarnieri was operating games—and keeping a portion of their revenue—all over the New York metropolitan area. That's the financial model: if you drop fifty cents into a pinball machine in a bar, it's likely that part of the money is going to the bar owner, part to an operator who owns games at several locations.

Guarnieri opened a series of amusement centers, one of which he sold in 1999 to someone who closed it in 2001. "It's funny," he reflects. "People buy a business that's . . . making money, and they get involved and change everything about it that was successful because they have their own idea about what it's going to be. People like that should start their own business. They shouldn't buy an existing business." Jersey Jack has a lot of ideas about what other people should do, and there's nothing wrong with that, except for the fact that other people don't always like to be told what to do. (I point out that 1999 may simply have been an inadvisable year to buy an arcade, and he reminds me that he started Jersey Jack Pinball in 2011. "That wasn't a good year, people would say, to start anything.")

Jersey Jack also started another company in 1999, PinballSales.com, later trademarking the company's motto, "We sell everything nobody needs." As the millennium closed out, Guarnieri started importing games from Europe to resell, and business picked up. Ford Motor Company listed a new Stern pinball machine called *Sharkey's Shootout* (2000) in its incentive catalog for salespeople, then approached Jersey Jack to fill the orders.

At the time, Guarnieri was not a licensed distributor for Stern Pinball, just a broker between private buyers and sellers, so on a whim he attended a trade show in Las Vegas to meet Gary Stern, a moment Guarnieri remembers as akin to "an audience with the pope." Stern wasn't interested in making Guarnieri a distributor—he already had two in New Jersey—so Guarnieri waited until Stern was more desperate for cash. "His words of wisdom to me were, 'Nobody wants to buy a pinball machine for their home, and you'll be out of business in six months, and this Internet crap will never amount to anything,'" Guarnieri recalls. "That was my congratulations and welcome to become a Stern distributor."

To boost sales, Jersey Jack sold *Austin Powers* games by making his own "gold" edition. He sent the metal legs to be colored gold, arranged for Gary Stern to sign the backglass, and numbered them one through ten. It's the classic business ploy of faux scarcity, the limited edition. I fall for it all the time in the candy aisle. "Dark chocolate Reese's cups are limited edition? If I don't buy them now, I'll regret it forever!" But some of Stern's other distributors became annoyed at the breach of protocol. Why did Guarnieri get to invent a gold edition anything?

Still, the ploy sold games, as did Guarnieri's attentive service. "When there was a problem with the game, we went out and fixed it for nothing for a while," he says. "You know, you just gave us two or three grand for something, and I'm not going to charge you a hundred bucks to fix a flipper. I'd rather have the goodwill in the bank."

Guarnieri tells me how, before a 2001 trade show, he decided to apply his limited edition magic to *Monopoly*, the pinball machine he said would "make or break Stern." Only instead of ten gold editions, Guarnieri outdid himself, mounting each of the forty title deed cards from a Monopoly board game on a platinum plaque, chroming most of the hardware, and soliciting signatures from Gary Stern, designer Pat Lawlor, artist John Youssi, and Alan Hassenfeld, the CEO of Hasbro, the company that sells the Monopoly board game. He auctioned off the Boardwalk edition and gave the proceeds to a charity called Boundless Playgrounds, which builds accessible play structures for children with disabilities.

Guarnieri's proactive sales approach and an article in *RePlay Magazine* earned him notoriety, both good and bad. Other distributors, he says, fought to keep up with him and copy his approach of selling to the home market. "It was a crazy kind of time because we could sell anything we could get," he says. "The economy was pretty good—people were taking home equity loans and stuff like that. They're buying hot tubs and home theaters and man caves and all that stuff, and that's where the money was going."

But some distributors, Guarnieri says, used their relationship with Stern to leverage other sales—when a customer would call asking about the latest Stern machine, the distributor would bad-mouth new Stern games and instead recommend "this used pinball machine I have in the back." Once Stern realized this was taking place, and that Guarnieri had remained loyal, even more buyers were directed to him. "I got every lead from the company. For years. And what did I do with them?" he asks himself. "I sold Stern pinball machines," he answers himself.

He recalls a day in 2006 when he sold one hundred *Pirates of the Caribbean* games over a nine-hour period while stuck in a lounge at O'Hare Airport. Jersey Jack became the biggest distributor of Stern games in the world. "In three weeks, I would do a million dollars' worth of business," he says. "So from Black Friday through Christmas Eve, I would be in my office from three in the morning until ten or eleven at night, running credit cards. Some days I ran more than $100,000 in credit cards. In a day. Selling pinball machines."

Guarnieri has very little love for his fellow distributors, characterizing them as charlatans who sold broken machines they wouldn't service. "Those guys put games out on the front lawn of their buildings, Christmas Eve, hoping to get some jerk [to] come by and buy some old piece of junk," he says. "And then if you called them for service a month later, they told you, 'Nah, we don't do that anymore.'"

Guarnieri was different. "People had problems with the playfield?" he asks. "People had problems with the cabinet? People had problems with something Stern didn't do? I gave 'em a free playfield. I gave 'em a free cabinet. I went out and did their service. Or I got somebody in Stumble Shit, Wyoming, to go do their service, and I paid for it. *That's* how I started Jersey Jack Pinball."

He names two competing distributors. "I crushed all those fucking guys," he says, shrugging matter-of-factly. "Every one of them. Because why? Because I took care of the customer. That's why."

But even Jersey Jack couldn't coast through the economic decline of 2008 and a vitriolic phone call with Gary Stern in which Guarnieri alleges that Stern yelled at him "like I was a two-year-old," claiming Guarnieri was delinquent on certain payments. Jack thinks the pressure of the collapsing economy made Gary act the way he did, but it's a conversation he's never forgotten. I don't know Jersey Jack very well, but I can tell from one day at his factory that he's someone who wants to be liked and admired. That's not a flaw—I think most of us feel that way—but it does imply a certain sensitivity to, say, getting unfairly berated by the Godfather of Pinball.*

---

* That moniker came from Stern Pinball's own press release for *CSI*. Interestingly, if you Google "Godfather of Pinball," you'll find the same honorific bestowed upon Roger Sharpe, Pat Lawlor, Pinball Hall of Fame owner Tim Arnold, Wisconsin-based tournament organizer Steve Tulley, someone named Kim who runs a pinball league in rural Ontario, game developer Steve Kordek, and a man called Berkeley Mac whose basement pinball parties partially inspired the creation of the Pacific Pinball Museum. I guess everyone wants to call someone the Godfather of Pinball.

It's around this time that I ask Guarnieri how much of our conversation he's comfortable with me putting in writing. "I'm a big boy," he assures me. "I know if I don't want to say anything, I don't say it, but I can't tell you anything that's not true. What I tell you is true, and it's factual. I have e-mails to back it up. There's a lot of shit I can't tell you, but the day you really want to write a book that's pretty fucked up, I'll tell you a lot of stuff that nobody could sue me over, or anybody else over, because it's all true." I promise him that when I want to write a book that's pretty fucked up, I'll call him first.

Guarnieri realized that relying on Stern could break his company as easily as it had fueled his success. "It was like somebody had poured a bucket of water over me and told me the party was over," he says. A week after his phone call with Stern, at a trade show in Las Vegas, a chance encounter led to him accepting a position as the CEO of a company called Elaut.

"They make cranes," Guarnieri says, "that I never operated." Based on this statement, I immediately misunderstand that Elaut is a company manufacturing construction machinery. As it turns out, Elaut makes the other type of cranes, the kind that charge a dollar in exchange for watching a weakly powered claw not pick up a plush SpongeBob. Guarnieri soon merged Elaut with PinballSales.com to form Elaut USA; in a year, he says, he had erased the company's $3 million debt. In another year, Elaut USA was turning a $1 million profit.

One of Guarnieri's accomplishments at Elaut USA in 2009 was inventing a popular *Wizard of Oz* "pusher," one of those machines full of tokens cantilevered over an edge that seem to defy gravity, enticing players with a payoff that's *so close* to falling. *The Wizard of Oz* pusher's rewards, and possibly a reason for its popularity, are collectible tokens and plastic cards that can later be exchanged for prizes.

"I created that game," says Guarnieri, "and it's probably one of the greatest redemption games ever made." He shows me a pack of cards, which he keeps in his desk drawer, from the machine. More importantly, the license to use *The Wizard of Oz* characters in the pusher game included an unexpected but important bonus: the license to someday produce a *Wizard of Oz*-themed pinball machine.

"In 2010, honestly, I was really bored—because as challenging as some things were there, they were too easy for me to solve," Jack says. "My biggest challenge was what I was going to eat for lunch that day." Every now and then someone would suggest that he start his own pinball company—not one reselling games but one that would invent and manufacture brand-new games from scratch, an idea he rejected immediately.

Guarnieri considers 2009–2010 a bad time for pinball. Stern still monopolized the manufacturing space, and the games they turned out were, in Guarnieri's opinion, uninspired. The economic crisis persisted, but he blames the games themselves for his substantial financial downturn that year. Previously, he had sold an average of about 1,500 Stern pinball machines per year. "In 2010," he says, "I think I sold forty-seven."

That was the last straw for Jersey Jack, who decided he would no longer rely on Stern to produce games his customers would buy. It was time to make the damn games himself.

Guarnieri's customer base was clamoring for a new game, a game more interesting than Stern's *Big Buck Hunter Pro* (2010), a pinball machine based on an arcade game. "They were like people in the desert that didn't see water," he says, "and they would drink out of any hole, anywhere, if there was a promise that water would be in that hole." Guarnieri declared to the world that he was going to personally end Stern's decade-long monopoly of the pinball industry, decided on the *Wizard of Oz* theme, and started digging his hole.

The theme was, in an important way, inspired by the 2006 Stern game *Pirates of the Caribbean*, a popular machine with a sinking boat, a treasure chest, and a centrifuge that spun balls around. "It was the only game that girls wanted their husbands to buy," explains Guarnieri. "Johnny Depp is on it: It's a Disney theme. It's not Iron Man, Batman, This Man, That Man . . ." The success of *Pirates* inspired Jack—Jersey Jack, not Captain Jack Sparrow—to create a game with a universally appealing theme. "If I make something, and women don't like it? Children don't like it? I'm eliminating 70 percent of the earth's population."

In that regard, *The Wizard of Oz* is a brilliant choice. "I liked it," he says, "because it was timeless, it was ageless, it wasn't men, it wasn't women, it wasn't boy, it wasn't girl, it wasn't young, it wasn't old—it was everything." It was a theme with universal appeal, and it became, he describes, "the pole that I want to put in the middle of my tent to start the company around."*

According to Guarnieri, Elaut USA could not have been less thrilled. They issued a press release officially wishing him luck but making it abundantly clear that Elaut USA was not in the pinball business. "Imagine you're partners with somebody in a business," he says, "and you read that in a press release. Nice."

The reaction from Gary Stern made Elaut look enthusiastic by comparison. "I told him what I'm doing," Guarnieri says. "He told me if I do that, we're gonna both be out of business."

Guarnieri's manufacturing difficulties began immediately. "Everything was a challenge," he recalls. "I mean, there was nothing that was easy." He would visit plastic vendors, for example, who would greet him with "Oh, you're the guy who's gonna go out of business next."

---

* In 2010, the Library of Congress named *The Wizard of Oz* the most watched movie of all time. However, despite this accolade, and perhaps as a lesson that no theme excites everyone, there are plenty of pinball-hungry locations where the film simply isn't a cultural cornerstone. Polish Pinball Association president Łukasz Dziatkiewicz wrote in *Pinball News* that, though he was excited about Jersey Jack's entrance into the pinball manufacturing scene, *The Wizard of Oz* "was never part of our culture" and may not be as beloved in Poland and Western Europe as it is in the United States. Poland, therefore, might even be a more difficult market for a *Wizard of Oz*–themed pinball machine than Stumble Shit, Wyoming.

Somehow, despite Guarnieri launching a company that had never manufactured a pinball machine in an era when it looked like one's potential customer base could be measured in dozens rather than millions, Jersey Jack Pinball managed to secure more than a thousand preorders, with pinball enthusiasts taking a leap of faith that their $6,500 prepayments would result in a beautiful pinball machine and not a sheepish, empty-handed Guarnieri saying, "Uh, so here's what happened."

For a while, deliveries seemed imminent. "We expect games to be rolling out of the building in great numbers by late spring or early summer," Guarnieri told the *Chicago Reader* in early 2012. When that didn't happen, he assured a reporter for *Slate* he'd begin shipping in January 2013. Then mid-March. On the Pinside forum, customers began sharing stories of their own patience wearing thin. Much later, Guarnieri would admit to *Pinball News* that "maybe we promised too much."

Delays are nothing new for a manufacturer's first attempt; everything is more complicated than it appears. However, Jersey Jack's delays came not only from start-up woes but also from Guarnieri's desire to make a pinball machine—and a pinball company—unlike any other. He wanted to reimagine what a pinball machine could be, and while certain tropes of the game were inescapable—pop bumpers, flippers, ramps—there were certainly areas that hadn't been updated in decades, despite advancing technology.

One of those changes is obvious. Recall the alphanumeric 1970s and '80s calculator-style score displays, which themselves evolved from mental math, followed by light-up scoring, followed by drum score reels. Then, in 1991, Data East manufactured a racecar-themed game called *Checkpoint* that used a dot matrix display in its backbox to communicate scores. This was a quantum leap in technology that allowed pinball machines to not only display scores but also tell stories, communicate complicated instructions, and show rudimentary graphics. Considering that most dot matrix displays are simple, 64 pixels high by 192 pixels wide, one could say it's remarkable how much the modern pinball industry has been able to do with them. That's the kind way of looking at it. Guarnieri would say it's shameful that, in 2015, we're still using the same displays that appeared on machines nearly twenty-five years ago.

The Wizard of Oz, unlike any pinball machine previously, boasts a twenty-seven-inch flat-screen monitor in its backbox. It's basically a giant iPad, and Jersey Jack uses it in every conceivable way—including showing licensed clips from the original film, gorgeous animations, and game maps that detail a player's progress through the various modes. Heck, you can even view the repair manual, a large PDF file, directly on the game's display—another first.

"Does anyone know why there's a twenty-seven-inch monitor in the backbox?" I once saw Guarnieri ask an audience. "'Cause it's the biggest monitor I could fit in the backbox."

The Wizard of Oz oozed innovation. It used special multicolored light-emitting diodes (LEDs); there were no more lightbulbs to replace. It contained an off-the-shelf computer with wireless capabilities. It had a seven-speaker sound system and even a jack on the front for players to plug in headphones. It packed everything onto an extralarge widebody playfield, the pinball industry's first wide-body since SuperPins were discontinued in 1994.

No detail was neglected. "It's artwork," Guarnieri says. "It really is. We thought about a lot of things with that game."

On April 29, 2013, Jersey Jack Pinball shipped its first truckload of *Wizard of Oz* games. In a YouTube video titled "SHIP SHIP HOO-RAY!," Guarnieri, wearing a black hoodie with his company's logo and attempting a cartwheel on wet grass, barely conceals his glee as the delivery truck pulls out of his parking lot.

The reaction to *The Wizard of Oz* was overwhelmingly positive. "I cannot see how it would be possible to make this game better," wrote a user named seanymph on the IPDB ratings board, and many players agreed. *Drop Target*, a now defunct five-dollar illustrated Kinko's-dependent pinball zine, calls *The Wizard of Oz* "a deep, engaging game that doesn't hold back on the bells and whistles, and in doing so, makes me really happy while playing it." So maybe, unlike Jack told *Pinball News*, he didn't promise too much—he just promised it too soon.

Two and a half years after "SHIP SHIP HOORAY!," at my visit to the company in the fall of 2015, Jack proudly announced that more than 2,500 customers had purchased *Wizard of Oz* machines, with another 1,500 already prepaying for *The Hobbit*, a machine that wouldn't begin production for another couple of months.*

•   •   •

One of Guarnieri's highest-profile poaches from Stern Pinball, his only competitor at the time, was Pat Lawlor, one of the aforementioned half-dozen godfathers of pinball and the designer of *Funhouse, The Addams Family,* and *The Twilight Zone,* whom Stern had lured after WMS closed. Lawlor had spent part of the 2000s designing games for Stern—*Monopoly* included—before publicly predicting in 2007, with disgust, that pinball would be dead in five years.

Perhaps that's why, when the offer came along, Lawlor jumped ship and joined Jersey Jack Pinball, a decision that Guarnieri says will probably render Lawlor a permanent defector from Stern. "Pat's last job in pinball will be working for my company," Guarnieri says, not without a note of pride, "when he's about a hundred years old and he makes his last game. He'll still be working for Jersey Jack if I have anything to do with it."

---

* Polish Pinball Association president Łukasz Dziatkiewicz is excited about *The Hobbit*. In the filmography of small, merry people, the citizens of Poland may not be fans of Munchkinland, but they love the Shire.

Watching Lawlor in action, moving metal ramps a fraction of an inch at a time around a bare wood playfield, obsessing over the tradeoff between gadgetry and flow, I think Guarnieri may be right. "Look at this guy," he says, showing me a photo on his iPhone of Pat with a new game's whitewood. "It's like he's six years old again. He's got his life back, this guy, he's got his fire."

For Lawlor, being six years old meant accompanying his father on his Schlitz delivery truck, playing coin-operated games at each stop while Dad sold beer. He codesigned his first game in 1987, a delightfully bizarre motocross-themed pinball machine called *Banzai Run*. Instead of a backglass with a glowing piece of art and score reels, *Banzai Run* had an entire second playfield, a vertical one, where the backbox normally is. Through a couple of neat tricks with magnets, the ball could move from the horizontal playfield to the vertical one and back again. It was the kind of machine a kid would dream up: "So, instead of this pretty backglass that doesn't do much, could we have, like, another pinball machine up there?"

"The reason I'm doing what I'm doing with Jack is that pinball fell into a rut," says Lawlor. "There's no other consumer product that you can describe . . . that stays the same over a period of . . . two decades. That's ridiculous. . . . Why are we still building these things as if it were 1992?"

Lawlor's passion to modernize pinball's dated feel—A dot matrix display? Really? When two-year-olds have iPads?—aligned perfectly with Jersey Jack's, though Lawlor's enthusiasm emerges in a much more measured way. Tall, lean, and soft-spoken, a Midwestern gentleman with a shy smile and clear blue eyes, Lawlor may have strong feelings about the industry's missteps, but you probably won't hear him openly disparage his rivals.

For a designer like Lawlor, who undoubtedly thought his glory days were behind him, the offer from Guarnieri must have arrived like a winning lottery ticket—the opportunity to return to the industry, leading his own team, once again making something grand and complicated of his own design. Finally, someone was making pinball disruptive—and he wanted Lawlor there, leading the charge. "When you hire Michelangelo," says Guarnieri, "you're not gonna tell him how to paint the Sistine Chapel."

"In the good old days, you'd have a game designer and a programmer and a standard game team of a mechanical engineer and an artist," recalls Lawlor. "Today I easily could have four programmers working full time on making that pinball machine come to life. Along with triple the artists, counting a video artist. Maybe two video artists. Animators." And unlike Stern's recent games—indeed, unlike Jersey Jack's first two games—no licensing is involved. Lawlor won't be beholden to the graphics or sound clips of a particular movie or television show; he can make whatever he wants, period. (At the time of my visit, everything about Lawlor's unlicensed game was a hugely hyped mystery. In late 2016, Jersey Jack Pinball revealed that the mystery game would be *Dialed In!*, a SimCity-ish cavalcade of technology that includes the ability to control the flippers from your own smartphone via Bluetooth and a "Selfie Mode," which takes and displays photos of the player during gameplay.)

An unlicensed game is a risky move. The '90s saw plenty of unlicensed games, like *Medieval Madness*, with its medieval theme, or the garbage-themed *Junk Yard* (1996). The theme of a game can dictate its popularity, regardless of whether it's a good game. Collectors often preorder pinball machines upon hearing what the theme will be—their favorite film, their favorite band. There are undoubtedly customers who immediately bought *Disney TRON Legacy* (2011) or *AC/DC* (2012) machines simply because they're fans of *TRON* or *AC/DC*.* In order to succeed in this day and age, a game with an original, unlicensed theme must be a *really, really good game.*

---

* Maybe not *TRON*.

And wouldn't you know it: some of the best games with original themes came from the brain of Pat Lawlor.

It's another way the industry has evolved. The first pinball machine licensed from a movie was *Wizard!* (1975), based on the film version of *Tommy*, and the next twenty-five years produced a blend of licensed and unlicensed games. That all stopped when Stern became the only pinball manufacturer on earth. The fact that there have been no unlicensed games this millennium—until *Dialed In!*—may be a symptom of pinball's loss of complacency. Why take a chance? Just make *Avatar* or *Wheel of Fortune* (2007) and guarantee yourself a little success.

An original game gives Lawlor a ton of freedom as a designer, since he's not stuck using artwork that had been purchased from Universal Studios or Disney. When you license a theme, you're buying a set art package, and if you want to redo any of that art—jazz things up, maybe change a font—you need to go back and seek approval, which may not be granted. For example, whenever Kili the Dwarf appears on *The Hobbit*, he's labeled with stylized text reading "Kili the Dwarf." Early critics of the *Hobbit* prototype artwork, which Jersey Jack posted to various pinball forums to seek feedback, pointed out that it's unnecessary to write "the Dwarf" with his name every time. But "Kili the Dwarf" is the piece of art that was licensed, and you legally *can't* just take out "the Dwarf."

The downside of designing an unlicensed game is that you start with nothing. "I [have] no video assets," says Lawlor. "Everything has to be built from scratch. And so I'm building a movie. I'm building animations. I'm building a pinball playfield. I'm building a world that I've envisioned that I have to make you understand as quickly as possible. So I've got a game team that's three times larger than I did twenty years ago, and I've become a movie director. The business has transformed radically."

Lawlor may be reenergized, but he knows the era of *Funhouse*, *The Addams Family*, and *The Twilight Zone*, his three games that each sold more than ten thousand units, isn't coming back tomorrow. "Right now, if we built a game that was every bit as good as one of those—and I fully expect we're building that game—we're not going to sell ten thousand of them," he admits, pragmatically. Not only does the demand not match that of 1992, but neither Guarnieri— nor, for that matter, Stern—has the capacity to churn out so many. The pinball factories are smaller, and even more important, the parts manufacturers—those who make plastic ramps, coin acceptors, and all the thousands of ingredients in each pinball machine—have slowed down their production. (These days, the magic number ten thousand is more than a lofty sales figure. It also happens to be the price threshold—$10,000—for a new game that collectors worry manufacturers will creep above. Jack's bells and whistles may be fun, but collectors remember the days when you could buy four or five new machines for that price. Whether or not the pinball community embraces the theme and gameplay of *Dialed In!*, there seems to be universal grumbling over its price tag, which ranges from $8,000 for the Standard Edition up to a whopping $12,500 for the Collector's Edition, thus smashing through the once-feared price ceiling.)

Thankfully, Lawlor's doom-and-gloom prediction that pinball would be extinct by 2012 clearly has not come to pass. "There was something that nobody quotes that I said [after] that," points out Lawlor, "which was *if nothing changes.*" In Jersey Jack Pinball, Lawlor has found a company that embraces change and that wants to dazzle players with complex games that look like they're from the future rather than the past, led by a hardworking pit bull of a CEO who knows that the only path forward is unrelenting innovation.

• • •

And, despite fears to the contrary, Jersey Jack's success has not meant Stern's failure. In fact, according to Guarnieri, not only did his own company not put Stern out of business, it forced them to keep up and may have even helped sustain Stern Pinball during a difficult time. Guarnieri, of course, expresses this a bit more starkly: "Left to himself, if I didn't start a company, he would've been out of business. Without question." Whether Stern's continued growth is a result of increasing their efforts to compete with Jersey Jack, or Stern's own hard work, or simply a happy accident of a rising tide is a question that may never be settled to the satisfaction of either Gary or Jack.

In January 2016, Stern Pinball tacitly acknowledged the influence of Jersey Jack and his cohorts in an article for the gaming website Polygon. "For the longest time we were the only ones making pinball tables," said Stern's marketing director, Jody Dankberg. "But now there are some boutiques making pinballs and they're using full color displays, and that gives us a little nudge."

As if Jack's nascent company doesn't have enough challenges, in December 2014, Elaut USA filed a lawsuit against Jack Guarnieri for $1.6 million, alleging he diverted funds to himself and to Jersey Jack Pinball during his time as CEO. Guarnieri immediately denied the allegations and continues to do so, calling the suit "utterly without merit" in a statement to *RePlay Magazine.*

But it hasn't been all bad financial news. In 2015, Miami-based ThinkLAB Ventures invested millions of dollars in Jersey Jack Pinball. That anyone with millions of dollars would choose to prop up pinball was amazing in itself—especially since they supported the company that had thus far only manufactured one machine—but even more impressive is the force behind ThinkLAB itself, entrepreneurs Leonard Abess and his son, Brett. Guarnieri walks me to his laptop and plays a YouTube clip from President Obama's 2009 State of the Union speech.

"I think of Leonard Abess," Obama declares, "a bank president from Miami who reportedly cashed out of his company, took a $60 million bonus, and gave it out to all 399 people who worked for him—plus another 72 who used to work for him. He didn't tell anyone, but when the local newspaper found out, he simply said, 'I knew some of these people since I was seven years old. It didn't feel right getting the money myself.'"

Guarnieri appreciates both the money and the vote of confidence from Leonard and Brett Abess. "That's Brett's dad," says Guarnieri, beaming. "That's something you don't see that often."

. . .

What I do see at a public open house inside the Jersey Jack Pinball factory in Lakewood, New Jersey, is a production facility not unlike Stern's. There are workstations, conveyor belts, boxes on wooden pallets. Half of the factory is a sight familiar to anyone who shops in the final room of Ikea, a high-ceilinged maze of categorized components—manufacturing a pinball machine must be like assembling the Hjälmaren towel rack from hell. At a wiring station, a monitor lists more than one hundred switches to test on a *Wizard of Oz* in progress, including "Crystal Ball VUK" and "Witch Melted." A table has piles of toys labeled "Witch Hut" and "Oz Face."

With around fifty employees, Jersey Jack Pinball can only produce ten machines per day. I say "only" because ten sounds like an "only" number to me. But I have been assured, repeatedly, that there's nothing "only" about building a pinball machine in a day, let alone ten.

Now that Guarnieri is actually shipping the *Wizard of Oz* machines his customers bought, his attention has shifted to *The Hobbit*, his sophomore entry into the world of pinball machines. Jack had told *Slate* he expected to have *The Hobbit* done by 2014, a deadline he's already missed by at least a year. Six weeks, he tells me today, in August 2015. Six to eight weeks. (It's not until mid-December that the Jersey Jack Pinball Facebook page shows photos of *Hobbit* playfields and cabinets being assembled, and even those customers who've sent Guarnieri a check for the full price of $8,000 had to wait until 2016.)

This time Guarnieri has managed to redirect the disappointment, taking less of a "Give us a break! We're new!" attitude and more of a "Quality takes time" approach. At Jersey Jack's open house, it appears the public has gotten the message. I stand in a long line to play a *Hobbit* prototype, and my fellow visitors standing behind me—who just want to play a good new pinball game and have no stake in Jersey Jack's success or failure—conjecture that the delays are because Jack wants to ensure he "hits it out of the park."

As a business, that's exactly what you want: people categorizing your inability to meet production deadlines as a virtue. Can you imagine, for example, fast-food customers pleased that their burgers are taking an hour and a half because they're certain that the chef is spending that time making them extra awesome?

On this particular day, Guarnieri has set up a question-and-answer panel for his game designers and engineers. He greets the crowd with a cheerful "What the hell?" He says this, smiling, because we've overflowed the folding chairs in the tiny lecture room. "Let's go in my office," he suggests.

Most offices are more intimate than a lecture room, but Guarnieri's eight-hundred-square-foot office can easily fit the crowd of fifty people or so. It's like a dream man cave/boardroom. There's a dark wood table with swivel chairs but also neon signs for Budweiser and the Yankees, *Wizard of Oz* paraphernalia, a jelly bean dispenser, and even a full-size Atari *Pong* video game—with serial number 17, meaning it was the seventeenth *Pong* machine manufactured and therefore, as a collectable, not cheap.

As the open house attendees find seats, Guarnieri starts a loud game on the *Wizard of Oz* pinball machine next to his desk, seemingly to make the point that he has one in his office, plays for a few seconds, then turns it off. He's clearly delighted to have so many people validating his event, and he fills many silences with off-color jokes. He interrupts a discussion about how to interest the next generation in pinball to throw small plastic bottles of water to people across the room.

Animosity toward Stern appears to be an accepted part of Jersey Jack Pinball culture. When Guarnieri discovers he has a few T-shirts from a Texas pinball show, he tosses them to audience members, laughing, "Let's see Gary do that!" (Not to take sides, but I'm pretty sure Stern is also capable of throwing T-shirts.)

In a 2014 interview for *Pinball News*, Jack was asked which Stern game was his favorite. He shot back, "When Gary Stern tells you which Jersey Jack Pinball game he likes, let me know."

"I want him to succeed," Guarnieri assures the crowd in his office, though no one has asked. "I want him to have a thousand customers a week. I want to have two thousand customers a week."

Later, lead software developer Keith Johnson tells the room that "everything [Stern has] done is just take money out of the game," meaning that they've sacrificed quality for cost savings. "We're just trying to make games people like." Johnson, himself a highly ranked competitive pinball player, has an extra reason to take a crack at Stern: he was one of the employees the company laid off during the recession.

Guarnieri has a lot to say about Gary Stern, and it's a strange blend of vitriol, admiration, passive-aggressive disappointment, and reassurances that if Stern knocked on his door tomorrow, he would be greeted with warmth. For the record, I asked Stern about Guarnieri, and here is the absolute verbatim entirety of what he chose to say on the subject: "He used to be a customer of ours." (Jody Dankberg, Stern's energetic and marginally more pugnacious marketing director, doesn't mind throwing a few numbers around, reminding *Inverse* in 2016, "They have produced one-and-a-half games in 6 years. We have done 22.")

Brett, the ThinkLAB Ventures coinvestor whose dad gave away his $60 million bonus, has traveled from Florida for the event. "We don't have an exit strategy," he says about his investment in Jersey Jack. "We just hope to make pinball machines forever." Massive applause; this audience likes that. Almost as much as they like when, shortly thereafter, someone's cell phone randomly makes a dying Pac-Man sound.

Guarnieri has entered full Jersey Jack mode. He's friendly. He's bombastic. He's jovial. He starts a lot of sentences with "Guess what." He needs to be the loudest person in the room. He invites three employees to do a Q&A, then answers most questions himself. He points out when someone's wife falls asleep. He calls out "Hello?" when someone's phone rings in the audience—every time. Jersey Jack has almost Trump-level self-assurance, and the more he answers his own questions, defends his strategy, and swears like a New Jerseyan, the more difficult it can be to tell exactly where his confidence ends and bombast begins. One could easily dismiss it as bluster—if it weren't for the fact that he has lived up to his promises and irrevocably disrupted the pinball industry.

Johnson, along with electrical engineers Butch Peel and Eric Meunier (who has a master's degree in medical robotics) reveal a reason *The Hobbit* has not yet entered production: When they began their licensing deal, *The Hobbit* was supposed to appear as two separate films. Then MGM decided to split it into three films, not two, and some of the best artwork—which Jersey Jack's designers wanted to put on the playfield—now could not be used until the third film debuted.

Every cubic inch of Guarnieri's games is a hard-won victory. Pinball, Lawlor says, is at a junction today, a junction at which it's sat for fifteen years. He and Guarnieri, along with a dedicated and talented team, are trying to push it as far as possible down the Yellow Brick Road.

"There's enough negativity in the world. We're trying to make a product that's fun," insists Guarnieri. "Who the hell wants to be negative? Not me! It's pinball!"

A few hours later, while I'm touring the Silverball Museum, thirty minutes north in Asbury Park, I happen to see Jack enter with his entire crew, still wearing their light blue Jersey Jack Pinball T-shirts from the open house.

That's right: this group of pinball manufacturers that spends every day building pinball machines, the folks who came to work at 4:00 AM that day and will be, as Guarnieri says, "putting shit away" at midnight, have taken a break to play pinball.

10

Backglass to the Future

"**A**RE YOU HERE FOR A PINBALL CONVENTION?**" asks the man renting me a car at Chicago Midway Airport, explaining that he just rented another car to someone with the same destination.

I confirm that I am, indeed, a thousand miles from home for four days to immerse myself in everything to do with the present and future of pinball. There will be lectures, a vendor hall filled with new and rare machines, and manufacturers even smaller and newer than Jersey Jack.

"I love pinball!" declares the agent with an enthusiasm that I allow to distract him while I quietly decline the optional collision insurance. "I wish there was someplace to play it!"

It's exactly like Tim Arnold, owner of the Pinball Hall of Fame, told the *New York Times* in 2008: "The thing that's killing pinball is not that people don't like it. It's that there's nowhere to play it." Or, to be depressingly precise, it's that no one *knows* where to play it.

Here's this Hertz employee, living in Chicago, a place Gary Stern calls "the capital of pinball machines," the city with one of the highest concentrations of on-location games—at the time of my visit,

PinballMap.com listed 458 publicly playable machines in 184 places—and though he'd love to play a game, he doesn't know where to go. And that, in a nutshell, is pinball's exposure problem.

Gary Stern once told me a story about his German colleagues from a company called Pinball Universe visiting a Chicago restaurant, where a waitress asked about pinball machines, "Oh, they still make those things?" The restaurant was down the street from the Stern Pinball factory.

In a way, the best thing that could happen to pinball is happening. It's becoming a haven for start-ups, innovators who aren't trying to conquer the market with thirty thousand games a year but who are trying to build at least a few hundred of their own new machines. If the manufacturing tier below Stern is Jersey Jack, who at least has a few dozen full-time employees, then the tier below Jack is the grassroots pinball manufacturing movement, a boutique craft for makers, the newly empowered generation of do-it-yourselfers that looks at a pinball machine and asks, "How hard could it be?"

"How hard could it be?" also happens to be Pat Lawlor's joke about the flippant attitude (we're almost done with the pinball puns, I promise) that has led far more of these start-ups—nearly twenty of them at the moment—to failure than to success.

I'm on my way up Interstate 294 toward the thirty-first annual Pinball Expo. I'm about to meet all the people in various stages of finding out exactly how hard it can be.

∗ ∗ ∗

Expo is an annual gathering of all things pinball: New games make their debut. Trading cards of pinball players and designers—yes, actual trading cards—are distributed and bartered. Stern and Jersey Jack host simultaneous events, probably on purpose. Designer Steve Ritchie autographs flyers, and Roger Sharpe poses for photos. There's a free-play game hall, a tournament, and an auction.

In the vendor hall, entrepreneurs sell everything from pinball memorabilia and replacement parts to custom pinball-themed lamps. The most prevalent vendors are those offering custom mods and art— there are graphics printing companies whose passion is finding bare spots on pinball machines to decorate. The metal lock bar on the front? The blades running down the sides? Hell, the legs? All prime real estate for decals.

I meet Pete Talbot and Ben Matchstick, for example, from the Cardboard Teck Instantute, selling the PinBox 3000 ArtCade Pinball System (all misspellings presumably intentional, or perhaps I should say instantentional). It's a pinball machine about the size of a desktop printer made completely from laser-cut, recycled cardboard. The product, which looks exactly like the Kickstarter project it is, is meant to provide a dream-it-and-build-it blank slate for kids to make their own minipinball machines.

The most interesting aspect of Expo may be the seminars. In one, Dr. Jim Schelberg, publisher and editor of *PinGame Journal*, screens the "sizzle reel" from *Pinballers*, a recent reality television pilot about the Texas pinball scene that unfortunately never progressed to production.[*]

In another, Art Kreisel of Pinball Perfection describes Sip-and-Puff technology that renders pinball machines operable by blowing into, or sucking out of, a straw. This would allow quadriplegics—for whom Sip-and-Puff might be their best means of physically interacting with the world—to enjoy playing the same games as everyone else. Kreisel recalls a company called Arcade Access that modified dozens of games for Sip-and-Puff tournaments in Pittsburgh in the '80s: "Not

---

[*] Reality shows about pinball are distressingly similar to reality shows about anything else. *Pinballers*, which would have been part *American Pickers* and part *Here Comes Honey Boo-Boo*, included "Shelley and Rusty the Socialites," a wealthy couple who loved to serve Jell-O shots at lavish pinball parties in their home arcade; "Jared the Promoter," who declared, "Bring an extra pair of underwear, because I'm about to show you something!"; and motorcycle-riding "Marc the Hunter," who burped a lot.

only could a kid realize a dream of playing a pinball machine, but they could play it against Franco Harris."

The 1946 *Three Stooges* episode "Three Little Pirates" is screened in the seminar room, to much delight. Set in some kind of Arabian-themed bar, the Stooges grapple with a pinball machine that bonks the player on the head with a giant mallet when one triggers "Ye Olde Tilt."*

More than just a pinball love-fest, however, Expo is—and has been for more than thirty years—the annual affair at which pinball manufacturers show off their latest creations. The year I visit, 2015, Stern launches *Game of Thrones*, and Jersey Jack, three months after my visit to his factory, brings a prototype *Hobbit*. I expected them to be the only two true manufacturers, since they're the only two companies actually building, selling, and delivering their games so far, right? There is, however, one more.

In the exclusive club of pinball manufacturers, it's easy to think of Jersey Jack and Stern as David and Goliath. But it's not just David and Goliath—it's David and Goliath and Charlie.

* * *

Charlie Emery, an impossibly agreeable father of two from Benson, Wisconsin (population 973), wearing a brown jacket and a porkpie

---

* Lest you think pinball machine sightings in ordinary television shows and movies are rare, Josh "Pingeek" Kaplan has meticulously chronicled every single appearance of a game on the small or large screen. As of this writing, his web page lists and describes pinball sightings in 455 films and 339 television episodes, along with the identity of the game and any contextual clues one might need—if one really wants to, say, locate the episode of *Mr. Belvedere* that aired on November 29, 1985, in which a Bally *Fireball* (1971) distracts the eponymous butler from his duties. Or maybe the January 3, 2009, episode of *Dave Attell's Insomniac Tour* in which comedian Dane Cook, playing a *South Park* machine, recalls, "My dad used to say, 'Life is like pinball. Sometimes you tilt, sometimes you're special, and sometimes you have an extra ball like me.'" Helpfully, Pingeek's "Pinball on TV" page lists the following disclaimer at the top: "Whatever you do, DON'T rent the 1976 ABC After School Special, 'The Pinballs.' There is not a single pinball machine in this program."

hat, is tired. His homegrown company, Spooky Pinball, defied the odds to become the third pinball manufacturer in a field of three, and it certainly didn't happen overnight.

Emery's journey began as innocently as the others: he and his nine-year-old son, nicknamed "Bug," tinkered with a machine for fun, changing the art to give *Firepower* (1980) a Godzilla theme. While showing off their creation at an arcade show called Midwest Gaming Classic, Emery suddenly found himself the center of fascinated inquiries about the game—it turns out he had used a digital printing process different from the one used by the rest of the industry.

While there, he met Internet celebrity Ben Heckendorn, better known in the hacking community as Ben Heck, a man renowned in certain circles for painstakingly dissecting video game consoles, like the Xbox and PlayStation, and stuffing them into custom laptop cases. After years of electronic tinkering, Heck took on the challenge of building a pinball machine from scratch—"not professionally," says Emery, "but out of whatever he could find." The process of making a pinball machine, which Stern and Jersey Jack can produce in around thirty hours, took Ben Heck from 2005 to 2010.

The game's theme makes the amount of time invested in construction that much sillier. You ready? It was called *Bill Paxton Pinball*. Yup. The game was based on the films and television shows of actor Bill Paxton, including *True Lies*, *Weird Science*, and *Big Love*. (Bill's three wives from HBO's *Big Love* are the multiball locks.) In a move that greatly pleased the pinball community, Ben Heck then turned around and sold the machine just to get it out of his garage.

Their complementary strengths made Emery and Heck a good partnership—Heck could code, program, and laser-cut, and Emery could professionally print artwork on wood and plastic. What began as a hobby, with Emery and Heck making one-off games, gradually interfered with Emery's day job, an intrusion he grew to welcome.

Like Pat Lawlor, who fell in love with pinball while his father delivered beer, Emery's first exposure came as something for a child to occupy himself with while the adults did things related to alcohol—in Emery's parents' case, drinking it. "It was nothing for them to sit in a bar for a lot of hours," he says, and doling out quarters for barroom pinball was a 1970s babysitting option.

"I would never do that with my kids," Emery is quick to assure me, and I get a picture of a man who—in response to his own upbringing—decided to become the awesomest dad ever. The kind of dad who builds monster-themed pinball machines for fun in the garage with his kids.

Emery was in his early forties when his father passed away. "I kind of started thinking about, well, you're not here forever," he says. So in 2012, he quit his job of twenty-one years, took $35,000 in savings, and devoted every waking moment to producing, on a commercial scale, Heck's latest game.

That game was called *America's Most Haunted* (2014), a ghost-themed machine that also begat the company name, Spooky Pinball, and its tagline: "We put the 'boo' in 'bootique pinball'!"

Emery and Heck set a goal of making and selling 150 games of *America's Most Haunted*. "When we set the number 150, we had sold maybe 30 games," says Emery. "We thought 150 is *so* far away we'll never get there."

For a year and a half, preorders gradually increased until they had sold eighty or ninety games. Then, as their reputation as a legitimate manufacturer began to precede them, at the Texas Pinball Festival in 2014, they sold the rest in a single weekend.

Spooky's website proudly declares it "The Best Pinball Company in Benton, Wisconsin!" That's a joke structure Emery and Heck don't seem to tire of—Heck called *America's Most Haunted* "the finest pinball machine ever made about paranormal ghost hunting," adding another time that "Roger Sharpe has called it 'the finest game called *America's Most Haunted* I've ever seen.'"

Actually, at Expo, no one is interested in *America's Most Haunted*, which already finished its production run by auctioning off its 150th machine to benefit the Juvenile Diabetes Foundation. They all want to know what Spooky Pinball will do next.

As, I'm sure, with many of life's turning points, this is where Rob Zombie comes in.

For those unfamiliar with Rob Zombie, he's a founding member of the heavy metal band White Zombie, known for their multiplatinum album *La Sexorcisto: Devil Music, Vol. 1*. In recent years, as a filmmaker, he's come to represent all things scary and gory, and his 2003 film *House of 1000 Corpses*, with its on-screen mutilations of four hapless travelers in so very exactly the wrong place at the wrong time, still creeps me out to this day.

For fans of the horror genre, Rob Zombie is something of a god, or a devil—whichever makes more sense. Emery came up with the idea to put him on a pinball machine.

There are many strategies for a pinball manufacturer to acquire a license to something cool without going bankrupt, one of which is what Jody Dankberg at Stern called a "halo project." All you have to do, Dankberg said, is convince someone—in his case KISS, in Spooky's case Rob Zombie—that having a self-themed pinball machine would be *awesome*.

Once he had Rob Zombie's attention, Emery pitched a game whose plot centered around the backstage goings-on at a Rob Zombie concert: players would work their way up from being a roadie to being Rob's tour manager. Rob Zombie hated the idea, instead requesting what Emery remembers as "a straight-up, badass horror game."

That's exactly what it became, an explicit gore-fest called *Rob Zombie's Spookshow International* (2016) that included, for the sake of customers with kids, a slightly toned-down "family mode."

"It will ship in family mode," Emery assures the audience at Expo, "and *trust me*, that's for a reason." (When the game is finally released in 2016, part of the reason becomes immediately obvious upon starting a non–family mode game: the machine greets players by yelling, "Go to hell, motherfucker!")

Since they're still in development at the time of Expo, none of the game's graphics have yet been publicly described in detail, but Heck's offhand description to the audience of how he programs says a lot about the game's content: "Put boobs here, make this ball blood, put the limbs here."

"And the ball save is absolutely horrific," adds Emery with a smirk. "Wait till you see it." Rob Zombie's band has, apparently, and it was so gory they laughed for an hour.

"There are no exposed nipples," Heck announces, before adding, with his thumb and index finger spread an inch apart, "close!" Sitting between the two on stage, Emery's wife Kayte widens her eyes, compresses her lips, and nods good-naturedly. She handles sales, cohosts their podcast, and, according to Spooky's website, "makes great French toast on Sunday mornings when she makes Charlie take a day off every week." Immediately their roles become clear: he and Heck are the overgrown adolescent scoundrels, and Kayte is the long-suffering but permanently smiling wife who hasn't had enough coffee yet today to deal with these two.

Charlie says that Kayte "was the sane one that held her job and kept the insurance for the family." After about two years, though, Spooky Pinball grew too massive for him to handle alone, so bye-bye insurance. Kayte is also a pinball fan; she grew up following her older brothers to arcades. "When I first wanted to get a game," says Charlie, "she didn't argue at all. She just said, 'Oh, cool! That would be great to have one in the house.'"

I'm just saying, Marina.

Benton, Wisconsin, is no Chicago—the nearest large city is Dubuque, Iowa. But the warehouse is affordable, the town is supportive, and wherever Emery goes in Benton, people gleefully recognize him as "Charlie the Pinball Guy."

Spooky operates on a much smaller scale than Stern or even Jersey Jack. While the former has nearly three hundred employees eating their lunches nuked in the twenty-two microwaves, and the latter employs around fifty, Charlie Emery has three. That's not counting himself and Kayte, plus thirteen-year-old Bug and his sixteen-year-old sister. "If you're an Emery," he says, "you're going to be making pinball parts."

Perhaps that's the way a boutique (or boo-tique) pinball manufacturer can survive: cheap land, reasonable production goals in the hundreds rather than the thousands of machines, and child labor.

"We're not profiting a lot right now," admits Emery. So I guess there's that, too.

In a certain way, smaller also means less vulnerable. "I think we're sitting in kind of a unique position where we don't have the overhead that [Stern and Jersey Jack] do," Emery says, "and we would be able to survive a bad pinball economy, so to speak. Maybe a little better than they can. I don't know. Let's hope we never find out!"

Unlike some of the other start-ups, Jersey Jack included, Spooky didn't accept much cash up front from interested customers—just $1,000, with the rest of the game's $6,000 price payable upon delivery. That decision helped mitigate some of the risk on his customers' end and some of the pressure on Spooky's. "What's the worst that's gonna happen at this point? We're not sitting on piles of people's money," Emery says. "If I did that, I don't think I could live with myself. I couldn't sleep at night."

"Our rewards will come later," he adds. "I'm not worried about that. I don't need a lot of money to be happy; I never have. I'm a happy guy now. If you give me more money, I'm not gonna get any happier." Emery laughs. "Be able to relax a little more, be able to hire people to do some of what I have to do every day, but no. Money doesn't make me happy, and it's not what drives me."

After hearing the same sentiment from pretty much everyone involved in pinball, it's not even slightly hard for me to believe him.

• • •

The attendees at Pinball Expo are like sharks smelling blood, and the blood they smell is the possibility of new games. Pinball is on an upswing it hasn't seen in years, and those who love the hobby have waited a long time for manufacturers to enter, not leave, the marketplace. Rumors fly about who's producing what and when it will be ready—after Stern, Jersey Jack, and Spooky, everyone wants to see where the next pinball machine will come from.

The answer might be Wales.

In a way, Andrew Heighway snuck into the pinball industry. In 2014, rum maker Bacardí asked him to produce a couple hundred weird little cocktail table games that resembled vintage bagatelles to be placed in bars worldwide, thus conveying the classic, daring, hipster nature of their beverages. The result was *Cuba Libre*, and while it isn't pinball—the game looks more like two small, adjacent roulette wheels stuck together in a handsome wooden cabinet—it got Heighway thinking.

Heighway is a former racecar driver, and let's get this part out of the way: yes, his name is pronounced "highway," and yes, it's kind of neat that someone with this name drove Formula 1 racers for ten years—though it's possible, he admits, that his name nudged him toward his profession.

In the early '90s, before his racing career left the starting line, Heighway managed a British McDonald's, sneaking off to a wine bar after work to play arcade games. One day, at age eighteen, he had what he calls a "eureka moment" in which he *got* pinball. Usually when an eighteen-year-old has a eureka moment, it's the postado-lescent swagger of someone who believes their epiphany more world changing than it probably is, but a quarter century later, Heighway is making his a reality.

Heighway initially chanced into the pinball supply business when he moved to Limerick and tried to buy two games, only to discover that no one was selling pinball machines in the entire nation of Ire-land. (He ended up purchasing a *Funhouse* and a *Bram Stoker's Drac-ula* [1993] from a distributor in Poland.) Before he knew it, Heighway was buying and reselling machines all over the Isles, taking a ferry between Ireland and the United Kingdom every month, ultimately abandoning other business ventures and volunteering to rescue the UK Pinball Party, an annual British pinball festival in need of a host. Somehow pinball had taken hold of his brain.

"I remember that golden two, three years when pinballs were magical to me," he says, "and I loved everything about them." He remembers his visits to the seaside town of Blackpool, where over the years the once ubiquitous machines dwindled to almost none.[*]

Now gray-haired, with a kind face, a bit of a beer paunch, and a reasonable, businesslike demeanor, Heighway has become the manag-ing director and CEO of Heighway Pinball, which proudly bills itself as "the UK's first ever major pinball manufacturer."

Heighway Pinball has invested a lot in manufacturing pinball machines—something, as of my discussion with Andrew Heighway over French fries, or "chips," in the hotel restaurant, it has not yet accomplished. They recently moved to a forty-two-thousand-square-foot factory in the very Welsh-sounding town of Merthyr Tydfil, where they devised a work-around for the crucial inventory supply problem

---

[*] Today the Pinformer database—which monitors "Where to Play in the UK"—shows Blackpool as a fair example of pinball's on-location scarcity. The city of Blackpool is home to thirteen pinball machines, of which eleven are in someone's home, and only two, a *Spider-Man* at a pub and a *Fish Tales* at an arcade, are publicly playable.

that plagues Gary Stern and Jersey Jack: Heighway Pinball became its own parts supplier.

They bought the equipment to manufacture their own plastics, as well as to cut, sand, and lacquer their own playfields. They installed a $150,000 flatbed printer. They hired employees to work in a factory the size of Jersey Jack's that, Heighway confesses, "could do with a lick of paint, but that's not at the top of the list." Thus they began, slowly, to manufacture prototype pinball machines.

Heighway's first machine's premise left the pinball world a little underwhelmed. To a community thirsty for quirky, original themes, Heighway Pinball introduced *Full Throttle*, a motorcycle racing game that, according to the company's web page, allows the player to "face off against arch-rival Francisco Valentino and force him to eat his taunting words." Even *Full Throttle*'s tagline feels a little lackluster: "Be the Champion, Become a Legend!"

I confess to knowing very little about sports, but . . . who the hell is Francisco Valentino? Why a bike racing game? In the history of pinball, there hasn't really been a shortage of motorcycle- and motocross-themed machines, including Pat Lawlor's brilliant, half-vertical *Banzai Run*.

Heighway is hoping for killer sales in Japan, where four of the five major motorbike manufacturers are located. He explains to a packed room at Expo that the Japanese love the tiny ball bearings careening around in pachinko,* "but if we can convince them that larger balls are better, maybe *Full Throttle* is the way to do that."

---

* Have you ever seen pachinko? It's full-on bonkers. Imagine the most confusing, brightly colored, cartoonish vertical pinball machine you can picture, then place hundreds of them in long rows like slot machines or Laundromat dryers on acid. Players purchase a tub of pea-sized silver balls, which they feed into a machine to watch them get instantly flung into trapdoors and weirdness, some of which results in the dispensing of yet more pea-sized balls. The modern Japanese pachinko parlor is not dissimilar in purpose from the American gaming halls of the 1930s; cash payouts are forbidden, but if you can make the machine give you more balls than you paid for, you can exchange your tub of balls

On the outside, Heighway's games are a little different from standard pinball machines. His backboxes look almost like a desktop Mac; they're a two-inch-thick rounded rectangle with silver edges and a black face, absurdly thin for a pinball machine. There's also a ten-inch video screen built right into the wooden playfield to display scores and animations. Then, because people seemed to want it, he built a version with a duplicate ten-inch screen in the backbox. And another with a much more Jersey-Jack-sized screen, which Heighway's ponytailed technical director Romain Fontaine reveals to the Expo audience by dramatically whipping off a sheet to a moderate amount of cheering.

But the real magic, Heighway says, is inside his machine. Imagine you own a beautiful new pinball machine and a solenoid burns out. To replace that solenoid, you need to know at least a little bit about electronics. An amateur can swap a lightbulb or two, but unless you know your way around a soldering iron, you can't rebuild a flipper coil.

Heighway Pinball, claims Heighway Pinball, has solved that. They've reimagined every component of the game and made them modular, exchangeable, plug-and-play. If your flipper mechanism on *Full Throttle* breaks, simply toss it and plug in a new one. The glass top of the game, usually painstakingly slid out frontward to search for a loose ball or clean the playfield, is now on hinges.

And that modularity goes beyond individual components. Once you've bought a pinball cabinet from Heighway, if you want a different game, you just need to buy a playfield, cabinet art, and a flash drive with the new software—then you can make the change yourself.

---

for prizes, some of which are medallions exchangeable for cash at the establishment next door. Supposedly some people make a living playing pachinko skillfully. I tried the game once in Tokyo in 1999. I put in 1,000 yen, watched some balls fly, continuously reinserting the balls I "won" until the total dwindled to zero. Then I returned the plastic bucket and left. Also, the crane machine at the arcade next door awarded actual live lobsters, and I encountered the Hello Kitty brands of both gasoline and meat. I freaking love Japan.

Heighway posits an "infinitely upscaleable system," an entire home arcade made from a single machine, plus a stack of playfields and cabinet art in the closet.

To top it off, Heighway is adding near-field communication technology so that you could pay for a game via your PayPal or Worldpay account on your smartphone, thus eliminating the need for quarters (or pence). And with pinball machines connected wirelessly to the web, players can compare scores head-to-head or instantly post scores on social media.

"We looked at every aspect of the pinball machine and said, 'Can we do this better?'" Heighway tells me, explaining that his games are meant to be a gentler introduction to the possibility of owning one's own pinball machine: "We're not trying to attract *us* back to pinball."

He shows me a YouTube video of a full changeover between games—the playfield and art panels come out, and new ones are dropped in. "You know how long it took to do that?" he asks. "Three minutes, twenty seconds." I decline to point out that, because Heighway Pinball has not yet made its second game, I've just watched a video of someone changing a *Full Throttle* into a *Full Throttle*.

The collectors at Expo have heard about *Full Throttle*. At a party tonight at a Hooters-like wing joint across the street, they'll get to play *Full Throttle*, and they'll walk away with *Full Throttle* T-shirts. But even though *Full Throttle* is not yet available for purchase, they're far more interested in Heighway's second game.

That game is *Alien*, based on the Ridley Scott movies. It will have a "chest burster" toy that captures the ball and flings it back toward the flippers, a giant "xenomorph" head whose spring-loaded tongue eats the pinball, and an animated screen that hides the alien queen.

"Would you all like to see the queen?" Heighway asks the audience mischievously, receiving a chorus of yeses. They clearly like this more than motorcycle racing.

So he shows a slide of Queen Elizabeth holding up the middle finger of each hand. It's the universal sign for "Fuck off, we know you want to see it, but we'll show it to you when it's ready."

Heighway has one more trick up his sleeve. Just as Jersey Jack hired Pat Lawlor to design games, Heighway announces that he has made successful overtures to another famous pinball designer, Barry Oursler.

A humble, practical Midwesterner with a light brown mustache, Oursler looks gratified yet baffled at being the center of attention. He was a Williams stalwart, starting work on the assembly line the day after he graduated from high school in 1970 and eventually rising through the ranks to design games like *PIN·BOT* (1986), *Doctor Who* (1992), and the amusement-park-themed trilogy *Comet* (1985), *Cyclone* (1988), and *Hurricane* (1991), which are all the names of fictional roller coasters. Oursler gave us *Gorgar*, the first talking game, and though he didn't directly provide Gorgar's voice, he can be heard through a speech-synthesizing vocoder on *PIN·BOT* and, with the help of helium-filled balloons, providing high-pitched giggles on *Jokerz!* (1988).

The late '80s were good to Oursler. He designed popular games for an expanding industry. When someone asks him which is his favorite, he wistfully replies, "It's like saying, what's your favorite kid?"

The late '90s were not good to Oursler: one day he returned from vacation to learn that his entire team had been laid off. At age forty-four, jobless, without a college degree, and possessing a skill valuable only within a soon-to-be-nonexistent sector, Oursler was in trouble. To support himself, he sold off his own collection of a dozen games, later accepting a job in the food safety industry. Food safety is important, of course, but it's no pinball. How in the world, Oursler wondered, would he ever have the opportunity to design another pinball machine?

Oursler's trip to Expo in 2015 is a kind of farewell—not to pinball but to the United States. In a few weeks, Oursler is moving to the

United Kingdom, where Heighway Pinball is copying Jersey Jack's strategy: after *Full Throttle* and *Alien*, Heighway's third game will have an original Barry Oursler theme.

Now, Oursler will not only take back his spot at the drafting table but also reenter pinball at a time filled with increasing optimism. "It'd be nice to have three or four companies like there used to be," he says. "Plus, if you've got competition, it's a lot easier to get a raise from your boss."

Oursler's boss can't wait for his new designer, his very own classic American game guru, to get to work. "We want to see it come back in a big way," says Heighway, "so we want to innovate as much as possible." And that, to make the understatement of the industry, is so very freaking much easier said than done.

● ● ●

Just ask Jaap Nauta, co-owner of Dutch Pinball.*

At Pinball Expo, while Guarnieri brags, Emery basks, and Heighway shows pictures of the queen, Nauta is in the awkward position of defending, to a packed seminar room, exactly why he hasn't yet delivered the game he promised several months ago—and for which many have prepaid a sizeable deposit.

"How many have been preordered?" someone shouts during the question-and-answer session. "Can you give a rough estimate?"

Nauta, who owns the start-up with his friend Barry Driessen, gives a small grin. He delivers both good and bad news with a pleased, upbeat Dutch accent. "I don't dare anymore," he says.

This is not what the question's asker wanted to hear. He sits back down and grumbles, "Good question-and-answer session."

---

* For the Dutch-impaired, "Jaap" is pronounced "Yop." According to an employee listing on the Dutch Pinball website, other workers at Nauta's company with extremely Dutch first names include Koen, Roel, Guus, and Freek.

In 2013, Driessen was a man with a dream: build a pinball machine based on the 1998 Coen Brothers cult classic film *The Big Lebowski*. He and Nauta started calculating whether there was any way this could be a viable commercial venture. They concluded it was—and today they're dealing with the results of that conclusion.

Step one: get money. More than two hundred people paid pre-order deposits of $8,500, in installments, to reserve a *Big Lebowski* on faith. That's a lot of faith. In part, customers trusted Driessen because of a previous project: along with programmer Koen Heltzel, he took a 1991 *The Machine: Bride of Pin·bot*, Oursler's classic sequel to *PIN·BOT*, and wrote new software, converting its dated alphanumeric display to a color dot matrix with animations, upgraded sound, and even new rules that made *Bride* play like a completely different machine. Called *Bride of Pin·bot 2.0*, Driessen and Heltzel's conversion impressed pinball players around the world.

But here at Expo, Nauta has some explaining to do. "Pinball is 5 percent fun and 95 percent frustration," he jokes with his audience, "and we all love frustration!" Except they don't. The attendees of Nauta's session would like to learn about the struggles he's faced in building *Lebowski*, but more than that, some of them want to know when they're going to get their damn games.

One reason for the delay has been a failure of communication. After successfully licensing *The Big Lebowski* theme from Universal Studios, Nauta and Driessen showed them some of the art they planned to use. Universal replied that they'd prefer some changes be made, a reply Nauta and Driessen interpreted as a request. "The Dutch and rules, we don't go well together," Nauta explains. "You can smoke weed. We don't care! Prostitution . . . in Holland, we don't care!"

Universal cared—about the game's art, not the weed and prostitutes—and it took some time before Dutch Pinball understood that Universal's request was more like a command. "In America," he explains, "it means 'You. Must. Change it!'" So the playfield art was held up while they worked, for example, to unblush Julianne Moore's cheeks. (Moore, now a L'Oréal Paris brand ambassador, which the Internet assures me is a real thing, apparently had to maintain a certain cosmetically consistent image, even in pinball art.)

Then there was a problem with the music. Dutch Pinball somehow acquired the rights to twenty songs from the film, like Bob Dylan's "The Man in Me" and "Just Dropped In (To See What Condition My Condition Was In)" by Kenny Rogers and the First Edition. What a treat, his customers thought, to hear snippets of the movie's idiosyncratic soundtrack while making shots.

At least they *thought* they had the rights. Months later, they would discover that the Dutch music rights authorities had "falsely informed" them—it turns out they had secured the rights to the songs but not as performed by their original artists.

So Nauta and Driessen began a quest to find covers of the same songs—only to learn even later that they could only use the songs uncut, beginning to end—no snippets. In a pinball game, that's impossible. No player wants to pause for three minutes and listen to a Dylan song every time he or she shoots a ramp.

Another unanticipated delay, and another apology to Dutch Pinball's presumptive customers. Finally, like the Stranger stepping in to give the Dude advice,* Roger Sharpe volunteered to interact with Universal and—at least for Driessen and Nauta—once again saved pinball.

Nauta has brought three prototype *Big Lebowski* machines to Expo, all available for free play. The game's goals include mixing a white Russian, bowling down ten miniature pins, and even unrolling the Dude's rug, which really ties the room together. The video clips on the color display (that's color dot matrix, a level more rudimentary

---

* The Stranger narrates the pinball machine as well, gruffly explaining that "multiball is lit" or declaring, "Let's go bowling," but it's not the real deep-voiced character actor Sam Elliott. Nauta tried to sign up Elliott but had to settle for a voice actor.

than Jersey Jack or Heighway's color video screen) look slick, with Walter telling Smokey he's over the line and (spoiler alert) Donny's ashes flying onto the Dude. Good night, sweet prince.

There's no denying it's a neat, nearly complete game with a popular theme—now there's just the small matter of manufacturing hundreds of them. Stern could probably accomplish this in a week, Jersey Jack in a month, Spooky in a year. As for Dutch Pinball, we'll find out.

"I'm sorry to my customers, our customers," Nauta explains to the audience, sounding validly contrite, "but we didn't make it. But we're *this close*."

• • •

Convincing customers to give thousands of dollars to someone who's never manufactured a game may be a strategy that will never work again. In May 2015, a post on the Bay Area Pinball website announced, "Pre-Order Pinball Is Dead," complete with a mock tombstone graphic. One of the biggest reasons was a man named John Popadiuk.

"I did not realize what it entails to run a company and get a machine designed and produced from start to finish," John Popadiuk wrote in May 2015 in an apology to investors in his company, Zidware. In the same letter, he made clear that no one should expect a refund, but if they'd kindly sign the attached legal document confirming that they won't sue, he'll try to get their machines manufactured by a "licensee."

Popadiuk never responded to my e-mails, and he's the center of some pretty fervent controversy, so I don't want to speculate on anyone's intentions. But what's agreed upon is this: Popadiuk, a designer who was fired from WMS the same time as everyone else, announced that he would take preorders for three brand-new pinball machines of his own design: *Magic Girl, Retro Atomic Zombie Adventure,* and *Alice in Wonderland.* Eager fans cheerfully gave Popadiuk their money, estimated at over $1 million total—after all, he had designed some pretty cool pinball machines while at WMS, including *Theatre of Magic* and *Tales of the Arabian Nights* (1996).

But the jobs of designing games and running the day-to-day manufacturing operations are sometimes incompatible for one individual, and Popadiuk ran out of money before even finishing a prototype of his first game, *Magic Girl*.

Around the same time, investors in Skit-B Pinball, a different start-up, run by Kevin Kulek and Aaron Klumpp, found themselves in a similar predicament. Kulek and Klumpp had taken preorder money for a pinball machine based on the film *Predator*, and, by all accounts, they physically developed their machine even further than Popadiuk had his, bringing a whitewood prototype—the undecorated barebones ramps and targets screwed into plywood—to gaming shows in 2012. But according to *Pinball News*, they had neglected one teensy detail: the license. Twentieth Century Fox not only refused to grant Skit-B a license for *Predator Pinball* but also asked Kulek on multiple occasions to stop working on the game.

Those who gave thousands of dollars to Zidware or Skit-B may have made an expensive donation to learn a valuable lesson: unless it's given to Stern, or maybe Jersey Jack, a preorder—even one accompanied by a check for thousands of dollars—guarantees nothing.

For good or ill, we've entered a new age of pinball, one in which a large company with a large factory isn't necessary to produce games, though it sure as hell doesn't hurt. *Pinball Magazine* maintains a "Who's Working on What?" page with, as of this writing, no fewer than seventeen companies attempting to develop games, from Chinese manufacturer Homepin, which is making a *Thunderbirds* game, to Quetzal Pinball, which has been working on *Captain Nemo* since 2009. There have always been both large and small pinball companies, with varying degrees of success, but never before has the proportion tipped so strongly in favor of the start-ups.

"That can't last," says Pat Lawlor, which is a pretty definitive declaration from someone typically judicious with his words. "The economics of what we do cannot allow those people to survive."

Zidware and Skit-B may represent the most public meltdowns of start-up pinball companies, but plenty of others start small, promise big, and either vanish or appear to be in the process of doing so.

"This business is littered with the carcasses of millions and millions and millions of dollars of people who thought they saw an easy way to make money and died horribly doing it," explains Lawlor, referring to all of the manufacturers who have come and gone. It's not that the pinball industry attracts rubes and charlatans—though from some of the comments on the Pinside forum, particularly from people who preordered games with Zidware or Skit-B, you'd think it was. It's that making a pinball machine is hard and expensive.

One way to deal with the expense, if you're only going to produce a few dozen or hundred units, is to slap a huge price tag onto your game. "At that point," Lawlor reminds me, "you're selling Rolls-Royces."

"Pinball prices are going out of control," agrees Heighway. "Eight, nine, ten thousand dollars, where does it stop? And that's what's going to kill pinball." His competitors might point out that, depending on the day's post-Brexit exchange rate for British pounds, $8,000 is about the price of a new Limited Edition *Full Throttle*. But after that initial investment, Heighway hopes his fans will enjoy buying Heighway Pinball's next games at half the price, since they'd only be buying playfields, art, and software, not a new cabinet.

Roger Sharpe agrees that "the price point of pinball has become somewhat silly." For players and collectors, there's no easy solution: they complain when there aren't new pinball manufacturers, and they complain when the games cost too much. I think what they really want is for it to be 1980 again.

* * *

Outside of the "Who's Working on What?" list is yet another stratum of manufacturers: those making machines not as products but as projects. The beauty of making a pinball machine is that anyone can do it, and not necessarily commercially. In addition to pinball players and collectors, Expo is filled with intrepid tinkerers who, like Ben Heck toiling for years on his Bill Paxton machine, have a dream, a garage, and a patient family.

Perhaps the best example of specialized homebrew pinball at Expo is a machine made by Josh Kugler, a middle-aged man who appreciates his patient family so much that he made them the theme of his pinball machine: *Kugler Family Pinball*. The cabinet is decorated with art, presumably of the Kugler family, including backglass line drawings and a collage of tiny photos. I give the game a try, and it's absolutely charming: Players can pretend to do the normal things the Kugler family does on a regular basis, like checking the mailbox or going to the mall. One mode is called Help Eydie Make a Bracelet. I suppose everyone expresses their love for their family in a different way; Kugler's way is to build a pinball machine.

It seems everyone in the exhibition hall has their own ideas about how to revolutionize pinball. A company called Multimorphic shows off *Lexy Lightspeed—Escape from Earth*, a game by designer Dennis Nordman and built for their P³ Platform—a standard-size pinball machine on which half of the playfield is a giant screen that can show, for example, aliens to squash when the ball rolls over them or smoke trails zipping behind the moving pinball. "The reception for the P³ and *Lexy Lightspeed* has been interesting," founder Gerry Stellenberg wrote to me in an e-mail. "Technical and forward-thinking people love it. Traditionalists are hesitant to give it a chance."

Perhaps that's because the giant screen in the playfield reminds them too much of computer pinball. But Multimorphic's game is more of a compromise between computer pinball and Heighway Pinball's modular—yet physically traditional—machines.

Also like Heighway, Multimorphic wants the P³ to be the Nintendo of pinball, a gaming system that can be used for any number of games; just buy a new cartridge. Only for Heighway and Multimorphic, the new cartridge is software, cabinet art, and a playfield—ramps, bumpers, targets, the whole shebang. Well, for Multimorphic, half the shebang.

Playing *Lexy Lightspeed* (the title character of which is a phaser-toting female "space adventurer" who has crash-landed in a Florida swamp) is fun, but Stellenberg is right—the differences between his game and traditional pinball take some getting used to. He admits it's "a different enough environment that it scares some people away," but he hopes it's not too many.

"Some get over that after three to five games," he wrote. "Some never do."

If pinball conservatives remain dubious of the P³, the fully virtual machines are outright pariahs. These house a flat-screen monitor facing the ceiling—and nothing else. It's like playing computer pinball, because it *is* playing computer pinball, only inside a full-sized cabinet—and it's probably the least popular offering in the room. That's how important it is to have a physical silver ball and not just a moving picture of a silver ball. (In response to an article about pinball using the Oculus Rift virtual reality headset, one pinball fan commented, "All simulated pinball is like sex with a condom.")

Indeed, as Pinball Hall of Fame owner Tim Arnold says in the documentary *Special When Lit*, what differentiates pinball from other forms of nostalgia is its inability to be reproduced digitally. A favorite old song or movie can be purchased from iTunes in seconds, and it's the same song or movie you once knew, but a favorite pinball machine can only exist as a well-maintained wooden cabinet containing moving parts.*

---

* If you want to play pinball at home, and you don't have a pinball machine, the closest you can come—besides the giant cabinets with flat-screens at Expo—is something called Visual Pinball, open-source software that faithfully re-creates classic pinball machines

In May 2016, a Fairfield, Ohio, company called VPcabs, which makes virtual pinball inside real pinball cabinets, appeared on ABC's *Shark Tank*. Creator Brad Baker delivered the standard pitch to the panel of investors, hoping one would purchase equity in his company: "Life is a buffet, and pinball can be, too. So, sharks, who's hungry?" Billionaire Mark Cuban probably caused pinball aficionados around the country to facepalm when he remarked, "This is actually better than traditional pinball." FUBU founder Daymond John was hungry and bought a quarter of the company for $200,000. But real estate mogul Robert Herjavec, who declined to make an offer, stole the show for me when he casually dropped the fact that he owns ten pinball machines. Then again, he's worth hundreds of millions of dollars, so he probably owns ten everything.

In a corner of the exhibition hall, Canadian manufacturer FAST Pinball shows that it's possible to requisition a one-of-a-kind pinball machine on any theme you'd like—as long as you don't mind waiting a few years and paying a hefty sum. One of their games, the sparse but artistically nice *Tattoo Mystique*, sold to the person who commissioned it for $25,000.

I'm a bit baffled, at first, by FAST Pinball's apparently magical success with licensing: their other half-finished games, essentially plastic ramps screwed into plywood at this point, have themes Stern or Jersey Jack would probably kill for. *Peanuts? The Muppets?*

This is the world of the one-copy license, the perfectly legal use of copyrighted themes as long as you're only making one machine out of them. And it's fun to see what people have built in their spare time. But something about it rubs Jay Stafford, senior editor of the Internet Pinball Database, the wrong way.

To him, there's an element of narcissism in bringing your home-brew game to a pinball show, because not only are you saying "Admire

---

on your home computer. Even the rules and scoring are identical to those of the real machines. Of course, it's still not the same.

what I built," you're standing next to the machine, implying, "Admire me." He likens it to bringing a classic car you've restored to a car show, then sitting next to the car in a folding chair all day to collect compliments. At a car show, he laments—unlike at, say, a car museum—"part of the experience of appreciating the car is appreciating the owner."

I also see Stafford's point in the sort of celebrity worship that has sprung up around pinball's famous designers and public figures like Gary Stern, Roger Sharpe, and anyone else with their own trading card or autograph session at Expo. Steve Ritchie can't sign *Game of Thrones* flyers fast enough, I had to register in advance for a twenty-on-one lunch with Barry Oursler, and Pat Lawlor is thanked for his service like a military veteran. In a way, Expo succeeds in maintaining enthusiasm for pinball by promising attendees something rare, something special, a chance to meet the hardworking geniuses behind the toys. But this new lionization of the builders and makers, says Stafford, is a trend that could lead to pinball machines focused more on hype and less on pinball.

I don't know. What I do see at Pinball Expo, for sure, is enthusiasm. People who bemoaned pinball's near extinction—essentially once a decade for the last three decades—are excited, because to them, this upswing feels different than the others. This time it's driven by the ingenuity of everyday people, and while they don't all realize their dreams, they're sure as hell trying.

It feels like pinball is reinventing itself organically. The companies manufacturing games at the time of pinball's major demise in the late '90s were all founded, or were divisions of companies founded, many decades previous—Gottlieb in 1927, Williams in 1943, Sega in 1960, Capcom in 1979. Of the companies making games now, all except Stern were founded in the past five years.

This doesn't mean that Stern's business model is outmoded or that the "last dinosaur" in the industry is unnecessary. "I don't believe we exist without those big fish in that pond, and we're the little guys swimming around below them," says Charlie Emery. His 150 *America's Most Haunted* machines and upcoming 300 *Rob Zombie* games will thrill the hell out of 450 people, maybe more if someone dares to install such a rarity in a bar,* but he knows Spooky won't dent the pinball market. "We're not capable of flooding the market the way Stern is, you know? We can't do a *Game of Thrones* or *The Walking Dead*. We can't afford those licenses. So I think it's incredibly important to our little company that those big guys are there."

Gary Stern agrees, of course: "We need a critical mass of product being produced, or it won't exist," he tells me, answering a question that I get the sense he's a little tired of answering, particularly because his answer isn't the "Rah rah support the underdog" response that most people, me included, naturally want to hear. "And without making multiple models a year, we won't have a critical mass." His point is clear, because at least today, there's only one manufacturer that *can* make multiple models per year, and that's him.

Jersey Jack Guarnieri may call this viewpoint monopolistic, but there's some validity to it. In most industries, competition invigorates innovation and pushes everyone forward, and in many ways, pinball is no exception. But the proliferation of start-ups can have a negative impact as well, by making consumers' spare cash unavailable while they wait for boutique manufacturers to deliver games—some of which will never arrive. Because there's only one big player in a uniquely precarious industry, if too many pinball machines are left unpurchased, the whole hobby could be jeopardized. Everyone talks about how difficult it must be for the little companies, the Heighways,

---

* I had my first sighting of an *America's Most Haunted* machine at the Silver Ballroom, a pinball bar in St. Louis. I had invited my cousin Kevin to join me there, and while we enjoyed the Silver Ballroom's famous meat pies, I bored him with the reasons it was so cool to see *America's Most Haunted* standing among the others. And yes, for those of you overly familiar with the cast of characters in the Who's *Tommy*, I'm aware of the irony of playing pinball with "Cousin Kevin."

the Dutches, the Spookies. It's easy, in that context, to underappreciate the big one.

"We are the only pinball manufacturer in the world," Stern told *Slate* in January 2013, back when that was true, adding that "pinball will survive if Stern Pinball continues to make pinball machines in a meaningful volume." He's right: while pinheads gossip about the new innovations from all the start-ups, if Stern Pinball vanished tomorrow, there would be no workhorse to keep the sport going.

So, what will kill pinball next? It seems like a mean question, but assuming pinball is eternal, that its ball saver is always flashing, is as naive as assuming the international economy will never endure another recession.

At this point, pinball has proven itself impervious to many potential sources of doom. Television didn't kill pinball. The Internet didn't kill pinball. Smartphones didn't kill pinball. Sledgehammer-wielding zealots, an aging customer base, bankrupt start-ups, successful but slow start-ups, hoarding collectors, the Xbox, public scarcity, daunting maintenance, and a societal tendency toward antisocial endeavors like solo Netflix binges didn't kill pinball.

Maybe pinball is here to stay. Maybe it's too integrated into our society to ever leave for good—certainly not a necessity for life but a nice thing to have. Like a smile.

"Were pinball not to survive, the world would continue," admits Stern at the end of *Special When Lit*. "But a little bit of the fabric of life would be gone."

Before that can happen, it's time for one more pinball event before this book is due to the publisher, one more attempt to see if I have any shot at seriously competing, one more time Marina will watch the kids as I gallivant off to an arcade: PAPA19.

11

PAPA19: Judgment Day

THE VOLUNTEER AT PAPA19 looks like she's in high school, and I think I'm scaring her. I'm trying hard not to inflict too much of my righteous, pinball-fueled indignation on her, but I think she can tell I'm close to losing my mind.

"I'm sorry. I'm really sorry," she tells me meekly. "I talked to the woman at the desk, and there's nothing we can do."

I'm not the sort of person with immediate access to rage, but at this point in the evening, my last shot at qualifying for the finals is about to disappear, and for no good reason. I'm about to unleash a tirade of dissatisfaction, but this volunteer, who has spent hours diligently tapping players' information into her handheld tablet, just like I did for a couple hours at PAPA18, looks *so scared*. She's pre-cringing. She looks like she's seen more than one older male pinball player fly off the handle after a mistyped score and is bracing for an explosion.

"But . . ." I say. And beyond that, I have nothing.

* * *

Let's go back to the previous morning. I haven't yet arrived at PAPA. I'm zooming across the Pennsylvania Turnpike in my Corolla, the Saturn having ended its fourteen-year run with a puff of smoke, a semimelted engine, and potentially a new life in the capable hands of National Public Radio's vehicle donation program.

This will be my final visit to PAPA, if Marina has any say in the matter, which she typically does. This is the last PAPA before my book is due, which makes it the last PAPA I'll have a reason, beyond enjoyment, to attend.

Once more over the Appalachians. Once more through the Allegheny Mountain Tunnel, and once more opening wide the double doors to Carnegie's glorious annual arcade.

The longest lines this time are for Stern's newest offering, *Ghostbusters* (2016), possibly timed to coincide with the release of the new film, even though the game art is based on the original. It's a deliberately retro callback that earns fairly universal praise; the 2016 *Ghostbusters* movie would not have been nearly as successful a subject, as it has no Egon, no Stay Puft Marshmallow Man, and there is no Dana.*

I've convinced my college roommate, Lee, to fly up from Atlanta and attend PAPA with me. Lee's wife, a pediatrician, is doing something very important with vaccines in Sierra Leone for a month, leaving him in search of time-intensive diversions.

Before boarding his flight, Lee texts me a photo of eighty dollars in quarters stacked on the airport floor, meticulously picked out from plastic bags of change he's been accumulating for a decade. "Game on," he texts. I reply that PAPA only takes tokens.

At PAPA, as Lee brings an outsider's perspective to the inherent weirdness of a massive pinball tournament and the wacky folks who play there, I realize somewhat sadly that I've become inured to the eccentricity. The physical quirks I identified during PAPA17 and

---

* Only Zuul.

18—golf gloves, fanny packs, abundant male ponytails, sweatshorts, cameras strapped to belts—now seem unremarkable. I see a man in suspenders and an Egyptian pharaoh hat, another in a *Star Trek* uniform, and still another with a raccoon tail dangling from his rear belt loop. I watch a woman dancing, literally dancing, for ten minutes straight while waiting in line to play, and I have to actively remind myself that this is unusual.*

During lunch, for example, at the next table, two women drink coffee concentrate (not coffee but *coffee concentrate*), eat matzo (it's not Passover), and—oh God, are they downing mouthfuls of bagged sauerkraut?

"Such an interesting slice of humanity," remarks Lee. *Careful*, I want to warn the pinball players, as Venkman did in the second *Ghostbusters* film. *You're scaring the straights.*

Lee is a perfect example of someone who could be nudged into the world of pinball. He's played a bit, but no more than your average boardwalk-goer. He's currently uninterested in competing, even in D Division, but he's having fun on the practice games, with me as the tour guide supplying an annoying overabundance of information about each machine.

"I'm trying to combo it from the left ramp to the right ramp or right loop," I tell him while slapping the buttons of *Johnny Mnemonic*, "and that lights throwing spikes, which will start super spinner; then if I can get quick multiball, I'll just pound the spinner."

Lee steps up to the machine. He points at the gap between the flippers. He says, "I'm trying to get it to not go *there*."

I have the same goal on my first entry in C Division—trying to get the ball not to go *there*—but you'd never know it. I launch my first ball on *Mousin' Around!*, a 1989 machine whose theme is aggression

---

* Maybe she's just excited: for the first time ever, PAPA has added a Women's Division, though they haven't named it MAMA. It's relatively successful—thirty-six women have signed up—and the winner will end up being someone named, pleasantly enough, Sunshine.

toward mice. It's a ball I've played over and over again in my head since PAPA18, because *this* is it, *this* is my chance to qualify for the finals, and it's *this* or nothing, and it all starts now.

Ball one on game one of entry one is the definition of touch-and-drain: launch, roll over one switch, then gone, for a score of 10,010. It leads to a shitty finish, then an even worse showing on *World Cup Soccer*.

Entry one reminds me what a long, expensive slog this whole process will be. Despite a fearless game on *No Fear* (1995), my five games in entry one place me twenty-first overall, which would be sufficient on Saturday night—it's the top twenty-four who qualify for the finals—but this early, my position will surely plummet as more people play.

Dinner takes place once more at the ersatz calypso restaurant Bahama Breeze, where the FSPA group clinks glasses of rum and wishes each other luck, then enjoys a spirited kvetch session about scorekeeping volunteers who stand too close to players' elbows.

Back by the tropically decorated bathrooms, I call Marina to wish the kids a good night.

"Say 'Good night, Daddy!'" Marina instructs Benjamin, now almost two years old.

"Good night, guy."

"Did he say 'Da-y,' like 'Daddy'?" I ask.

"No, he said 'Good night, guy.'"

I know Benjamin didn't intend this, but it feels like a demotion.

Entries two and three mirror the theme of entry one. I now have the second-highest scores on each of three machines—one on each entry. This accomplishes little. Sweaty and vexed by the ignominy of helplessly flapping at a tiny ball, I know I'm doing this wrong.

As evening turns to night, Lee says he wants to go back to the hotel. I want to stay until they kick us out at midnight, but I'm Lee's ride.

"It's been a long day," he cajoles. "You started driving early." It's certainly true; my day began what feels like a lifetime ago, over two hundred miles away, waking up early to shower before the kids got up, pulling laundry out of the dryer, then trying (unsuccessfully) to convince Maya that she didn't need to wear a Belle costume to breakfast.

But there's something about Lee's tactic that gives me pause. He's not saying we should go to the hotel because he's tired; he's saying we should go because *I'm* tired. All my life, people have been trying to convince me that I'm tired. I'm not tired! I want to play pinball.

Telling someone he's tired is like telling someone . . . I don't know, that pinball is silly. That it's not worthwhile to invest your time and energy in a game you know is ultimately inconsequential but that, nevertheless, has a special pull for you. It's a way of mainstreaming the obsessives, of convincing us what is and isn't rational to desire. But you know what? We obsessives are just fine, thanks.

Instead of getting into my car, I challenge Lee to a game based on cars, *Corvette*, and when he scores seventy million, I score over seven hundred million.

"Now who's tired?" I ask with a huge grin.

"Me," says Lee.

Fair enough. At this point, my best entry has drifted down to thirty-second place, but tomorrow is a new day. And a crucial one. This book is due in two months—on, how neat, the 40th anniversary of the relegalization of pinball in New York City, not to mention the 145th anniversary (plus one day) of the issuing of Montague Redgrave's patent for "Improvements in Bagatelles." Marina is unlikely to support another visit to PAPA until the kids are legal adults. If I want to qualify for the finals, tomorrow is the *only* day.

"Hi," I grumble to the hotel desk clerk. At this point, Lee and I are both beyond exhausted. "Reservation for Ruben."

"All we have left is a smoking room," he says.

"Seriously? But I have a reservation for a nonsmoking room," I tell him. "I made the reservation three months ago. Here, I can show it to you on my phone. And I called tonight to say I'd be arriving late."

"Don't know what to say," shrugs the clerk, more interested in his own smartphone than anything I could show him on mine. "We gave away the room. We had a lot of people come in—there's some kind of Ping-Pong convention."

. . .

I feel more prepared the next morning for entry four. While Lee showers, I watch Bowen Kerins's tutorial videos, marveling at the man's ability to assess the value and the potential danger of every shot. His brain is a databank of rules, which he can combine and evaluate in a fraction of a second.

At PAPA, lights flash, solenoids fire, and sounds overlap: the usual. This morning I'm trying to achieve a Zen-like state, even though I don't really know what one is or whether it would help me. *Calm down. You know how to do this. You're well rested. One bad ball is just one bad ball. One bad game is just one bad game.*

And, as I learn from entry four, five bad games are five bad games. I keep hearing a new idiom from frustrated players: "shit the bed," as in, "I really shit the bed on *Iron Man*." I don't know whether the phrase implies soiling one's sheets or physically defecating an entire bed—a significantly worse outcome, medically speaking—but either way, entry four shits the bed.

As I start my fifth entry, the lines for each machine have grown longer, and I have a pounding headache. I think it's from focusing fully on a game, getting the blood flowing, then standing behind two or three people to wait for the next game. *Go go go focus focus now stop and wait, and wait, and here we go this is it go go focus focus.* My hands shake from repeated adrenaline withdrawal.

Entry five shits the bed.

Then I notice someone familiar. He's tall and comfortable, with short dark gray hair and stubble, all made practically unnoticeable by his sky-blue eyes and giant smile. He's wearing an untucked button-down denim shirt, playing *Stingray* (1977), and laughing with some friends.

Oh my God. It's Ed Robertson.

The lead singer of Barenaked Ladies is playing pinball at PAPA.

I'm not a celeb stalker. I don't read *Us Weekly*, and I don't watch *TMZ*. But to me, there's always been something so, I don't know, *separate* about those in the limelight. Something palpable. Something that makes me nervous. Which is all to say that when I'm in the vicinity of someone well known, I enter Famous Person Mode. It is not a pretty sight.

In 1997, for about fifteen seconds, I met then president Bill Clinton. He asked me two questions while shaking my hand. The first was my name, which I told him correctly. The second was where I would start college in the fall. I told him—and this is verbatim—"Uh . . . I forgot."

Lee agrees to help me pinball-stalk Ed Robertson, which means we just "happen" to pick a game to play near where Robertson is playing while I try to build up the nerve to talk to him. I've actually been e-mailing Robertson's agency for months, trying to see if I could interview him for this book, so I feel like I have an in, but . . . gah. I don't know.

My half-minute conversation with Robertson is a blur. I tell him about this book, he writes his e-mail address in my little notebook, and for some reason, I mention that I enjoyed his New Year's Eve concert in 1998 at the Spectrum outside Philadelphia.

"That part was lame," Lee says when I gleefully recall my thirty seconds with Robertson and show off his e-mail address. "But other than that, good job!"

I relate the good news to Marina on the phone, much to Maya's delight—apparently the phone was on speaker, and I have now caused

Maya to run around the house, laughing and yelling, "Daddy met a bare naked lady!"*

Having dispensed with the lameness and made the evening a little more difficult for Marina, it's time for entry six. It doesn't shit the bed, but it doesn't do whatever the opposite of shitting the bed is, either. It's not enough.

Lee, at this point, says he's "getting a little pinballed out" and goes to the café area to sit and read. The clock ticks closer to midnight, when qualifying ends. My arm hurts. Don't care. I'm thirsty. Don't care. There are hundreds of pinball machines between me and the water fountain, so I'll never make it there without stopping to play anyway.

Entry seven includes a score of 150 million on *The Twilight Zone*. Ordinarily that's a decent score, but with player after player putting up scores on these machines, the bar continues to rise, and a score of 150 million is now worth essentially zero. By the time entry seven finishes, I'm still in forty-third place, and there's only time for one more entry before midnight.

Lee has gone back to the hotel. It all comes down to this. Over the course of the last three PAPAs, I've put in a total of twenty-three entries, and this one—entry eight tonight—will be my twenty-fourth and last. In my notebook, I write, "DO NOT BE BAD."

---

* Robertson later told me in an e-mail about a pinball-related encounter he had with actor Patrick Stewart while filming an episode of *The View*. Robertson told Stewart he was a big fan, to which Stewart asked a "bullshit detector" question: "Really? Which of my roles is your favorite?" Robertson cleverly avoided saying "Captain Picard" or "Professor Charles Xavier" and instead endeared himself to Stewart by naming an obscure BBC adaptation of a Shakespeare play. Having cleared the first fanboy hurdle (I guess even famous people have Famous Person Mode), Robertson felt comfortable telling Stewart, "Actually, I have a confession to make. My favorite line of yours is 'All hands prepare for multiball,'" citing the often-heard line of dialogue recorded on the *Star Trek: The Next Generation* (1993) pinball machine, which Robertson owned. This sparked a discussion of Stewart's pronunciation of "multiball"—in his version, the central syllable had a long *i* sound, as in, "mul-TIE-ball," not the traditional "mul-TEE-ball"; Stewart insisted his own pronunciation was correct. This is probably the most satisfyingly nerdy celebrity-meets-celebrity story I've ever heard.

My first of five games is *Mousin' Around!* I don't know why I keep choosing this machine—I'm not playing it well—but compared to some of the other games, I at least know the rules on *Mousin'*. This time I drain with a score of 2.6 million. Hmm. On this machine, that's not bad.

Next is *World Cup Soccer*, which can be a fast, frustrating game. My strategy is always to advance toward multiball, which can be started by shooting the ball into a notoriously difficult-to-hit scoop, a metal strip that guides the ball into a hole. I try to light that scoop early via a series of other shots, making multiball available, then spend as much time as possible trying to bury the ball in the scoop. Sometimes it works right away. Often it doesn't.

This time, it does. Oh, wow, it truly does. I have multiball. I'm *scoring* during multiball. I'm having not just a good game but an epic one, surely one of the top few games in this contest, a game that culminates in a score just over one billion. The volunteer shows me her tablet, and I confirm my score.

I can still blow this, but I'm two good games for two—on pace to qualify. However, while in line for the third game, *No Fear*, I check my entry-in-progress on my phone to see where that *World Cup* score ranks.

Uh . . . something's wrong. My score is listed as 280 million, a zero on *World Cup*, not one billion. That's not my score.

I flag down the high school volunteer I'm about to intimidate. She apologizes but explains that there's a reason they ask us to confirm our scores on their little tablets before moving on to the next game. Now I see the reason: When something is incorrectly entered, it becomes the player's fault, not the volunteer's. When I confirmed my score, was I even looking at the tablet? I don't remember.

This is not happening. No no no. This is my last entry of my last trip to PAPA, and everything is falling into place. I will *not* be thwarted by a clerical error. I scored over one billion on *World Cup*. I don't want to be difficult. But I think I need to be difficult.

Losing my place in line for *No Fear*, I find a purple-haired woman at the main desk and explain my issue. I'm definitely not the only person who's ever had this problem—it's bound to happen when they're trying to manage thousands of entries in real time. But why me? Why now?

She can't reassign my score, she says, because what's to stop anyone from approaching the desk and claiming they had a billion points?

With a little research, I see the source of the error: my high score was most likely switched with the score of someone named Kody. He has my billion, and I have his 280 million. To fix my score, the purple-haired woman concedes, I'd need to find Kody, bring him to the desk, and have *him* agree to swap scores.

I don't know who Kody is. I don't want to yell, "Does anyone know Kody?" in the middle of the tournament, so I can only look at every player's nametag and hope to encounter Kody. This is more difficult than it sounds, since Kody could be anywhere in the facility or maybe in the parking lot, or maybe he's gone home—and if he's playing a game at the moment, I can't exactly lean over the playfield glass to scrutinize the tag hanging from his neck.

Kody. Kody, Kody, Kody. Where the hell are you?

Roger Sharpe partially credited serendipity for his magic plunge in 1976. Serendipity is a wonderful phenomenon in that it needs no cause, like divine intervention, nor a trend, like luck. It just needs the right thing to happen at the right time. And sometimes it does.

The first person whose nametag I look at, standing right there by the C Division games, is Kody. *Bingo.*

Even better, Kody himself just noticed his unexpected billion on *World Cup*, and, honest guy that he is, gladly approaches the information desk with me to fix the mix-up. Kody, wherever you are, thank you.*

After a decent showing on *No Fear*, my next game is *Full Throttle*, Heighway Pinball's much-anticipated first game. The presence of a *Full Throttle* machine at PAPA means that Heighway has officially become the fourth manufacturer of pinball machines, joining Stern, Jersey Jack, and Spooky.† Lines for *Full Throttle* are especially long, since the game is enough of a rarity that everyone wants to play it.

I need a score of at least thirty million to secure my spot in the finals. I watched Kerins's *Full Throttle* tutorial video this morning, in which he scored over two hundred million in less than seven minutes. Starting a multiball is key. It's 11:20 PM, I'm on-offing adrenaline, and, as fate would have it, I happen to be wearing a *Full Throttle* T-shirt.

Fate sucks. I never start multiball and drain with only twelve million.

Which means I have one chance left, one game between me and the end of my last entry, or else I'll once more fall short of qualifying for the finals. That game is *The Twilight Zone*. It's the game I played regularly in grad school and my secret weapon in pinball league, the game whose rules I know better than any other, even *Johnny Mnemonic*. It's probably my best game, but even on my best game, sometimes I just tank. We all do.

I hate the pressure. Oh, how I wish I'd done well on *Full Throttle* and could relax with some insurance that I was already in the finals. I need two hundred million on *The Twilight Zone*. There are three balls between me and the end of the night. Here we go.

Ball one is a joke. Three million. *Three million.* It's possible to make a skill shot and score triple that much in the first five seconds

---

* Maybe he also took my hotel room. In which case, screw you, Kody.
† Only a week later, Dutch Pinball will announce that they've started shipping *The Big Lebowski*, making them the fifth pinball manufacturer in the world—recall that only three years earlier, the entire industry was Stern and a bunch of talk.

of the game. Ball two hoists the score to thirty-five million, but still, it's a long damn way to go from thirty-five million to two hundred million on one ball. This just isn't meant to be. I'm going to choke while coming *this close*, just like I did at PAPA17 and 18. And, for that matter, before Maya and Benjamin were born, at PAPAs 8 and 12.

Then ball three gives me the chance to start something called Fast Lock Multiball, an instant multiball mode that can rack up points as long as you keep the balls in play and occasionally bury one in the jackpot hole. I'm completely focused on the playfield, on the flippers, on keeping the balls out of the drain. I can't even look at the score display. Doesn't matter. *Control what you can control.*

The multiball ends with a multidrain, a simultaneous loss of both balls that feels more frustrating than any single drain—one down the left outlane, one down the center. The score display has already moved on to adding my bonus, the extra points awarded at the end of the ball. It's only when my score is fully tabulated that I see the grand total: 233 million.

And so it comes to pass that on the last ball of the last game of my last entry, in what is probably the last time I'll attend PAPA in the foreseeable future, I did it. I finished in nineteenth place, which qualifies me for the finals.

Tomorrow I'll have a chance to blow it all over again, but for now, I'm done, and I'm happy. PAPA closes at midnight, and back at the hotel, I tell my story to a pinballed-out Lee, who probably wants to go back to sleep. I know I need to rest, too, before the finals. But let's be honest: I'm just not tired.

● ● ●

Sunday morning at PAPA is different for the handful of players in the finals. For the first half hour, we're allowed to scrutinize the machines we'll be playing but not to touch them. People bend over games like they're museum artifacts, peering through the glass and pointing out useful minutiae.

I join the pack and assess the games, hands on hips, as though I can really glean useful information by inspecting machines that are turned off. It's a different bank of games from yesterday. I know some games very well, like *Bram Stoker's Dracula*; others, almost no one seems to know.

Target Pool (1969), for example, is the lone game from its era in the bunch, and a gray-haired man—who looks like he played it when it was new—begins telling a friend the rules and strategies. Immediately the other players flock around him, desperate for the information.

At every machine, competitors seek advice from their friends. "Short plunge, live catch, every time," someone's friend says at *Avatar*. "Upper playfield is bullshit." Competitors relish these tidbits. The ten words this player just heard may dictate his entire strategy on *Avatar*. After all, the finals are head-to-head, so today players don't need epically high scores to succeed. Like campers escaping a grizzly, they don't need to outrun the bear; they just need to outrun each other.

Terminator 3 (2003) is in my bank of potential games, and I don't know the rules well—but since there are a few other *T3* machines around PAPA, I decide my time is best spent playing these instead of squinting at games that aren't on.

"Judgment day is inevitable," growls Ah-nold Schwarzenegger, who provided custom speech for the game. Indeed it is, Ah-nold. Indeed it is.*

---

* At another point in the game, in a sound bite so classically awkward that it's become a running joke among pinball players, Ah-nold offers the following lackluster and unclear advice: "Shoot here and here." The only game I can think of with a more ambiguous call-out is *Star Wars: Episode I*, in which Anakin Skywalker suggests, "Plunge the ball, and use your flippers!" Good advice, Ani.

"Players, please go to your areas," booms the loudspeaker. "Or—I suppose you're already there. God bless you."

At this point we are allowed to play the machines. We're supposed to be testing them, probing for valuable information, learning that this particular kickout always feeds the ball to the left flipper, that tilt bob is set tight, and this game is sloped so steeply that the right ramp is hard to hit.* We're not playing entire games, just a ball or two, then getting in line for the next machine. At least, I'm told by a grumbling player that this is the expected etiquette. He sighs loudly as he waits in line for *Attack from Mars*, displeased that his opponents aren't rotating through machines fast enough.

I practice *Target Pool*, from which I learn that I do not like *Target Pool*.

Then PAPA official Ed Williams calls over our group of twenty-four players to review the rules, which include such I-can't-believe-they-need-to-say-this-but-it-must-have-happened-before examples as "no hitting other players."

My group of four, which will play three games in this round and eliminate two of us, doesn't really do much to tout pinball's diverse appeal. We're all men in our midthirties, and we're all wearing black T-shirts and jeans, two of us with black hoodies on.

"Hey, good luck, everyone," says Williams before sending us to our first games. "I hope you all play well."

My group starts on *Avatar*: short plunge, live catch every time. Upper playfield is bullshit.

---

* The slope of the playfield of any pinball machine can be adjusted, making the gameplay faster or slower. The industry standard incline is 6.5 degrees, but it's not a hard-and-fast rule. At tournaments like PAPA, operators frequently set the games steeper to reduce the possibility that a champion player will occupy a game, and thus hold up the entire contest, for a long time. In other words, since the industry standard isn't hard-and-fast, they'll set up the games to play hard and fast.

Right away, I defiantly ignore Williams's advice—not about hitting other players but about playing well. No one is playing well on *Avatar*, and a single multiball could spell the difference between a first-place and a last-place finish. *Avatar* offers two different multiballs. But I start neither, and by the time I've tilted my last ball in a frustrated attempt to save it—*no no no no!*—I'm at the bottom of my group.

Why, *Avatar*?

And why *Avatar*? Can't Ed Rojas—the top-seeded player in my group, who therefore chooses the games we play—pick one I'm familiar with?* Something I've played hundreds of times before? Something like *Bram Stoker's Dracula*?

"Game pick for the second game?" asks Williams.

"Let's do . . . *Drac*," says Rojas.

It's the break I've been waiting for. I have a strategy on *Drac*: Shoot the left ramp five times in a row, then the upper scoop. The third ramp shot starts Bats, a countdown mode that offers fifty million points, with the value diminishing until your ball hits fifteen switches. Since it can take a while to hit fifteen switches with a single ball in play, the fifth ramp shot will light Mist Multiball, which the scoop shot starts. Multiball can pick off fifteen switches in no time, and the Bats award carries over to all future balls. So if, on ball one, I make these six shots in order—hell, five of them are the *same* shot—I can lock in a score of at least 150 million, which will probably win.

That's the value of knowing a game's rules. Six shots, I win. *I am here in Carnegie*, I tell myself, *to make these six shots.*

Or maybe I'm here in Carnegie because of the beautiful scenery and abundant culture, because—*fuck fuck fuck fuck*—it doesn't happen. I pull off the first two shots to the left ramp, heart pounding—*I'm doing this*—but I never make the third, starting no modes at all and

---

* Between the musician, the tournament official, and my opponent, there are three people in this story named Ed. Sorry for any confusion. I guess three Eds are better than one.

earning a total score under twelve million. Just like on *Avatar*, I've yet again locked in last place.

At this point, my path to the quarterfinals has narrowed to a single option. In our third and last game, *if* I win and *if* the guy currently in second place happens to finish last and *if* I win the tiebreaker that would arise from this outcome, I'd advance. I feel like Maryland governor Martin O'Malley in a conference room with his political advisers, mapping strategies to the 2016 Democratic nomination: "Well, sir, we're not saying it's *impossible*, just very, very unlikely."

There's a long wait before our last game to let the other groups catch up; *T3* needs repair mid-game (though, as Ah-nold promises, he'll be back), interrupting everyone playing either *T3* or the adjacent *Metallica*.

Once the games are restored, Rojas chooses our final machine, a game that will end, for me, in either a miracle or heartbreak. The game is *X-Men* (2012).

I remember the last time I played *X-Men*. In October, after a conference in Philadelphia, a few of my coworkers and I visited a downtown bar, where an *X-Men* machine sat in a corner.

My boss, who knows of my propensity for pinball, watched as I played a couple games. I tried to narrate my basic strategy to him: "It says three more shots over here to light lock, so that's what I'm trying to do." I then played terribly, losing most balls quickly down the outlanes, probably leaving my boss to wonder why I thought I was good at pinball.

Now *X-Men* is my last stand, but before I can touch the game, there's another delay. It seems that the game has pre-awarded one of my opponents 1,110 points before he even launched his ball. Since his score ought to be zero, he waves for Williams to issue a ruling.

This may seem like the epitome of nit-picking; 1,110 points will probably not matter in the grand scheme of millions. But if the game awarded the points because of a misregistered switch hit—in other words, if it thinks he already launched the ball and hit something—he may have lost his ball saver, the magical resurrection that recovers an early drain like preprogrammed pity and can make a difference of a lot more than 1,110 points. It's worth asking.

Like it or not, tournament players have to defer to the officials' rulings. They strive for consistency, of course, but the simple fact remains that a machine with over 3,500 parts and a computer can malfunction in all kinds of unfamiliar ways.

Williams examines the game, then issues the ruling, a very pinball-esque dismissal both simple and unsatisfying in its conciseness: "It does that."

My first two balls shit the bed. But on ball three, the very scenario I need has presented itself: my opponent currently in second place overall has an abysmal score on *X-Men* and is likely to lose the game. I have three million, and my other opponents have finished their games with eight million and sixteen million.

So if, with this one ball, I can top sixteen million, I'll win the game, and we'll go to a tiebreaker. Forget the six shots on *Drac*, I've come to Carnegie for *this*: to find thirteen million points on *X-Men*, to rally a clan of mutants, to snatch victory from Wolverine's adamantium claws of defeat. I'm calm. I'm thinking clearly. And once the ball launches, I start—finally, finally—hitting the shots I want. *I'm the Juggernaut, bitch.*

There's a mode called Hellfire Multiball. Since ball one, I've been trying to start it, and now—with one shot to the left loop—I do. Suddenly balls fly around the playfield, down to the flippers, up the ramps, back down again, fed to the flippers through the inlanes. I've got the rhythm now, sinking shots, gliding around loops. Jackpots announce themselves, and each is a step closer to first place. I'm so wrapped up in playing that I can't watch the score increase; I can only catch and shoot and flip and save and sweat.

The balls drain, and I finally lift my eyes to the display to see my score: 6,083,720.

Six million. Not sixteen million.

It does that.

Thus ends my run at PAPA19. Two weeks from now, I'll receive a check in the mail for fifty dollars, my prize for finishing twenty-third in C Division. With travel costs and entry fees, over the course of the last three PAPAs, I think I spent over $1,000 to get it.

Lee pats me on the back. "Pinball, she giveth," he says, "and pinball, she taketh away."

•   •   •

It's Sunday, several hours until Lee's flight back to Atlanta, and we each hold jingling cups of tokens in a warehouse with more than five hundred pinball machines. I suppose there are worse fates.

Despite the loss, I'm surprisingly jazzed. I may not have won, but each game included instances of *wanting* something, then achieving it. Like hitting the left ramp on *Drac*, at least the two times I hit it. Or starting Hellfire Multiball, even if it didn't pay off.

It's a satisfying feeling, like I had on *The Twilight Zone* last night, like I had in the league finals, that I did what I needed to do when I needed to do it. Not *every* time I needed to do it, but each minisuccess was its own achievement that promised more. And maybe that's how pinball makes us all feel like we could win: I didn't make my shot every time. But I know I *can*.

In the late afternoon, we watch the A Division finals from the bleachers. This time Kerins has crapped out in tenth place. Instead of a PAPA victory, the highlight of his weekend, told and retold around PAPA, will probably be the time an excited fan approached him during a conversation with Barenaked Ladies singer Ed Robertson.

"Oh my God!" the fan shouted. "It's really you! It's such an honor to meet you!"

The fan then put his arm around Kerins—not Robertson—and smiled. He even handed his phone to Robertson: "Would you mind taking our picture?"

I love that story.

The four finalists this time are Zach Sharpe, two guys I've never heard of named Jim Belsito and John Replogle, and the twenty-seven-year-old autistic Canadian prodigy Robert Gagno—none of whom has ever won PAPA.

"They spent two years filming Gagno on his quest to be world champion," a man in the bleachers tells me. "Wouldn't it be funny if he became world champion the year after?"

He's talking about *Wizard Mode*, a recent documentary about how Gagno finds comfort—not to mention frequent success—in competitive pinball. In the film, Gagno's challenges at a pinball competition are not limited to playing the game; he also has to remind himself to congratulate other players and engage in similar social niceties. Tall and lean with unkempt curly hair, thin-rimmed glasses, and a wide smile, Gagno competes in pinball tournaments around thirty weekends each year, often traveling with his dad.

John Replogle, with his beard, ponytail, roadie physique, and a T-shirt reading "KEEP CALM AND PAPA ON," is the unlikeliest competitor in the final four—primarily because the thirty-nine-year-old local is less than two years into his recovery from maiming his hand with a chainsaw while cutting a branch. (Replogle's painful accident is gorily immortalized in a trophy at PAPA's information desk, labeled the John Replogle Memorial Trophy: an elaborate, gold-painted chainsaw cutting into a fake hand.) But it's also because, only a few years ago, Replogle was competing in C Division. Just like me.

By the time they reach their last game, the two favorites, Sharpe and Gagno, are far ahead. Sharpe selects *Flash Gordon* (1981) for the final game. In a lengthy play-by-play in *Pinball Magazine*, Tommy Skinner describes *Flash Gordon* as a game with "out-lanes that seem as wide as the Rio Grande, in-line drops that are crucial to big scores but have destroyed more players than they have helped, and exposed pop bumpers that can send a ball down the middle in the blink of an eye." It's a hard, cruel game, but you'd never know it from watching Gagno, who coolly builds his score until he's topped the other players—without even playing his third ball.

Sure enough, the documentarians behind *Wizard Mode* would have been wise to wait a year. The crowd rises to its feet to applaud Gagno, the tall Canadian with noise-canceling headphones and a huge smile.

A tournament official carries out Gagno's gigantic trophy, topped by a bronze figurine of one of the aliens from *Attack from Mars*. "The new world pinball champion," he announces grandly, before a dramatic pause, "is me!" He fake-runs a few paces, pretending to abscond with the trophy, then returns, grinning. "Is Robert Gagno!"

At the after party, which I missed but experienced vicariously through Facebook, the large flat-screen monitors delightedly flashed the PAPA logo above the words "ROBERT GAGNO, WORLD CHAMPION" before changing to "ZACH SHARPE, NOT WORLD CHAMPION." It was Josh Sharpe's suggestion.

* * *

According to *Pinball News*, twenty-three of the top twenty-five players in the world attended PAPA19. (Notably absent was the number-one ranked player in the world at the time, Jorian Engelbrektsson of Sweden, who chose to stay home with his new baby. Another one bites the dust.)

I can't match the dedication needed to succeed here. I just can't. Even if I were as good as the A Division players, which I'm not, I'd need to travel for pinball every weekend. Just looking at the records of some of these players is dizzying—not because of their impressive wins but because of the sheer number of cities they visit in a short period of time.

I once asked Josh Sharpe whether the birth of his two children curtailed his pinball-related activities. "Ohhhhhh hell yes," he wrote in reply. He and Zach used to travel to a major tournament in a different city every month, but now he's had to limit his pinball to local events, major championships, and competitions he helps to run. His wife, he wrote, has watched in horror—supportively, but in horror—as his position running a college pinball league in 2001 gave way to the IFPA, the tournament scene expanded fiftyfold, and the games in his personal collection multiplied from two to twenty-three.*

I arrive home from PAPA close to midnight. While I'm cleaning up some toys from the living room rug, a bleary-eyed one-year-old Benjamin pitter-pats down the dimly lit hallway in his Dr. Seuss pajamas.

"Hi, Benjamin!" I say gently but warmly, kneeling, arms outstretched. "It's Daddy! I'm home!"

He pushes me out of the way with a small, sleepy "No" and runs to Marina, who scoops him up. Completely oblivious to my presence, he rests his cheek on her shoulder and shuts his eyes.

Well. That would have happened anyway.

I could be the C Division winner. I could be the PAPA world champion. I could be the top-ranked player in the world, hopping between tournaments and consistently clobbering all opponents, crowds gathering to watch my live catches and slap-saves and bounce passes.

But I could never be Mommy.

I started this book to learn whether an ultimately ordinary player could flip with the greats. And now I don't think that matters so much.

---

* Zach is now the better player of the two, as evidenced both by their respective tournament records and Josh's own admission, which he conceded to me in an e-mail followed by a smiley emoticon and the phrase "Fuck you Zach."

Obsessions are fun to indulge, and don't get me wrong: I love pinball. But to become great, obsessions require time, and time is finite.

"It takes a lot of determination, passion, and just really, really wanting this so much that you'll do everything in your power possible to get it," Robert Gagno says in *Wizard Mode*. Thirty weekends a year, this guy competes. Thirty. I guess . . . I don't want this that much.

I guess.

Epilogue

Insert Coins to Continue

———————

CHECKING THE PINBALL ENTHUSIASTS GROUP on Facebook one morning, I stumble across (or, I guess, scroll to) a post from a player in crisis: "I need some serious help," he writes. "Over the past six months I've been starting to lose passion and interest in pinball. I don't know if people have been through this before, and if so, how did you get through it?"

Admittedly his request for "serious help" is a somewhat ridiculous first-world problem to have. But the Pinball Enthusiasts community is quick to offer solutions, everything from taking a break to joining a league to obtaining, ahem, "a new set of balls." One reply, however, is beautifully simple: "If you're not having fun you're doing it wrong."

There was a moment during league finals when I felt physically ill. I had just drained my ball on *Medieval Madness* in the most frustrating way while trying to control the ball and cradle it on my left flipper. I *had* the ball. I could have whacked it up the playfield, but I tried to get cute, to be masterful, to be Bowen Kerins. And in the process, the ball dribbled slightly upward, paused just out of reach of my flipper tips, and then fell between them. It was 100 percent my fault.

I smacked the flipper buttons, even when it was too late, then screamed something impolite and walloped the game—not on the glass, of course—with my open palms.

Then I felt a wave of nausea, actual nausea, and for a split second I sank to my knees and experienced a sensation I've only ever felt when inhaling pool water through my nose. You know that feeling? A second or two later, it passed, and I doubt anyone noticed. Still, now I understand something crucial about that moment: I sure as hell wasn't having fun. I was doing it wrong.

I think pinball has a future for two reasons. One is that it continues to evoke such intense emotions from those who alternately love and hate it, sometimes within the same minute. As long as pinball can make players feel so game-wallopingly frustrated and so high-fivingly exultant, all it needs is a stream of players willing to seek it out.

The second reason has more to do with pinball's current trajectory, the fact that there were 145 manufacturers in the 1930s, then twenty-three in 1980, then only three by the late '90s, then one, then nearly zero during the financial crisis—but now, just in the last few years, the count is back up to five. The influx of boutique manufacturers may be problematic in some respects, but it shows something incontrovertible: that pinball can *adapt*.

Pinball has reflected the zeitgeist of the eras it's passed through, from the *salons de jeu* normalizing the pursuit of leisure to the tug-of-war between gambling and puritanical overreach to the public miniexhibitions of innovation in the arcade age to the individualization of entertainment that shifted pinball machines out of corner stores and into basements to what we're seeing today—a reempowerment of the small-time creator, using tools formerly only available to large companies, to make and distribute pinball machines.

We live in an age of unprecedented resources for individuals to *do stuff*. You can become a taxi driver for Uber or Lyft, own a bed-and-breakfast with Airbnb, manage a store on eBay, and crowdsource start-up funds. It remains to be seen whether this is a realistic business model for pinball manufacturers, but I think it says something that people at least want to try it.

"The forces of change and development are relentless," wrote Roger Sharpe in 1977, "and some people worry that the classic pinball machine may evolve into something less beautiful and appealing than it is today." Whether his concern has been borne out over the past forty years is a matter of opinion; some would say that today's sleek machines are more fun to play than the silk-screened beasts of the Carter years, while others believe that pinball peaked at some juncture in the irretrievable past—as, often, did the players themselves. But even though pinball can't always adapt to what everyone wants, it's shown a remarkable ability to do what's necessary to stay alive, despite facing serious challenges.

When I started writing this book, I had no idea I'd encounter anything beyond surface-level controversy. I was naive, though, and I soon discovered that the pinball world, like every other part of society, is sometimes roiled by major acrimony and abrasiveness. While many people I've talked to were simply happy to bask in the fun of a complicated game, others seemed to spout controversy with every sentence.

Multiple people ordered me to stop my iPhone's voice recorder function before they'd continue talking. (Once, for no reason at all and without me noticing until much later, my iPhone's voice recorder stopped itself ten minutes into a two-hour interview. Many thanks to Jay Stafford of the IPDB for being a good sport about this.)

"This isn't for your book," someone told me about their last statement, eyes narrowed, "and if you print this, I'll deny it." (I didn't print it.) I even had someone deliver a Facebook message diatribe about another person's fiscal mismanagement/embezzlement that led me to enlist a computer-savvy coworker to dig through public tax records— only to learn that I have no idea how to interpret public tax records.

Part of the reason for the secrecy and the subterfuge is, maybe, a general fear of claiming to know where pinball is headed next. No one wants to publicly misjudge the future, especially in light of the consequences for those who've misjudged the past.

"It is hard to predict the future for a game that has endured so many ups and downs," wrote Marco Rossignoli in *The Complete Pinball Book*. Rossignoli wrote this in 2000, when, as I mentioned, we all thought virtual reality helmets were the future.

"Imagine a virtual reality pinball where one can pick out their favorite pinball from any era, just like songs on a jukebox," Rossignoli muses. "Insert the money, step up onto the game arena, pick the pinball, and put the visor on."

The good news for Rossignoli, and undoubtedly for some others, is that this is already possible. In March 2016, Jessica Conditt reviewed something called *Pinball FX2 VR* on the tech blog *Engadget*. It's simulated pinball using the then best commercially available virtual reality headset, the Oculus Rift, and since a virtual world fills the player's entire field of vision, it feels much more immersive than a regular computer game. The bad news is that most pinball players would still rather spend time with a physical game, no matter its age, than in a virtual arena, even a good one.

"Nothing will ever beat playing a real-life pinball machine in a dark, sticky-floored arcade," wrote Conditt, whose byline calls her a "professional nerd," "but *Pinball FX2 VR* is a close, gratifying second."

"I think pinball will always be around," says Dan Toskaner, the admittedly biased general manager of the Silver Ball Museum. I'm willing to agree that pinball will always be around at the Silver Ball Museum, as long as kids—both the regular kind and the technically adult kind—need something to do at the beach in the evenings between dinner and ice cream. But what about the rest of the world? Will pinball ever again be as ubiquitous as it was forty years ago? Will there be a pinball machine in your barbershop? Can you play a game while waiting for an oil change? Or ordering pizza?

"Pinball deserves a better fate than it currently has," laments Roger Sharpe in the documentary *Pleasure Machines*. The good news is that he said this in 2009, and just a few years later, pinball already has a better fate. Whether or not it will ever be as widespread as it was in 1934 or 1982 or 1992, pinball already has a new direction. I, for one, can't wait to see where it goes.

• • •

Everyone who likes pinball seems to have their own unique pinball-associated comfort memory. Pinball reminds Pat Lawlor of his dad's Schlitz beer truck; Andrew Heighway thinks about sneaking away from McDonald's; Ash Preheim at Beercade pictures a gas station game room; and when I hear Raul Julia's voice from *The Addams Family* say, "Keep the ball! I have a whole bucketful!" I'm eleven years old again, banging flipper buttons on the Rehoboth Beach boardwalk, blissfully unconcerned about work deadlines, or preschool schedules, or paying my mortgage. I'm a child once more, and when my last ball drains, that's okay because Dad said we can stop at Dairy Queen on the way home.

I've been trying to figure out what it is about pinball that gets inside people's heads. And I can make up any number of answers about what, objectively, makes the game brilliant. But obsession and fascination are hardly unique to pinball.

Pinball happens to be my "thing," but around the world, millions of people caught up in random fandom spend nights and weekends addicted to thoughts of their "thing." I have a former editor who's obsessed with high-end audio equipment. My dad is a life master in bridge, which he's now played for fifty years, and he says that when he returns from a tournament, his active brain—shuffling decks and pondering moves—won't let him sleep. He's using as much of his retirement as possible to bounce between bridge tournaments. Heck, just this morning I parked behind an SUV with the license plate "DOCKDOG" and a vinyl sticker declaring a dog named Harry to be the 2011 champion of what Google tells me is "the world's premiere canine aquatics competition." While I'm reading a Pinside discussion about Stern's newest game or learning the finer points of a flick pass on PAPA TV's YouTube channel, someone nearby is sitting at his or her desk dreaming about bringing a chocolate lab to the wildcard qualifier at the Old Florida Outdoor Festival, digging into a heated Internet forum debate over the rules of the speed retrieve event.

Whatever force picks out our hobbies for us—be it socialization, memories of comfort, coincidence, skill, love—everyone has their own passion. That's what makes humanity so varied and eclectic and magical and interesting. I'm glad mine is pinball.

● ● ●

In May 2016, a new pinball-and-pizza joint opens in Bethesda, Maryland, about a fifteen-minute drive from my condo. It's called VÜK, the acronym for the vertical up-kicker that returns a pinball onto the playfield after it's settled in a divot. The reason for the umlaut over the *U* is unknown, at least to me, nor can I figure out whether it makes the name rhyme with "puck" or with "work." (As it turns out, according to an e-mail from the owner, it rhymes with "spook.")

Regardless of the linguistic function of the diacritical mark, the weird thing about VÜK, which sells only a few types of pizza and has basically bet the farm on pinball, is the fact that it's in Bethesda. This is not a quasi-funky, pitcher-of-beer town—it's freaking Bethesda. In 2014, the real estate blog *Movoto* ranked Bethesda as the richest small city in America, with a median household income of $141,817 and easy proximity to a polo field, luxury car dealers, a private airport, and plastic surgeons. Businesses in downtown Bethesda are fashion boutiques; they're jewelry stores, they're hot yoga studios, and they're handcrafted olive oil emporia. They're not pinball arcades.

VÜK is the brainchild of Scott Nash, the CEO of MOM's Organic Market, a local grocery chain. An April 2016 article in *Bethesda Magazine* trumpeting VÜK's arrival had a mixed, somewhat confused reception in its comments section. "Oh goodie!" someone wrote. "Just what we need in a high-rent, upscale, highly-paid, and highly educated area, a pinball and pizza shop."

Exactly, I thought. *For all the reasons you listed, this is indeed just what you need.*

I'm itching to visit VÜK the moment it opens, but kids, but work, but life, et cetera. Then, one Sunday night, as we're thinking about what to do for dinner, I float an idea.

"Hey, Maya," I ask my daughter, now five years old, "how would you like to go play pinball and have pizza with me?"

It's a yes. Pizza is always a yes. I could have asked if she'd like to have pizza and a rotavirus vaccination, and she would have said yes.

Inside VÜK, nine games are lined up against one wall; on the opposite wall is a television showing, for whatever nostalgia-inducing reason, the 1986 documentary *Heavy Metal Parking Lot*. I ask Maya which game she'd like to play first.

"That one!" she says, pointing to *AC/DC*. She's never played pinball before, and she certainly has no idea who AC/DC is, but I guess to a five-year-old, a game with flashing lights is a game with flashing lights.

We start from square one. I explain how to insert quarters, how to press START, how to launch the ball, how to flip. Maya kneels on a chair, staring at the vast kinetic expanse under the glass.

"Here it comes!" I say when the ball rolls toward her. "Flip! Flip! Keep it out of the drain!"

Maya's flailing at the flipper buttons, and most of her balls last just a few seconds, but she's having a blast. I find myself wishing, more than ever, that I knew what was going on inside her head. What *is* this busy-looking gigantic toy? What do all of these lights and sounds mean? And—maybe?—so *this* is what Daddy was doing all those times he left us.

I don't know whether Maya will one day remember her first pinball trip, but the skill she masters immediately is feeding quarters into the coin slot. If there's anything kids can do well, it's spend their parents' money.

We take turns. Maya plays while I watch, then I play while she watches. In my mind I'm impressing her with my live catches and rule set knowledge, but probably not. Playing pinball with Maya watching is like playing pinball any other time, only with someone asking every few seconds, "Now can it be my turn?"

We take a pizza break. In addition to pizza, VÜK offers soft-serve ice cream.

"Daddy," Maya asks, "can I have ice cream if I finish my healthy meal of pizza?" I see what she's trying to do here. But sure, why not? Nothing wrong with tacking one more positive association onto Daddy's hobby.

After dinner, back on *AC/DC*, Maya's flipper flapping somehow sends the ball to the right place, and suddenly the fun intensifies: Maya's first multiball! Why isn't there a page for this in her baby book? First smile: six weeks, at Marina. First solid food: six months, rice cereal. First multiball: five years, *AC/DC*.

"So what did you think of your first multiball?" I ask afterward.

"I like it," says Maya, smiling. "A lot." That's my girl.

Driving home at the end of the evening, I ask Maya what her favorite part was. If you have kids, you know this is a good way to guarantee you'll hear the answer you don't want.

"The pizza!"

"But besides the pizza, if you—"

"Daddy, I have an idea. You say something, and then I'll say it after you say it."

"No, Maya, I really want to know your favorite part."

"No, Maya," she repeats, "I really want to know your favorite part!"

There is no winning this game. Believe me, I've tried. So I say, "My favorite part was spending time with you."

"My favorite part," Maya repeats in a silly squeal, "was spending time with you." Then she relaxes out of her mimicry voice and says, "That's what I was going to say, too."

Kids can be sweet when prompted.

We drive for a few more minutes in silence. Maya stares out the window, watching the trees and storefronts and houses swish past. Then she asks, "Daddy, can we go back to pinball pizza?"

I promise we will.

Updates

I N THE PINBALL INDUSTRY, as in a pinball game, so much happens so quickly.

During the year or so since I finished writing the book, Stern Pinball has continued to dominate the industry. Perhaps inspired by their competitors, Stern's game *Batman 66* (2016), based on the campy fifty-year-old television series, became their first machine with an LCD screen in the backbox. It was followed in 2017 by *Aerosmith*, continuing the series of games themed after bands that Jody Dankberg likes, then *Star Wars*.

Jersey Jack Pinball premiered *Dialed In!* to generally rave reviews from those who've played it and some bafflement from those who haven't. (After waiting years to see how brilliantly Pat Lawlor can design a thoroughly modern machine of his own devising, no one really expected that theme to be "cell phones.")

Spooky Pinball edged away from the spookiness when a major pizza chain commissioned them to manufacture *Domino's Spectacular Pinball Adventure* (2016), then returned to their roots with *Alice Cooper's Nightmare Castle* (2017).

Heighway Pinball's infinitely replaceable playfields can still only substitute a *Full Throttle* for a *Full Throttle*, but their second title, *Alien*, has reached the preorder-and-prototype stage, with production moved from Merthyr Tydfil to the almost Welsher-sounding town of Ebbw Vale. In June 2017, Andrew Heighway announced he would step down as CEO.

Dutch Pinball continues to sell *The Big Lebowski*.

Astounding the pinball world and especially their customers, Zidware—whose *Magic Girl* pinball machine never materialized, famously squandering both money and goodwill—started actually delivering the promised machines. Under president Dhaval Vasani, a new manufacturer called American Pinball (whose director of software engineering happens to be Josh Kugler, the man whose homebrew *Kugler Family Pinball* I admired at Expo) stepped in to make *Magic Girl* for John Popadiuk, in exchange for Popadiuk designing a second game. The delivered *Magic Girl* machines were described as visually attractive but mechanically incomplete. Customers finally had their promised games, but they weren't really playable, rendering *Magic Girl* what one Pinside commenter called "little more than an extremely expensive Christmas tree." With *Magic Girl* behind it, sort of, American Pinball has embarked on its next game, *Houdini: Master of Mystery*, bringing an increasingly functional prototype to pinball shows and promising delivery by fall 2017. More than one Internet commenter has made the same cautionary joke about how *Houdini* will make your money disappear.

PAPA20 marked the last pinball competition inside Kevin Martin's warehouse in Carnegie; Martin announced that he's moving future events, starting with PAPA21, to an even larger and better venue. Sweet.

There can be no more inspiring story about the future of pinball than the shocking outcome of PAPA20. After surpassing the usual group of luminaries (including Cayle George and both Sharpe brothers) in the semifinals and finals of A Division, Bowen Kerins faced off in a tiebreaker against Escher Lefkoff—age thirteen. Kerins was once the youngest PAPA world champion himself, winning PAPA4 at eighteen years old, and at PAPA20, he lost that title on a game of *Skateball* (1980) to Escher Lefkoff. Streaming PAPA TV shows Kerins draining his last ball unexpectedly, falling to his knees, and an overjoyed Lefkoff jumping into the arms of his dad, Adam Lefkoff—who himself took seventeenth place in A Division, losing in the first round to his son.

It was an invigorating outcome for pinball, a sign that the youth are ready to receive the torch. Nor was Escher Lefkoff the only young pinball prodigy at PAPA20—the B Division winner was sixteen years old, and the D Division winner was eight. I think pinball will be all right.

Maya, now age six, often asks to go to VÜK, or as she calls it, "pinball pizza." I love to tell her yes.

Appendix

S O YOU WANT TO PLAY PINBALL, or at least learn more about it. Here are some useful resources and some awesome places and events to visit. All are current as of this writing. Bring quarters.

Magazines

Gameroom Magazine, www.gameroommagazine.net
Pinball Magazine, www.pinball-magazine.com
Pingame Journal, www.pingamejournal.com

Blogs

The Gameroom Blog, www.gameroomblog.com
Pavlov Pinball, www.pavlovpinball.com
Pinball News, www.pinballnews.com

Podcasts

Coast 2 Coast Pinball, www.podcastgarden.com/podcast/coast 2coastpinball

The CoinBox Pinball Podcast, coinbox.libsyn.com
Dead Flip, www.deadflip.com
Gameroom Junkies, gameroomjunkies.com
Geek Gamer Weekly, www.geekgamer.tv
The Pinball Podcast, www.thepinballpodcast.com
Spooky Pinball Podcast, www.spookypinball.com/podcast-2

Pinball Museums (United States)

Ann Arbor Pinball Museum, Michigan, vfwpinball.com
Asheville Pinball Museum, North Carolina, ashevillepinball.com
Coney Island Pinball Museum, El Cerrito, California, www.playland
    -not-at-the-beach.org
Lone Star Pinball Museum, Hockley, Texas, www.lspinball.com
Museum of Pinball, Banning, California, www.museumofpinball.org
Pacific Pinball Museum, Alameda, California, pacificpinball.org
Pinball Arcade Museum, Wisconsin Dells, Wisconsin, www.facebook
    .com/DellsPinballArcadeMuseum
Pinball Hall of Fame, Las Vegas, Nevada, www.pinballmuseum.org
Pinball Perfection, Pittsburgh, Pennsylvania, www.pinballperfection.com
Quarterworld, Portland, Oregon, www.quarterworldarcade.com
Replay Amusement Museum, Tarpon Springs, Florida, www
    .replaymuseum.org
Roanoke Pinball Museum, Virginia, www.roanokepinball.org
Seattle Pinball Museum, Washington, www.seattlepinballmuseum.com
Silverball Museum, Asbury Park, New Jersey, and Delray Beach,
    Florida, silverballmuseum.com

Pinball Museums (Europe)

Budapest Pinball Museum, Hungary, www.flippermuzeum.hu
Dutch Pinball Museum, Rotterdam, Netherlands, www.dutchpinball
    museum.com

Krakow Pinball Museum, Poland, www.krakowpinballmuseum.com

Paris Pinball Museum, France, www.pinball-gallery.com

Museums with Pinball but Not Solely Dedicated to Pinball

American Classic Arcade Museum, Laconia, New Hampshire,
    www.classicarcademuseum.org

Coney Island Museum, Brooklyn, New York, www.coneyisland.com

International Arcade Museum, Pasadena, California, www.arcade
    -museum.com

Marvin's Marvelous Mechanical Museum, Farmington Hills, Michi-
    gan, www.marvin3m.com

Musée Mecanique, San Francisco, California, www.museemecaniquesf.com

National Videogame Museum, Frisco, Texas, www.nvmusa.org

Retro Arcade Museum, Beacon, New York, www.retroarcademuseum.com

Route 66 Arcade Museum, Atlanta, Illinois, and America's Playable
    Arcade Museum, McLean, Illinois, www.vintagevideogames.com

The Strong National Museum of Play, Rochester, New York, www
    .museumofplay.org

Supercade, Los Angeles, California, www.facebook.com/supercade

Online Resources for Locating Pinball in Public

Pinball Map (with smartphone app), pinballmap.com

Pinball Rebel locator, www.pinballrebel.com/locator

Pinball Spot, www.pinballspot.com/web

Pinfinder (with smartphone app), www.pinballfinder.org

Pinformer (UK only), www.pinformer.co.uk

Other Online Resources

International Flipper Pinball Association (IFPA), www.ifpapinball.com

Internet Pinball Database (IPDB), www.ipdb.org

Pinball Bash forum, www.pinballbash.com

Pinside forum, www.pinside.com

Professional and Amateur Pinball Association (PAPA), www.papa.org

Rec.Games.Pinball Forum, groups.google.com/d/forum/rec.games
.pinball

Tilt Forums, www.tiltforums.com

Tournaments, Shows, Events, and Conventions

California Extreme, Santa Clara, www.caextreme.org

Free Play Florida, Orlando, wp.freeplayflorida.com

Louisville Arcade Expo, Kentucky, www.arcaderx.com

Lyons Pinball Spring Classic, Colorado, www.lyonspinball.com

Michigan Pinball Expo, Rochester, www.mipinball.com

Midwest Gaming Classic, Brookfield, Wisconsin, www.midwestgam-
ingclassic.com

Northwest Pinball and Arcade Show, Tacoma, Washington, www
.nwpinballshow.com

Ohio Pinball Show, Cuyahoga Falls, www.ohiopinballshow.com

PAPA World Pinball Championships, Carnegie, Pennsylvania,
papa.org

Pinball at the 'Zoo, Kalamazoo, Michigan, www.pinballatthezoo.com

Pinball Expo, Chicago, Illinois, www.pinballexpo.net

PinFest, Allentown, Pennsylvania, www.pinfestival.com

Pintastic Pinball and Game Room Expo, Sturbridge, Massachusetts,
www.pintasticnewengland.com

Portland PinBrawl, Oregon, groundkontrol.com/category/portland
-pinbrawl

Replay FX, Pittsburgh, Pennsylvania, replayfx.org

Retro Gaming Expo, Portland, Oregon, www.retrogamingexpo.com

Rocky Mountain Pinball Showdown and Gameroom Expo, Denver,
Colorado, www.pinballshowdown.com

Southern-Fried Gameroom Expo, Atlanta, Georgia, www.southern-friedgameroomexpo.com

Texas Pinball Festival, Frisco, texaspinball.com/tpf

Vancouver FlipOut Pinball Expo, British Columbia, www.vancouverflipout.com

White Rose Gameroom Show, York, Pennsylvania, theyorkshow.com

These are just a few of the major events in the United States and Canada. For plenty of others, and events outside the United States, see www.pinballnews.com/diary. Also see a list of IFPA-sanctioned tournaments at www.ifpapinball.com/calendar. And for a list of IFPA-sanctioned leagues, see www.ifpapinball.com/leagues.

Manufacturers

Dutch Pinball, Reuver, Netherlands, www.dutchpinball.com

Heighway Pinball, Ebbw Vale, Wales, www.heighwaypinball.com

Jersey Jack Pinball, Lakewood, New Jersey, www.jerseyjackpinball.com

Spooky Pinball, Benton, Wisconsin, www.spookypinball.com

Stern Pinball, Elk Grove Village, Illinois, www.sternpinball.com

Accessories, Parts, and Mods

Bay Area Amusements, www.bayareaamusements.com

Coin Taker, cointaker.com

Marco Specialties, www.marcospecialties.com

Mezel Mods, mezelmods.com

Pinball Life, www.pinballlife.com

The Pinball Resource, www.pbresource.com

Pinball Swag, www.pinballswag.com

The Pinball Wizard, www.thepinballwizard.net

Planetary Pinball Supply, www.planetarypinball.com

Pinball Charities

Pinball EDU, www.pinball-edu.org
Pinball Outreach Project, www.pinballoutreach.org
Project Pinball, www.projectpinball.org

Acknowledgments

———

NO TWO WAYS about it, Marina is a saint. Thank you for picking up all of the household tasks, double child care included, during each of my trips to some far-flung pinball destination. Thank you even more for editing this book.

I'm equally indebted in the latter regard to Marina's mother, Vicki, for her extensive edits, and to Roger Sharpe, for fact-checking the entire book and providing a lot of valuable historical context.

So many people were generous with their time in granting me interviews and answering questions that it would be impossible to thank them all, but I'll try. In alphabetical order: Duncan Brown, Jody Dankberg, Bill and Linda Disney, Barry Driessen, Charlie Emery, Steve Epstein, Jack Guarnieri, Andrew Heighway, Dan Hosek, Ken Kalada, Bowen Kerins, Pat Lawlor, Jody Levchuk, David Marston, Ben Matchstick, Scott Nash, Constance Negley, Barry Oursler, Kevin Perone, Ash Preheim, Ed Robertson, Paul Rubens (no relation), Joe Said, Jim Schelberg, Joe and Julie Schober, Daniel Spolar, Jay Stafford, Gerry Stellenberg, Amber Streath, Josh and Zach Sharpe, Gary Stern, Pete Talbot, and Dan Toskaner.

Thank you to my agent, Laurie Abkemeier, and my editors at Chicago Review Press, Jerry Pohlen and Lindsey Schauer, for all of their help in making this book a reality. Thank you to Mike Freeman for Googling "pinball league" in 2003 when searching for a birthday present for me, and thank you to Lee Hadbavny for joining me at PAPA19.

Finally, thank you to my family for our numerous trips to the pinball arcades of the Delaware seashore. If you want to go back, just let me know. I'm ready anytime.

Index

About the Author

ADAM RUBEN is a humor writer, comedian, and molecular biologist helping to develop a vaccine for malaria. He is the author of *Surviving Your Stupid, Stupid Decision to Go to Grad School* and the monthly humor column "Experimental Error" in the journal *Science Careers*. Adam has appeared on several TV networks and hosts *Outrageous Acts of Science*, the most popular program on the Science Channel.